Memoirs of a Counterrevolutionary

Memoirs of a
COUNTERREVOLUTIONARY

ARTURO CRUZ, Jr.

D O U B L E D A Y

New York   London   Toronto   Sydney   Auckland

PUBLISHED BY DOUBLEDAY
a division of
Bantam Doubleday Dell Publishing Group, Inc.
666 Fifth Avenue, New York, NY 10103

DOUBLEDAY and the portrayal of
an anchor with a dolphin are trademarks of
Doubleday, a division of Bantam Doubleday Dell
Publishing Group, Inc.

Library of Congress Cataloging-in-Publication Data
Cruz S., Arturo J. (Cruz Sequeira)
Memoirs of a counterrevolutionary / Arturo Cruz, Jr.
—1st ed. in the United States of America.
p.   cm.
Includes index.
ISBN 0-385-24879-2
1. Cruz S., Arturo J. (Cruz Sequeira)   2. Nicaragua—
Politics and government—1979–   3. Nicaragua—Politics
and government—1937–1979.   4. Counterrevolutions—
Nicaragua—History—20th century.   5. Military
assistance, American—Nicaragua—History—20th
century.   6. United States.   Central Intelligence
Agency.   7. Counterrevolutionists—Nicaragua—
Biography.   I. Title.
F1528.22.C78A3   1989
972.8505'3'092—dc20   89-11828
CIP
Copyright © 1989 by Arturo Cruz, Jr.

Printed in the United States of America

First Edition in the United States of America
BG

To my grandparents
Adela and Julio, my mother Consuelo,
and my sister, Consuelo Teresita.
With Love.

Acknowledgments

Many people helped me gather my thoughts and prepare the manuscript for this book. I cannot name them all, but I would like to especially mention my close friends, Mario Castillo, Carlos Ulvert, Leonel Gomez, Bruce Cameron, and Eugenio Leal. I would also like to mention my late friend Dennis Volman, from the *Christian Science Monitor*, whose company I miss very much. And also, I can never forget the warmth of my friendships with "Zelayita," "Manuel," "Malicia," and dear "Nafre"; these boys were all Sandinistas who became contras, and are now dead. If I had not lived with them, I could not write this today. I owe special thanks to Raphael Sagalyn for piloting me through the shoals of the publishing world. There I found the finest harbor imaginable. Patrick Filley, my editor, is a marvel who combined the highest professional talent with great human sensitivity. Gene Stone is my friend without whom I could never have written this book. Finally, I would like to mention Rogelio Pardo-Maurer and James LeMoyne, who have introduced me to the joys and pains of writing.

Contents

Preface

My youth in Jinotepe and Granada was filled with tenderness.

Of those years in Granada, I recalled the garden in the house of my grandparents, the old walls of the neighborhood of Jalteva, the neighbors and their recollections, and mass at nine every Sunday morning.

The mornings I spent walking up and down a single street that ran between eight corners, excited by the doings of the people and wishing that midday would come and the siren of the firemen would sound announcing the hour for lunch. Sometimes I journeyed beyond this frontier. I went walking past the convent of San Francisco, where I took the byways of the neighborhood of Santa Lucia and crossed to the main avenue with its mango trees that took me to the wharf filled with smells from the province of Chontales, which lay across the broad expanse of Lake Nicaragua, whose waters nurtured and cooled my hometown Granada.

At sundown, after this journeying, I would return to sit in the shadow of the entryway of my grandparents' house and felt as if I had completed an expedition to the ends of the earth.

When I first went to Leon, more than sixty miles from Granada, it was like going to the moon. I made this trip to be with distant relatives, to see the colonial cathedral and its main altar, and to touch the famous marble statue of the lion reposing on the tomb of Rubén Darío, Nicaragua's greatest poet. There my grandparents left me for an entire week, complaining about the food, suffering the sweltering heat of the surrounding cotton fields, and seeking relief in the coolness of the bishops' chapel in the dark cathedral. On my return to Granada, I badmouthed the poor people of Léon and swore I would never go back to their city.

When I was sixteen, my parents tore me from Granada. They took me to a country where they promised me snow would fall. I was taken to Washington, where, on arrival, I suffered my first deception. The heat was unbearable, as suffocating as the cotton fields of Léon, and at that moment I longed for the cold relief of the promised snow.

From the moment I left Nicaragua I was tormented with the thought of returning. But within months I was fascinated by the new experience of cold weather, and in December, when the trees of the neighborhood were covered with snow, I had my first dream in English. According to my cousin Luis Fernando, now a revolutionary, but who at that time would visit us from Exeter Academy, my English dream was cause for joy. He prematurely perceived that it meant I could already speak the new tongue, that I was thinking in English. Only months away from Nicaragua, Nicaraguans were telling me to adopt a new language.

A year and half after that memorable dream I returned to Granada. By that time I truly was speaking English, but with an accent. My childhood between the street corners of Granada was etched so deeply that I was not willing to permit myself to lose my Nicaraguan accent. I continued to be a Nicaraguan, still seated on the old walls of the neighborhood of Jalteva. But at the same time, I was beginning to metamorphose into a hybrid of two cultures—and in the years since that return visit to Granada, I would live pinned between two worlds: one here, one there. One, close and open; the other, distant and discreet.

With the passing of the years I had moments of confusion. At times I did not find pleasure either in the culture that weaned me, or in the culture of America. These moments of confusion were always present within me, and they would be with me in my years as a young Sandinista and later on in my years as a Contra. To leaven this duality, I decided to become a bridge between the two cultures. For Americans I would try to decipher the rituals of Nicaragua, and to Nicaraguans I would try to explain the rituals of the Americans, especially the "secrets" of Washington, seat of the empire.

There were occasions when I wanted to feel that I belonged to my borrowed culture and to rid myself of the nagging punishment of my duality. Those were my worst moments, truly awful moments when I thought I could be an American—only to rudely realize that you always belong to the mystery and liturgy of your tribe. It was then that I finally understood that, if only in your imagination, you have to return, return to Granada, to Léon, to wherever your home may be, but return all the same.

Several years ago, on the border between Nicaragua and

Costa Rica near the San Juan River, the Nicaraguan poet José Coronel Urtecho warned me that the beckoning of home is inescapable. During a visit to the hacienda of his wife, María Kautz, he would not desist repeating to me that I was not going to fit in the United States, that the Americans were always going to see me as a foreigner. In the midst of his warnings, Don José always referred to Salomon de La Selva, the Nicaraguan writer who, in the years that he penned *Tropical Town and Other Poems*, sometimes wrote for the *New Republic* magazine. Salomon, Don José used to say, wanted to be American but finished up in Mexico, alone, old, and exhausted.

Each time I returned to see him, Don José referred to the experience of Salomon—the Nicaraguan who tried to become an American. And, like all good Nicaraguans, who are obsessed with origins and blood ties, Don José would bid me farewell, noting that we were family, related on the side of the Cabistan sisters.

Nicaragua was already living its revolution at the time of my meetings with Don José. The country was at war. It had Sandinistas. It had Contras. Don José, after having passed through a youth of Somocista idiocies during his accumulated eighty years, now found himself supporting the Sandinistas. And I, not yet thirty years old, found myself on the other side of the San Juan river border supporting Edén Pastora, the rebel commander who, like me, had initially supported the Sandinistas but then grew to oppose them. Don José was willing to tolerate the confusion I felt, pulled between two cultures. This confusion did not threaten him. But he could not understand what I and Carlos, his favorite son who also supported Pastora, saw in the anti-Sandinista rebel commander. According to Don José, Pastora was at best an uncontrolled adventurer who might still be capable of salvation. At worst, he said, Pastora was a Contra of little talent who was a tool of the CIA.

Like many of my generation, I had expected perfection of

the Revolution. In our sectarian dream, the Sandinista Comandante in olive green symbolized the best of the Nicaraguan spirit—triumphant idealism at last sanctified in power.
The Comandante represented the valiant peoples' warrior,
the tortured martyr whose passion and suffering guaranteed
that he would only do good with power. With the Revolution,
corruption would end; there would be no more hidden plots,
large and small; and there would no longer be a ruling court
with its courtesans. Strongmen's mistresses, wielding hidden
power, would disappear forever. And the powerful would
not use promises of a scholarship abroad as a bribe to seduce
us. If errors were committed in the Revolution, and if crimes
occurred, the Comandante could not be at fault. Ah! If only
he had known! Others had to be at fault, the Russians, or an
ambitious wife, or a scheming priest, or some miserable intellectual made small with intrigue. But never could the good
Comandante of the good Revolution knowingly do wrong.

But what old Don José did not and could not see, was that I
supported Pastora because he continued to symbolize my secret dream of an unblemished, pure Revolution of the "good
revolutionary," he symbolized the man who embodied mo-
rality, who would never let himself be seduced by the corruption that accompanies power. Because of this naive idealism
I spent two years with Pastora, only to be deceived again,
only to choose other paths that I would travel without my
former arrogance. Born down by the weight of my experiences, I had finally been tamed, as the Cuban poet Heberto
Padilla says, by that word "history." It was with Pastora that
my secret hopes began to die, that I began to "mature," dis-
carding my small acts of rebellion in order to have ambitions. I started to remain silent, to be prudent, to be empty so
nothing could affect me as I patiently survived, convinced
that personal conduct no longer mattered, that Nicaragua,
my country, could not find solutions.

In the years after my time with Pastora I went in other
directions. I came to know the combatants in the Contra re-

bel movement, those peasants whom I once secretly despised as inferior, antihistorical kulaks. These peasants who had reason to resist the Sandinistas, died barefoot, died without boots, even as they were deprecated by Americans whose government tried to support the peasant fighters. I also got to know those Nicaraguans who once were supporters of the dictator Somoza, with their worries, their hatreds, and their painful nostalgia for Nicaragua. I entered the world of mirrors of Nicaraguan exiles, their family squabbles, their old feuds, their fear of anything foreign and terror of being anonymous nobodies in this overwhelming country of laws and taxes.

I moved among the agents of the CIA, the majority of them decent men, patriotic in their manner but also inept, strangers in their own house who were filled with the cultural arrogance of chauvinism, still living in the age of the Panama Canal. In the midst of all of this, I met Oliver North, the man with the historic ego, the liberator who saw himself as the father of the Contras. He was the very embodiment of the American who lives in the imagination of all Nicaraguans when they speak of the Americans of old, the "Mr. Yankee" of the days of empire under Calvin Coolidge. A time when U.S. presidential envoy Henry Stimson told Nicaraguan General José María Moncada, "General, the United States never makes mistakes."

For ten years I traveled these confusing paths, between two cultures, paths of dogmatic hopes on which I felt secure in the shame of always keeping a safe distance from the real war. I was with the Sandinistas, I was with Pastora, only to end up being with the Contras. And journeying on these roads, I found that I had turned into a chronicler, a chronicler who lived one of the saddest episodes in the history of my country—which I discovered is not the land where snow falls, but rather the land of my youth, the land of the street with eight corners, the wharf filled with smells and of the Revolution led by corruptible men who did bad as well as good. I found that my country, with all its sadness, is Nicaragua.

Pastora's older brother, Don Felix Pedro Pastora, used to like to say as he firmly stuck his pistol in his belt: Nicaragua is a land where brave men grow like wild grass, where it means nothing when people die. When Don Felix said this, he spoke with weight of Nicaragua's history, a history of war, soaked with the blood of peasants. Three years after achieving independence more than a century ago, Nicaragua was already drowning in the first of countless wars, so vicious that other Central Americans were terrified by the accounts of the ferocity of the fighting and the intensity with which Nicaraguans hated each other.

But with this most recent war among Nicaraguans, even a scarred warrior like Don Felix Pastora began to have doubts. For the first time we Nicaraguans began to fear a war because too many had died. The people yearned for a return to normal life, longed for the ordinariness of everyday existence. It no longer mattered if this normality was Somocista, the peace of a dictator. Let the Sandinista Ortega brothers remain in power for forty years. The older brother, Daniel, takes the presidency, and Humberto, the younger brother who is a general yearning to be a field marshal, gets the army. Just so long as there is no more war.

In some later time, my country will come to dream again. But for now we seek refuge in our tradition, our punishments, and the search for our salvation. I write this as a Nicaraguan who, since his lost youth in a Nicaragua that no longer exists, has lived other lives but is still a child of a land where it never snows, a land I pray will now heal.

—Arturo J. Cruz, Jr.

Memoirs of a Counterrevolutionary

Growing Up
in Nicaragua

I spent much of my childhood in Granada, the city of my mother's family. I was my maternal grandparents' first grandchild; my parents, who lived in the smaller city of Jinotepe, loaned me to them for several months of each year.

In Granada, Monsignor Mejía y Vilchez, the priest of the Church of La Merced, would sit outside the parish house and hold court every afternoon. Joining Father Vilchez were the old men of Granada: Héctor Mena Guerrero, called

"Doctores," for he had degrees in medicine, pharmacology, and law, and he had never worked a day in his life; William Hurtado, nicknamed the "Tyrone Power" of Granada because of his handsome features and his dark, perfectly coifed hair, who could not attend Father Vilchez' mass because he was married to a divorced woman; Anselmo Ximenez, my great-uncle, the eternal cardplayer; "Calambre" Benard, one of the many grandsons of Adolfo Benard, the Sugar King of Nicaragua, some of whose many descendants were so lazy that it was said they rented an ambulance to drive to their hacienda so they could travel supine; Juan Sequeira, the brother of my grandfather, who claimed he was a great bullfighter when he studied in Spain. We never knew for sure because there was no Spanish-style bullfighting in Nicaragua.

These men were vigorous adherents of the Granadan art of indolence. By four in the afternoon, as the sun grew pale, a light breeze blew over the town from Lake Nicaragua and refreshed the city's soul. The mood lightened. The men sat on small rocking chairs and I would settle down on the ground next to them. They talked of everything but almost always Father Vilchez would recall the glorious day in Rome when he served as an acolyte to Pope Pius XII. And almost always Calambre Benard would scoff, Oh, come on, Father Vilchez. This place of yours, this Europe—this place is only an invention.

Calambre was not the only one who thought this way. Our world of family, mannerisms, and nostalgia was purely Nicaraguan. I too knew the rest of the world was an invention of Father Vilchez. These men might discuss America, Europe, or Panama but Granada was the center. If anything else existed at all, it existed only in its distant effect on us. Granada was the sun. Paris, London, and America were small moons. My childhood in Granada was made more of fantasy than normalcy.

Granada in the 1960s was a glorious city of 24,000, or

26,000, or 30,000. We debated the statistics relentlessly. Granada was settled either in 1523 or 1524. The city's great historical rival, León, was also founded in 1523 or 1524, which led to a never ending controversy over which of the two was the Second City of the Western Hemisphere. Veracruz, Mexico, was founded in 1519, although it did not have a mayor for some time afterward, lessening its importance in our eyes.

One of the Nicaraguan cities was next. Both were established by the conqueror Hernandez de Córdoba, who was sent to Nicaragua at the request of the governor of Panama, Pedrarias. Pedrarias was famous for his iron coffin, which he had brought over from Spain, as he was almost eighty when he arrived in the New World and traveled fully prepared to leave all worlds. In time Pedrarias thought Córdoba was plotting against him and so the octogenarian journeyed to León and jailed Córdoba. He soon had him decapitated.

Settlements in Panama also predated León and Granada but we didn't consider these towns cities such as ours, especially Panama City, which was burned to the ground by Morgan the pirate and had to be rebuilt, thereby losing its historical claim. Nor did we regard as competition Santo Domingo in the Dominican Republic, which was an island and to be discounted.

The streets in Granada were wide, the squares were grand, and the churches, painted a special grayish white, dated from colonial times. In October 1856, after his defeat in the battles of San Jacinto and Masaya, the American adventurer William Walker set the city ablaze, destroying many residences. The towers of the cathedrals burned but the shells remained intact.

The center of Granada was dominated by old one-story mansions which belonged to the landed gentry, the Spanish descendants of the conquistadores or, some said, of whores and pirates. They were surrounded by little Florentine palaces built by the nineteenth-century merchant class to re-

3

place the burned houses. These merchants filled their houses with chairs imported from Austria, marble tables and staircases from Genoa. The tradition was to buy four paintings, one of each season, to hang in the living room. In the dining room would be a picture reflecting a dead tableau from nature, unless the inhabitants were unusually pious, and then a picture of the Last Supper was hung. The one-story houses were furnished in a more austere style.

Several major avenues crossed the center of Granada—La Calle Real, La Atravezada, and La del Consulado. The middle of the city was dominated by a central park, with a fountain, small alligators, turtles, and mango trees, and by the bishop's palace and the social club of Granada. Granadans traveled through the city in carriages which are still in use today. In funeral processions the casket is carried in a black carriage drawn by white horses covered in black crepe.

It is a city of traditions. Granadans dislike change.

My grandparents talked to me always of how life once was. In Granada everyone talked about the city's past—it was the obsession of all Nicaraguan bourgeoisie, to live a life of nostalgia and memory, beautiful but embalmed—because the town had long ago entered a permanent state of decline. The rise of Managua eventually doomed Granada. León and Granada had fought for power over the centuries; neither would allow the other to be chosen as the country's permanent capital. Thus, by the mid-nineteenth century, when a capital was necessary but still not yet chosen, the dusty village of Managua, between the two cities, was selected. Over time most of Granada's mercantile families moved to the capital. Managua was an emerging city and León, which was geographically too far from Managua for an easy escape, flourished. It was also the city of President Anastasio Somoza's wife, who allowed it constant favors throughout the mid-twentieth century. Granada's riches were her memories.

For me, the keeper of those memories was Don Enrique

Guzmán, whose grandfather Fernando, the illegitimate son of a priest, was once President of Nicaragua. Don Fernando's niece was married to Tomás Martínez, a general who had fought against Walker, following which he served two terms as President and wanted another. The fact that he had himself re-elected once was a problem. Twice would have been a catastrophe.

Martínez installed Don Fernando, his wife's uncle, in the post, expecting to retake it after Fernando's term expired. However, he didn't wait until the term expired before he started agitating to regain his job. Don Fernando resisted and eventually defeated Martínez in 1869. He then resigned after his four-year term, and in so doing established a continuing tradition of non-re-election, which only lasted until 1891.

Don Fernando's son, Enrique's father, was also called Enrique. He was a famous journalist, renowned for his irreverence and iconoclasm and for his conspiracies, among which he included as a target his father. In the 1860s the senior Enrique joined with the great Liberal of Nicaragua, Máximo Jérez, against Don Fernando and the Conservative forces, although at the time he was working as his father's secretary. He did not prove a successful adversary: Jérez lost.

As Enrique grew older, he became quite conservative. Because of this political shift he became known in Nicaragua as "The Spirit of Contradiction."

By the time I knew Enrique's son he was already in his mid-seventies, living with his sister, a saint who never married and who endured her brother's terrible temper. Don Enrique was a physically unattractive man, which made life difficult in a city obsessed with appearances and facades. He was my neighbor, and he was also the local distributor of a magazine called *La Revista Conservadora,* which was essentially an archive of Nicaragua's historical families. Through the magazine, which my grandfather read regularly, I became obsessed with the past. I was a terrible student in school, but hearing about the past from those who had lived it enthralled me.

Enrique would talk to me for an hour each day. He told me of famous Granadans, particularly of my maternal grandfather and his family, the Arellanos, to whom the magazine had once devoted an entire issue. Many Arellanos, he confided, were demented.

Don Enrique took me to visit my Uncle David, who had attempted in previous years to memorize the dictionary of the Spanish Royal Academy by heart. In Nicaragua, where an obsession with intelligence had endured through the centuries, the two indications of mental prowess were thought to be the size of the brain and the size of the memory. This was said to stem from the fact that the greatest of all Nicaraguan poets, Rubén Darío, had possessed both a huge memory and a remarkably oversized head.

Uncle David was haunted. I met him when he was already mad, as he explained to me. He had always been very intelligent and remarkably verbal. Blond, blue-eyed, and preternaturally thin, David looked like a crazy man—intense circles ringed his eyes; his clothes were in disarray; he lived with his sisters and allowed them to take care of him. It is not uncommon in Nicaragua for the leftovers to live with their sisters.

My family was not troubled by David and his obsession with memorizing the dictionary. It was a harmless pastime and occupied a temper that otherwise might have become violent or unsettled. The family became perturbed, however, when David stripped off his clothes and climbed naked to the top of the house. From that vantage point he shouted random entries from the dictionary stored within his brain. There was little anyone could have done to help, so the family continued their daily lives while David wailed the dictionary out from the roof.

He didn't spend all his time outside; when he grew tired of words he climbed down again and told me stories from his memory. (He claimed his memory was so prodigious that during World War II he worked as an agent of the O.S.S.; Granada's German and Italian residents were closely monitored, and his job was to listen to their stories and repeat them verbatim to his superiors.) It was David who told me about the first renowned member of the Arellano family, a family which had lived in Nicaragua since 1768. In 1828, Narciso Arellano, a handsome womanizer, was Minister General of Nicaragua after Central American independence in 1821 (the third position of importance in the country, after Chief of State and Vice Chief of State).

While in office Don Narciso, only in his early twenties, was married to a member of the aristocratic Chamorro clan and had three daughters by her. He also had a stable relationship with his mistress, who produced two sons, Faustino and Indalecio. (My family descended from both the illegitimate sons and the legitimate daughters.) But then Don Narciso fell in love with Damiana Palacios, commonly referred to as "The Panamanian." Damiana's husband, Juan Francisco Casanova, was a Colombian who had been shot in 1828 because he had been implicated in an alleged plot to link Nicaragua with the plans of the Great Liberator, Simón Bolívar. The Panamanian believed the Chief of State was responsible for the assassination. So, it was said, she became the lover of Don Narciso because she wanted to persuade him to plot with the Vice-Chief of State against the Chief of State. Their affair produced a little girl—later known as "The Daughter of Revenge."

In 1829, Cerda was shot by Arguello. Don Narciso, to everyone's amazement, resigned his post in protest. Uncle David said that Don Narciso's lover, Damiana, was wrong to have sought the assassination. It hadn't been Cerda who had shot her husband, but rather Don Narciso himself, who had spotted The Panamanian from a distance, fallen in love with her, and so contributed to his execution.

Damiana left the country for Colombia and entrusted her

daughter to a branch of the Sacasa family living in the town of Rivas. She did not return to Nicaragua for many years, until she was traveling to the United States and her ship stopped at the port of San Juan del Sur. The Sacasas took the girl to see her mother, but Damiana could only touch her daughter's face, for by this time she was totally blind.

My Arellano ancestors continued to flirt with high drama. In 1843, while on a journey to Quimichapa, one of his cattle ranches, Narciso suffered a sudden attack of appendicitis, which at that time meant certain death. He was terrified. He carried within his soul the horrible sin of having secretly murdered his mistress' husband. The failure to confess could hurl him straight down to hell. So Narciso dispatched one of his cowhands to Acoyapa, the closest town, to locate his friend Juan Alvarado, a priest. But it took the cowhand two hours just to find the priest and then two hours to return him. Every hour on the hour Narciso sent a different cowhand to inquire what could be happening to the other cowhands and the priest.

Finally the priest arrived, just as Narciso lay dying. The man entered the room and said, How are you, my beloved Don Narciso? Narciso shouted back, Here you have me, Father Alvarado! I am here waiting for you as anxiously as King David with the weight of horrible sins on my conscience and, like King David, crying, full of remorse. You must forgive me before I die.

Standing next to her father, listening to the entire scene, was my eight-year-old Great-great-great-aunt Elena. She was profoundly affected by the revelation of past family sins. At that exact moment she offered her virginity and her soul to the Lord.

I decided I would dedicate my matrimony to the Lord and my wealth to the Church and the poor, Elena later said, in order to erase the sin of my father. There were no convents in Nicaragua at the time.

The Arellano fortunes began to decline, partly due to this

incident, and partly because Narciso's only sons were illegitimate. Elena, however, prospered. She was responsible for bringing the Salesians from Italy to Nicaragua, to replace the Jesuits, who had fallen out of favor with the Managuan government for protecting the Indians in Matagalpa.

The telegraph was the instrument of the future. In 1879 the government of Nicaragua decided to extend the telegraph out to Matagalpa, and the Indians were drafted to install the poles. They weren't paid for their labor, however, and so were less than interested in the work. At this time thirty-six Jesuits had come to Nicaragua seeking refuge from the liberal revolution in Guatemala, and Matagalpa became their hub until their expulsion in 1881. That winter, after the Jesuits were expelled, the rains began and seemed as though they would never end. The Indians believed that the deluge was caused by the ouster of those they called the "little fathers"—that when the Jesuits left, God left with them; that whenever God leaves, the Devil and his evil angels take His place. The telegraph, the Indians whispered, was bad witchcraft.

On August 4, 1881, the authorities came to inaugurate the telegraph line. Before they did, they attended church to prove that they were not godless people. But when the service ended and the ceremony began, the telegraph did not work. Six of the poles had been cut down by the Indians. In the next few days more than three thousand Indians, chanting death to the government and drunk on the notorious *chicha*, swarmed through Matagalpa until reinforcements from Managua crushed them in battle, killing five hundred. The telegraph worked from then on.

The Jesuits had not acted without self-interest, for the Indians were also busy building the Jesuit church in Matagalpa. The national government had entered into an alliance with local priests, who also wanted the Jesuits out of the country. The corrupt local priests felt threatened by their more ascetic brothers. The power of the priests and the government doomed the Jesuits. After their banishment they spent a month with my Great-aunt Elena and then sailed for Ecuador.

Elena then went to work. She had already journeyed to Rome on behalf of the Salesians. Now she traveled there twice more. On her first trip she asked John Bosco, founder of the Salesians, for a mission to replace the Jesuits. On her second trip she met with Pope Leo XIII. She was received at the Green Palace and on May 15, 1912, the Salesians arrived, twenty-four years after Elena had last visited Rome and five months after she died.

Elena is presently being canonized, the only such individual in Nicaragua's history.

Don Enrique Guzmán recalled his stories of the past for me only after 5 P.M., because he spent his early afternoons at the social club of Granada waiting to receive word of the current state of affairs. Years earlier, the club subscribed to one copy of *La Prensa*, the country's newspaper. Like everything else in Granada, the social club had enjoyed an auspicious past but now could afford only one subscription. The men sat in their rocking chairs on the terrace and discussed the world until the train carrying the newspaper arrived. The men read the paper in order. Carlos Cuadra Pasos, father of the poet Pablo Antonio Cuadra, who eventually became coeditor of *La Prensa*, was the eldest and therefore the first. Number two was José Barcenas, the Deputy Foreign Minister in the Conservative government during the 1920s. Don Enrique followed somewhat later.

As four o'clock approached, the daily conversation was repeated, like the chorus of a song. Has the train blown its whistle? Cuadra Pasos would ask José Barcenas. No, not yet, Carlos, Barcenas would reply. The men would rock. Has the train blown its whistle? Cuadra asked again. Not yet, was the reply. Now has the train blown its whistle? Yes, it has, José Barcenas would now say. Has *La Prensa* arrived yet? Cuadra would then ask. No, it has not, Barcenas would say, and the question was repeated until the answer was finally yes.

Upon its arrival, the paper was handed to Cuadra Pasos, who would scrutinize it thoroughly and then pass it along to Barcenas, who would then pass it to Don Enrique and so on. And according to Don Enrique, José Barcenas more than anything in the world wished and prayed for the day when Cuadra Pasos would die so that he could become number one.

Don Enrique talked to me of the personalities of Nicaragua. He never talked of the politics. He told me stories of how people worked, but never of their institutions—because there were no institutions. He said that Nicaragua had nothing to do with ideas. The country was all about faces. Not ideologies but personalities. He used to walk me through the walls of Jalteva, formerly the Indian neighborhood of Granada, and show me the history of the city by telling me the stories of its people.

For instance, at the walls of Jalteva he once told me how his father, Don Enrique, became a Catholic. In 1880 Don Enrique was shot point-blank by his cousin after a dispute arising from a newspaper article. He took one bullet in the leg and one in the chest, and spent seventy-two days under the care of Doña Elena. Don Enrique had been a famous radical, which in Nicaragua meant an anticleric. Doña Elena took advantage of his condition and for the first time since his childhood Don Enrique made a confession; he was immediately pinned with two medals, of Pius XI and the Virgin Mary Immaculate. Don Enrique then began to attend services at La Merced, and eventually the man known as "The Spirit of Contradiction" denounced liberalism.

Don Enrique, the son, also told me of President José Santos Zelaya, the man who seized power in 1893 and kept it until the threat of an occupation by the United States Marines forced him to abdicate in 1909. He spoke of how Zelaya considered the Miskito Indians of the Caribbean coast an annoyance and how, in 1894, he decided to remove their leader, Chief "King" Clarence, from power.

The British, since 1640, had considered the Caribbean coast their own domain. In 1670 they took a Miskito Indian, Oldman, to Jamaica and crowned him as king. The event was so overwhelming that Oldman was panic-stricken. He observed the elaborate preparations and assumed that the foreigners must be planning his death. So he sought refuge on top of a coconut tree until he was coaxed down to the ground. Afterward the Miskitos maintained some autonomy over their land with British support. But in 1894 General Zelaya took Bluefields, the major city of the Miskitos' homeland on the Caribbean coast, and rid himself of Chief Clarence. The chief went into exile in Panama.

The British were furious. The Nicaraguans, it was rumored, had roughed up the British consul. So the British dispatched warships to Bluefields and the Nicaraguans were forced to retreat. (Eventually, as the United States became the area's hegemonic power, the British departed.) But the Nicaraguans were called upon to settle accounts with the British, who asked for fifteen thousand pounds sterling, to redress the abuse of a civilized man by a small, half-civilized country.

The incident infuriated Granadans, rich and poor alike. It was a slight to Nicaraguan honor. Granada's local playboy, "Cabo" Hilario, a Liberal and a pro-Zelaya man, had been a sailor who lived for some time in England. He played billiards all day and wore pants that reached only to his mid-thighs and he had what Don Enrique called "happy eyes." He was crazy for women. He boasted tirelessly of his conquests, and when he returned from England he mentioned offhandedly that he had been the lover of Queen Victoria.

Everyone in Granada believed him. And so when the protests against the English swept through the town the placards read, "Down with the Mistress of Cabo Hilario."

By early evening Don Enrique tired of telling me stories. He would then walk purposefully to a small room between his living room and the dim bedroom, where he stored a rotted wooden trunk, which held the collected remnants of his life: old letters, his father's articles, the presidential sash once worn by his grandfather. From inside the trunk he would retrieve an ancient picture of an angel and a naked woman. The woman was touching the angel's genitals but Don Enrique's eyesight failed him so he could only remember the picture. He could not see it. Each day he would ask, my child, is she touching his organ? Yes, I would say. Ahh, he'd reply, and then he'd fall back in his chair and drift into sleep.

In Granada neither social prominence nor craziness was dictated by money. Both were rampant, although lunacy was more so.

Across the street from my grandparents lived the four Urbina sisters. This particular street was the Avenue of the Funerals, where at 4 P.M. funeral processions used to march past. The Urbinas' house dominated the block. We called them "Picos," for they always had beautifully painted lips and powdered white hair and lovely dresses. We also called them *niñas*, because they were either unmarried or widows. As regularly as the rising moon, late each afternoon they appeared outside their walls to sit and watch the funerals pass. Death in Granada was frequent and when we knew a funeral was planned we would race the streets to discover who had died, although almost always Miguel, the shoeshine man at the corner, knew. Miguel was very, very skinny, he always wore a baseball cap, and though he spent his days working on others' shoes, he never wore them himself. His wife later died giving birth because he could not convince a doctor to leave a baseball game and attend to her.

The gathering on the corner was also joined by "El Poeta" Suazo, who was called a poet because he never worked a day in his life. El Poeta arrived at the funerals smelling like roses, as this would be his first activity of the day after awakening and soaking in a scented bath. He always watched the funerals and would ask, of no one in particular, "Why is it that we never see a Chinaman buried in Nicaragua?"

The Cuadra sisters set our town's standards for mourners. The colors of mourning progressed from black to gray to white. The two Cuadras were descendants of the family of Carlos Cuadra Pasos and they were very wealthy. When they were children they were given presents every hour in order to alleviate the boredom of the town. Eventually they lost their money through mismanagement.

I have never seen people suffer so much as they did when their mother died. Their grief was so profound, it did not allow for a wake. Our wakes tended to degenerate into social gatherings and the Cuadras did not wish anyone to enjoy himself at death's expense. They wore black for six years. Each day they went to mass twice—they received special permission from the bishop to receive communion twice a day. Then one day they switched to white—I remember the morning because I was the first to announce that the sisters had changed colors. They wore white for four more years. None of us could ever match this grief.

The Urbina family was noted for the remarkable crime of their brother Manuel. He had murdered his brother Coronado. For years Granadans said that Manuel's wife had been carrying on an affair with Coronado. Don Manuel was a very proud man. He never owed a cent to anyone, and his home was huge but more austerely furnished than his neighbors' houses because he was a solid, humorless man. He always wore a pistol and settled his disputes the honorable way—by dueling.

Coronado Urbina was the opposite of his brother. He was gay, happy, witty. Don Manuel loved Coronado very much.

One Saturday afternoon, according to the story told by Don Manuel, the brothers were going to the cockfights. Don

Manuel decided to discover whether it was true his brother was having an affair with his wife. So he instructed Coronado to return home for the cock spurs, which Don Manuel feigned to have forgotten. He then followed his brother.

The spurs were kept on top of the *ropero*, a cabinet so high that Coronado had to lift his sister-in-law off the ground to reach the top. When Don Manuel arrived at the unfortunate time, he saw his brother holding his wife and this was enough proof for him that the rumors were true. He instructed Coronado to leave town immediately, or he would kill him. Coronado did not believe his brother. Two days after the warning, Don Manuel spotted Coronado riding in a carriage near his house. He walked over to the man handling the carriage and instructed him to stop. He then drew his pistol from his holster and shot his brother dead.

Don Manuel kicked his wife out of their home and never mentioned her name again. Every day he would talk about Coronadito as though he were alive. Have you seen Coronado? he would ask. No, people answered. You shot him. Then Don Manuel's reality realigned. If he ever comes back I will kill him again, he would say.

Don Manuel was never put in jail. He was never tried because he was never arrested. He had committed a crime of honor. So the law did not reproach him. Crimes of honor were seldom prosecuted. Besides, he was a Somocista, a follower of Somoza.

But the Urbinas were marked for life. Everyone always remembered them as the sisters whose brother killed their brother.

Don Manuel never liked me but he tolerated me sufficiently to advise me on the faithlessness of all women. He wasn't rich enough to send his sons to the United States for their education, so he sent them to Mexico. One of them, Chester, married a woman named Mecha in Mexico and brought her back to Granada, where she gave birth to three children. Not long after her arrival in Granada, Mecha began to have an affair: Freddy, Don Manuel's youngest son, saw the man entering their house while Chester was working. Freddy told Don Manuel. Don Manuel went to the house with a pistol and pounded on the door until the man had to climb out on the roof and run naked down the street.

As a result of this incident it was decided in Granada that Mexican women were whores. Then another young Granadan, a dentist, traveled to Mexico and returned with a Mexican wife who gave birth to eleven children and proved to be faithful while her husband carried on numerous affairs. At that moment Mexican women were rehabilitated, from whores to saints.

Granada's Father Vilchez was always convinced that Coronado had indeed had an affair with his brother's wife. Coronado's mass took place in the Church of La Merced, with Father Vilchez in charge. During the ceremony, while he was pouring the holy water on the coffin, Vilchez muttered to himself, quite audibly, what am I doing wasting my time with this son of a bitch? He is going straight to hell.

My father and mother lived in the small coffee town of Jinotepe, with a population somewhere between ten and fifteen thousand. To grow coffee the land must be shady and the altitude high and so the air in Jinotepe was fresh and pure. Huge trees shaded the coffee fields around the city and the temperature was cool. Jinotepe, because it was less wealthy than the larger cities, did not suffer the same social divisions as Granada and León—it was a town of small property owners and the newer professional class such as my father, who ran the local branch office of the Nicaraguan Bank, the first major private bank in the country.

My mother's family was more of the gentry, my father was of the emerging bourgeoisie. My mother believed life centered around the family, whereas my father looked beyond the family to the institution and the concept of public service independent of family needs. I grew up torn between love of the family and the obligation to serve the country.

My father seldom lied, even to children. At Christmas, when I would wonder why only the rich children received presents, he simply told me that *Niño Jesús*—our equivalent of Santa Claus—did not exist. He instead explained to us the causes of poverty and the need for change.

He tried to make us contribute in any way possible. For a time the family lived in Honduras. While we did, my father would buy all seven of us children an ice cream cone every Saturday. Then, each week, one of us would have to give his or her cone away to a poor child. I admired my father greatly for six of every seven weeks.

Despite the increasing complications of public life, he preferred simplicity. He felt happiest when he was taking care of a small plot of land in the middle of Jinotepe, where he tried to grow fruit. He was a terrible gardener. Inundated by his inner thoughts, he was the sort who often forgot whom he was addressing or what he was doing. Office work, however, held him in thrall; he could work for hours longer than anyone else. So often did he work through the weekends that my mother started hiding his shoes on Saturdays to keep him home. Instead he went to work in sandals.

All seven of us children appeared within the space of ten years. We compared our rapid appearances to the quick rhythms of the marimba. I was the first beat of the marimba and so, when I wasn't being loaned out to my mother's relatives in Granada, I was sent off to relatives in Jinotepe—the Asenjo sisters.

My great-grandmother was an Asenjo, one of the few wealthy local families. I think my mother hoped that if I behaved myself properly I would become their heir. Even though my parents lived a few blocks away, I spent many days with these sisters. Aunt Angela I don't remember well, for when I was only a year old she was already dying. To make her feel better the sisters used to lay me in her deathbed for hours to let Aunt Angela feel the warmth of life yet to be lived as she passed to the next world.

The Asenjos' riches derived from their father's skills as both a merchant and an exploiter. He was famous in town for two things: the way he cheated his peasants and the way he raised his daughters. Both peasants and daughters lived in abject submission. If Cleto Asenjo owed a peasant ten pesos, he would pay him, one peso for you, one peso for me, until he had paid the man five pesos.

Cleto Asenjo's house reminded me of a convent. His daughters were its nuns and men, especially young men, were its enemies—I was too young to be considered a man. It was a dramatic home, filled with old women who seldom saw a man. The only masculine presences in the house were the two old gardeners and they were dismissed every day at six o'clock.

Serving the family women were the "Daughters of the House," the daughters of local peasants who were given to the Asenjos so they could be provided with a rigorous Christian education and social manners in return for their service. It was an inexpensive method of recruiting domestic help.

One of the Asenjo maids gave birth to a daughter, who was raised in the Asenjo home as though she were an Asenjo. When the daughter sat at the table to eat, her mother could wait on her but could not talk to her.

According to family legend, once, in the early 1900s, Cleto Asenjo had to leave Jinotepe on business, to sell his merchandise in El Salvador. As always, he departed leaving strict orders that the doors of the house should not be opened at night, not for anyone, not at any time.

Cleto Asenjo drove his mules off to El Salvador at 4:00 P.M. Toward nightfall, an immense rainstorm broke out and the muddy roads became impassable. Instead of continuing his trip Cleto Asenjo decided it would be wisest to return home and start again the following morning. It took him over three hours to reach his front door. By that time the house was totally dark and the doors were locked tight. Open the doors, Cleto Asenjo commanded. Nothing happened. Open my doors, he shouted. But the doors remained shut. Cleto Asenjo spent the night in the rain, waiting for the daughters to obediently reopen their gates the next morning at dawn.

Of the six Asenjo sisters, three eventually married, only two of those for love. One of these was Isabel Asenjo, my great-grandmother. Her marriage to Nicolás Ximenez took place against her father's will. He had decided that none of his younger daughters would be permitted to marry until the oldest had completed her vows. The problem with this was that no Asenjo girl could ever become betrothed since the eldest daughter, Angela, was so ugly as to be legendary throughout Jinotepe.

Cleto Asenjo also raised four boys, blond, nice-looking boys, young men who were sent to study medicine in Germany. None of them returned. One of them, Máximo, according to Jinotepe lore, became the doctor of Adolf Hitler.

The sisters' days were enveloped in prayer and meditation; but it was whispered through the town that behind the closed gates they sat and accumulated their capital. The town imagined that the sisters were so rich that every day at four in the afternoon the daughters of the house brought dozens of baskets brimming with paper currency out from the house into the gardens to let the money see the light of day. Otherwise it would rot.

The women's conversation was filled with animated talk about the dead. Spirits were very real to these women—and therefore to me. When the sisters described the flames of hell, they saw them in front of their eyes, burning and smoking. They believed that the Devil roamed the streets of Jinotepe at night. During Holy Week they would drape medals over my body to protect me from the Devil, who for those seven days prowled the streets looking for young boys to abduct into hell. During rainstorms, they gave me small straw crosses to protect me from random lightning.

Most of all, the sisters made me pray for the soul of my Uncle Pancho. Pancho married my Aunt Innocenta when the couple were both in their sixties. He had a reputation as a sinner and womanizer, but he was a good man and, once married, a reformed one. "Chenta" dominated Pancho. He loved to play cards with his friends. When he stayed out past seven in the evening Chenta would send her maid Victoria to fetch her husband. Tell him it is time to go, Chenta would say, and then she would give Victoria Pancho's hat and umbrella, in case it was raining. Pancho always took the hat and umbrella quietly and followed Victoria back home to Chenta.

The sisters did not have a radio nor did they go out to see movies. They did nothing every night except pray for the souls of their father, their mother, and Pancho, who died when I was seven, in 1961. Even though he had redeemed himself through marriage, he had accumulated so many previous sins that prayer was needed to reduce the amount of time he spent in purgatory. I prayed with the sisters nightly and so in my life I have prayed more for the soul of the womanizer Uncle Pancho than for anything or anyone else in my life.

My Great-aunt Sipria, the sister of my Grandmother Adela, married a gentleman from León. This is the ultimate sin that can be committed by a daughter of Granada. When I was a teenager, I used to visit her in León. Through these visits I learned to understand the rivalry between the two great cities.

Granada was situated by Lake Nicaragua with access to the sea. It was an outward-looking city, active in international trade. Granada knew how to turn leisure into an art. It was a city of hedonists, iconoclasts, and merchants, a city built to live in rather than to work in.

León, seventy-five miles away, was totally isolated from the rest of the world. It was a more reverential city, in love with formal processions and pomp. The men of León were hard-working. They had earned rather than inherited their wealth. They had less imagination and less time to dream. Granada was inventive, León industrious; Granada was luxurious, León pragmatic. Granada was where projects were initiated, but León was where they were carried to fruition. Even the great family of León, the Sacasas, came originally from Granada but flourished in León.

Léon was also famous for its duels. Its citizens had violent tempers and resorted frequently to guns. Not a Sunday went by without someone being shot. The Granada cemetery was beautiful, graceful. The León cemetery was slowly sinking, the Leonese said, because of all the lead in the corpses.

Sipria's house in León was close to the cathedral. She lived next to an old colonial mansion once owned by Colonel Zavala, who was infamous for his cruelty to the Indians. The house was rumored to be haunted and was filled with old papers and even original manuscripts by the great Rubén Darío that had been abandoned to time by his relatives, who had long since left the city.

Zavala was rumored to have employed Indians to dig huge holes in his cattle ranches near Lake Managua in order to bury his treasures. After the Indians had dug the holes, he killed them. The legend continued that after his death, as his soul was not permitted to enter heaven, Zavala rode a horse through León in the middle of the night to guard his treasures, returning to the dead at daybreak. During my childhood the milkmen of León were cowboys who rode into town from the country every morning. They would enter the city at around five, and we would say, Listen to that, Zavala is making a huge racket this morning—he must be very angry.

Sipria's main function in life was to clean the wooden

saints in the cathedral, the biggest in Central America. The cathedral's size angered Granadans, who used to say that the real plans for the cathedral were lost on their route from Spain, and this one, obviously designed for the finer city of Lima, Peru, mistakenly replaced them. Sipria was in charge of buying dresses for the saints, cleaning the statues, and also for washing the laundry of the priests and bishops. She adored her work. She was religious, obsessed with cleanliness and whiteness, and always carried an umbrella to protect her fair head and white hair from the sun.

On my third visit to León, I arrived just as the poet Alfonso Cortés was dying. It was 1969, during Holy Week. The entire town turned out for the seventy-six-year-old man's funeral. A lyricist, the tender, introspective Cortés had never left Nicaragua. He had been the sole male in his family, and he was not permitted to forsake his sisters, all unmarried, with whom he lived. He could not go out to work without leaving his sisters alone, so he didn't. He soon became insane to escape from the boredom of day-to-day life in León.

His lunacy eventually became unmanageable and for many years his family stored him in a Managua madhouse until the gentlemen of León decided to return the poet to his sisters. They placed him in a room where he was provided food through a little window in a wooden door, and through the window he could see a patch of sky beyond. In one of his most famous poems he wrote:

A little piece of blue more intense than all the sky.
I feel that there lives, flowering, ecstatic happiness
    and desire.

A wind of spirits passes far beyond my window, carrying
    a breeze that stirs the flesh of angelic Diana.

And in the spilling sweetness of these signs,
    drunk of azure, I sense boiling up mad pretext,
    that being here, from there, they beckon.

In the historical mind of León, the 1916 funeral of Rubén Darío—who had returned to Nicaragua in order to die at home—was *the* great Nicaraguan funeral, the one which set an example for all to follow. At the time Santiago Arguello, the greatest living Nicaraguan intellectual, gave a speech widely considered the apotheosis of funeral oration. Now everyone in León wished to give a similar speech, wished to be remembered as the great funeral orator.

But Cortés died slowly; as the city waited until the end, more and more signed on to the list of orators to bid public farewell to the poet. The head of the federation of poets, the federation of workers, the federation of artists, the men of the great families, the mayor, the doctor, all signed on to speak.

In most of Nicaragua, two speeches framed every funeral —one when the funeral party left the house, and one at the burial itself. But in León there was a speech for every occasion. And so when Cortés finally passed away, the town's official list of orators was interminable. Even on the way to the cathedral men would halt the funeral procession and say, Stop. How can the poet go without my saying farewell? And yet another speech was given.

Cortés was finally buried in the late afternoon. Fortunately, after his interment his skull remained fully intact, unlike Rubén Darío's—whose brain had been removed. Darío's superb intelligence haunted Nicaragua's educated classes, who became obsessed with the size of his head, which was considered abnormally large. After his death his wife, Rosario Murillo, authorized the removal of her husband's brain to allow scientists to study the organ. The brain was subsequently stolen from the doctors. A debate still rages over the whereabouts of Darío's brain.

Darío had left Nicaragua for Europe and South America to find fame and recognition. But he returned home to die. As he lay on his deathbed the worldly poet who had abandoned religion for his art called for a priest. He wanted to make a final confession.

His friends tried to dissuade him but Darío was determined. He had returned home, after all, to die in the shelter of his Nicaraguan past, comforted by a priest, an expression of the world he had once rejected, who stood over him and then closed his eyes.

2

Dealing
with the Dictators

My grandfather on my father's side, Arturo Cruz, was from the same town as the Asenjo sisters, Jinotepe. He was a self-made man. As a boy he had sold newspapers in the street and eventually worked his way up into business. My grandfather was very thin, he always wore a Spanish beret, and he was obsessed with biblical history. He was so taken with Israel that he became a biblical scholar. When he wasn't studying Israel, he studied Wilson and Franklin Delano Roosevelt. He was staunchly pro-American.

Like the Somozas, his family was from the region of Carazo, the province which provided many of the men who dominated the century's politics. President Zelaya's ascent to power at the end of the nineteenth century symbolized the end of the long hegemony of Granada and León. Somoza's family came from San Marcos, General José María Moncada from Masatepe, General Augusto César Sandino from Niquinohomo—all small towns, geographically close, all men with similar backgrounds, they were rural petit bourgeois, and all members of the Liberal Party. My grandfather left the Liberal Party when it was taken over by Somoza.

People always used to tell me how much my grandfather and the first Somoza resembled each other. It wasn't until years later that I discovered the two men were, in fact, second cousins—my great-grandmother was a Sánchez, her other name was Reyes, and Somoza's father was her cousin, Anastasio Somoza Reyes.

No one in my family ever discussed this relationship because my grandfather was such a rabid anti-Somocista. He did not consider it a contradiction that he loved the United States and hated Somoza. The Americans' support of Somoza, he thought, simply stemmed from the stupidity of the local American ministers, with whom he could never maintain a good relationship.

My grandfather also reviled Sandino, who he felt was simply one more bandit, scarcely a serious man of the people; he said both Somoza and Sandino abused power. My grandfather was in love with the concept of parliamentary procedure and citizens' rights.

He could never fathom the reason for the popularity of his enemy Somoza. During every Somoza rally in Jinotepe the revelers would gather in front of my grandfather's house and shout insults at him. My grandfather would enter the garden, survey them with disdain, and then calmly re-enter the house.

The Somozas understood how to forge friendships when

they needed them. They had helped create and then aided the newly emerging middle class. As the national budget grew, so did support for the Somozas. If there was anything that each of the three ruling Somozas never let anyone else handle, it was the budget patronage. Each Somoza oversaw even the appointment of the most obscure teacher or electrical meter reader. Everything economic was an act of personal politics. As the budget grew, as its payroll grew, so did the number of Somoza's supporters and the enmity of my grandfather.

In part this was caused by the death of my Uncle Adolfo, my grandfather's son-in-law, who was killed in 1954 after an assassination attempt on the general failed. The legend is that my uncle was killed by Somoza's son Tachito, and then his body was burned. A wooden box in my Aunt Lilian's room contained his ashes, but we really never knew what, if anything, the box contained.

The city of León continued to flourish after Managua was chosen as the new capital, not only because of its location and its more industrious nature but also because Somoza granted continual favors to the city. León was the home of his wife; Granada was the home of his enemies. Somoza himself had come to León as a young man to find his fortune. In the 1920s one of the richest families in the country were the Sánchezes, who had become wealthy from land, usury, and intelligent marriages. Somoza was a nephew of the Sánchezes. When he arrived in León he looked up his relatives and they found him work in the electrical company. Not long after his arrival Somoza met Salvadora Debayle Sacasa, the daughter of a French doctor from León's foremost family. Somoza fell in love.

Salvadora's father was horrified at the prospect that his flower of the aristocracy might marry this tolerably handsome but penniless upstart from the country. The young girl was rushed off to Philadelphia to live there with two women from León, Ernestina and Tulita. They happened to be members of the Sánchez family, however, and proved to be more sympathetic to the cause of "love" than the whims of the Sacasas. Somoza got his Sánchez uncle to send him to Philadelphia to study. He started to date Salvadora and the affair was consummated. Salvadora became crazy for Somoza, who, returning to León, asked Dr. Debayle for the hand of the princess of León.

Dr. Debayle said no.

Thereupon Somoza went to his uncle, Fernando Sánchez, who in turn called on Dr. Debayle. How are you, Doctor? He asked. Fine, was the answer. Well then, Sánchez continued, if my nephew is not good enough for your daughter, my money is not good enough for you. He called in his outstanding debts. No, no, no, said Dr. Debayle. You misunderstand me, we would be overjoyed to have your young Mr. Somoza join our family. And so the marriage between the city and the countryside, between old money and new, took place and the debt was forgiven. The grip of the historical cities on the towns was loosened and Somoza entered the aristocracy without ever being assimilated into it.

In 1933 Salvadora's uncle, Juan Bautista Sacasa, became President of the country. Somoza was made head of the National Guard, a force which had been created by the United States Marines in their own image, to maintain order in their absence. Sacasa needed a trusted relative for the position, but his family was not distinguished by a reputation for bravery. Somoza was convenient; he was already in the army and was married to Sacasa's beloved niece. It was also widely believed at the time that he was having an affair with the wife of the American minister to Managua. It was said that the minister under the influence of his wife, approved the appointment. Three years later, in 1936, Somoza overthrew Sacasa and took over the government.

León was the epitome of clan politics in Nicaragua. The Sacasas, the Argüellos, the Herdocias, the Salinases, all played with the power of politics: they appointed judges, mayors, clerks, and tax collectors. Somoza allowed the locals of León to maintain control of their patronage during his reign, so as to keep his wife's relatives content.

Crisanto Sacasa, the grand old man of León, was a cousin of the first Somoza's wife and the uncle of the last two ruling Somozas. I remember Don Crisanto as an old-fashioned gentleman. The Sacasas did not resemble other Nicaraguans but were considered more like the Costa Ricans, in both physiognomy and temperament. Nicaraguans tend to equate politeness with hypocrisy. We say what we think. Costa Ricans are much more polite and much less honest. The Sacasas always had a kind word for everyone, young or old, rich or poor. We assumed they were hypocrits.

Don Crisanto used to hold court in his house throughout the day with the exception of his lunch, his siesta, and his supper. He was the chief of the political department of León but he never went to his office. Depending upon social standing, petitioners were allowed into different rooms of the house. Every day flocks of people waited patiently to see Don Crisanto, sitting in different chambers throughout the residence, talking, reading, gossiping—some in the corridors, some in the private rooms.

In the older cities of Nicaragua, inside the cavernous bedrooms, a cloth hammock was used for siestas, rather than the bed. Or before going to sleep in the bed a brief rest in the hammock prepared the body for the mood of sleep. The most socially acceptable petitioners were received by Don Crisanto in his hammock, in his bedroom. My Aunt Sipria's husband Manuel was among those. During my pilgrimages to León I would be taken into Don Crisanto's bedroom where I would watch him swing languidly in the hammock. The man spent the entire day in his V-necked cotton pajamas (the Leónese were too miserly for silk), parceling out favors, distributing scholarships, getting people out of jail. His favorite pastime was to grant permissions for church processions.

Don Crisanto's sister would stand outside the house to watch who came and went. Once I joined her and her friends, all sitting on comfortably stuffed chairs in the mild daytime heat. At one point I remember a peasant woman selling fruits walked past. Don Crisanto's sister said, oh, hello, my dear, dear love. How is your mother doing? She just died, was the reply. Oh, my God, my God, the sister said, I am so sorry. Please give my love to everyone in your family, you mean so much to me. After the fruit seller left, the sister turned to us and asked, who on earth was that woman?

After Somoza deposed his wife's uncle, the Sacasa family split into pro-Somoza and anti-Somoza camps. Most Sacasas became Somocistas, although a few had the dignity to resent the betrayal. Both sides of my family were anti-Somocista, but for different reasons.

My mother's family was related to the former leaders of Granada, who constituted the bastion of the Conservative Party which had ruled the country from 1858 to 1893. All these presidents from this era were modestly wealthy men who conceived of the office of the presidency as a burden; they were reluctant to assume the responsibilities of state. My mother's grandfather viewed the Liberal revolutionary President Zelaya as an abomination; the man belonged to neither León nor Granada.

Zelaya was Nicaragua's first true despot, the first to create the apparatus of the organized state—a permanent bureaucracy, a modern army, a bicoastal navy, with small boats in the Caribbean and the Pacific. He was also the first to struggle with the only national institution, the Church. Zelaya took from the Church and gave to the state the social responsibilities the clerics had come to consider theirs during the Conservative administrations. By the same token, Zelaya also created the first significant national debt, as the government did not have the resources to pay for these services.

The numerous civil and foreign wars during his tenure also contributed to the huge deficit.

My Grandfather Cruz thought well of Zelaya, and one of his brothers died fighting in one of Zelaya's wars. But my grandfather could not abide Somoza, who he thought represented the death of the liberal state. Somoza represented the triumph of personal over constitutional rule. My mother's side of the family was repelled by Somoza's geographical origins, my father's family worried more about the democratic system of checks and balances.

My father learned to loathe Somoza from an early age, just as I did. He was at Georgetown University in Washington, D.C., at the time of the Marshall Plan, which he thought was the most glorious moment of American foreign policy. He felt he had lived through the American re-creation of the world.

Somoza jailed my father for the first time in 1947, the year he placed a puppet in the office of the presidency (while remaining head of the National Guard). America, triumphant in World War II, expressed its dissatisfaction with surviving dictators such as Somoza by recalling its ambassador from Nicaragua in 1947. Somoza had to respond with a gesture of democracy, so he appointed a grandee of the Liberal Party, a man named Leonardo Argüello, to succeed him as President.

Argüello did not prove to be quite as docile as the general had thought. But, luckily for Somoza, he was not as astute either. Argüello announced on the day of his inauguration that he was prepared to send Somoza to Europe as a diplomat. I.e., into exile. It would have been difficult to find a better way to alert Somoza to his agenda. Within a few weeks Somoza mounted a successful coup against Argüello. Several men, including my father, joined Argüello in the futile struggle against Somoza.

The primary conspirators were the Aguirre brothers, two young, ambitious men who were close to Somoza, responsible for logistics of the National Guard and internal security.

They organized the coup efficiently; and it might even have worked had it not been for Argüello.

In old Managua the President's residence and the home of the head of the National Guard stood next to each other, the President to the left looking toward the lake, the National Guard's commander to the right. That night in 1947, three weeks after Argüello's inauguration, the Aguirres and Argüello invited Somoza and his family to a formal dinner.

Somoza was said even by his detractors to possess one great virtue: he listened to everyone, regardless of how humble their position. If the maids talked to him he sat and he listened. Once a week, as he was being shaved, anyone in the National Guard, of any rank, could come and talk to the chief and he listened.

Now, on the way to the limousine waiting to drive them the one-minute route to the dinner—walking was in poor taste—one of the lesser National Guardsmen approached Somoza and said, Boss, you should not go to that house.

Somoza asked why.

Because, the man answered, there are some men in the gardens waiting for you with submachine guns.

Somoza asked his son Luís and his aide Luís Ocón to check the story. Upon their return they corroborated it. Somoza walked back into his official residence as commander-in-chief of the National Guard and called every military installation in the country to make sure he was still in control.

In the meantime, those at the President's house kept calling. Where is Somoza? The dinner is getting cold. The President is waiting.

The Somoza residence informed them that the party was almost ready. Any second. In a moment. On its way. One more minute. Finally, when Somoza was ready to surround the President, he did. And at 3 A.M., Somoza called the American embassy to inform him that he was asking Argüello to resign.

My father, one of the conspirators, was thrown into prison for four months.

The Somoza rule was marked by these incessant coup attempts and by such incidents as the sinking of the largest boat on Lake Granada, the *Victoria,* which belonged to the Southern Pacific Railway Company. Somoza decided he wanted a boat on Lake Nicaragua. He had one brought overland and christened it the *General Somoza.*

The lake has no fog and no obstructions on its entire 8000-square-kilometer surface. Nonetheless some years later the only two boats on the water managed to collide. The *General Somoza* sank and the superstitious Somoza became terrified because everyone was saying to him, General, your time must be over.

Somoza went to the lake, examined the wreck, and launched a rescue operation, eventually raising the ship from the lake bottom. It was never really the same, although when I was younger we used to visit the lake on Sunday afternoons to see the wreck of the *General Somoza.*

My father was also involved in the 1954 coup attempt, in which my Uncle Adolfo was killed. Every Sunday morning Somoza used to go visit his sugar mill in Montelimar, near the Pacific, where the mill was being modernized with equipment from Europe. To get to Montelimar, Somoza had to drive over the Southern Highway, a road which twisted up through the coffee hills and then back down to the ocean. Twenty would-be assassins were waiting for him ten miles down the road.

For hours the men waited in the cool coffee groves. It turned out that Somoza was indeed touring his sugar mill but had learned of the plot. He returned with his son Luís in a plain black car which belonged to his relative, Luís Pallais —an engineer at Montelimar—instead of traveling in the presidential limousine.

Nearby, in one of Somoza's summer houses, the family

was celebrating the birthday of a Somoza grandson. Among the would-be assassins was a Honduran named Jorge Rivas. He knew the location of the house and suggested they transfer the assassination party to the summer house and kidnap the children. My Uncle Adolfo refused. He did not want children to be hurt.

Someone had walked into El Hormiguero, the notorious police headquarters, earlier that day and told the authorities of the plot. They hunted down the conspirators and Uncle Adolfo was captured in Las Cuatro Esquinas, as he was trying to go to Costa Rica; he had disregarded my father's advice to seek refuge in one of the embassies in Managua. When they captured him, the officers hadn't a clue what to do with him. Adolfo had been an army officer, he had studied at Guatemala's Polytechnic, the best military academy in Central America, and Somoza had loved him. He'd once served as Somoza's personal aide.

Luís Pallais was notified that his friend Adolfo had been captured and went to see him. Adolfo gave Pallais his ring and gold cross and asked him to give them to my Aunt Lilian. Pallais then went to Managua and asked Somoza not to kill Adolfo. Somoza agreed. Pallais then waited outside Somoza's office through the night. Adolfo was to be transferred, said Somoza, to the Presidential Palace from Las Cuatro Esquinas.

Early the next morning Somoza stormed into Pallais' room, shouting, those sons of bitches, they have killed Adolfo! Some people still think Somoza's son Tachito was responsible. Who else could reverse a Somoza edict? But others say Somoza himself was only acting as though he were upset.

My father, who had managed to get back to Jinotepe, was sent to jail for the second time, for fourteen months. That was the way it worked. A man who was captured in the city was jailed. A man caught in the countryside was killed.

The assassination took place in 1956. At the height of his

rule, Somoza traveled to León for a party in his honor at the workers' club. The intelligence agents of Captain Oscar Morales, a favorite of Somoza, alerted him to the possibility of an assassination attempt. Morales implored Salvadora Somoza to have her husband skip the party. She tried but Somoza felt invulnerable. He had survived a dozen coups, the Americans had made their peace with him, a cordial Eisenhower was in the White House, the economy was robust, and Perón of Argentina was turning out to be a good friend. Somoza even refused to wear his bulletproof vest; it made him feel too claustrophobic.

To plot the death of Somoza was the national pastime. It was a national anthem that the revolution would come any minute. The rumor in 1956 was that former President Figueres of Costa Rica had sent a hunchback to Nicaragua to kill his old rival Somoza. The week Somoza went to campaign for an election in Ocotal, a northern Nicaraguan cattle town, the head of the government security apparatus had ordered that any hunchback sighted would be shot first and questioned later. It was just another rumor.

Rigoberto López Pérez was a poet, a mystical, religious man, an anarchist with a touch of romanticism, a man overwhelmed by a sense of mission. The mission was to kill the tyrant. Rigoberto was the one who finally shot Somoza. He came from the El Calvario neighborhood in León and had lived in El Salvador for many years, where a dissatisfied émigré cadre of National Guard officers bought him a .38 revolver and gave him the names of the Leónese who would aid him.

Rigoberto decided to trade his life for Somoza's. Money was collected by telling people that a man had come from El Salvador to kill Somoza. To prove that he was serious Rigoberto would display the .38 with its five poisoned bullets. He would also prove his sincerity by indulging in constant rehearsals. The conspirators would hail a taxi and drive from León to the seaside resort of Poneloya, where they re-

peatedly walked into the countryside and practiced by shooting a silk handkerchief. They shot low, as though firing under a table. By showing the shot-up handkerchiefs, they
raised more money for more bullets.

The conspiracy was talked about throughout León but everyone was always talking about killing Somoza. The officer
in charge of the León barracks paid no heed.

Early in September Somoza traveled to Panama for a
meeting of the Central American presidents. Rigoberto went
along too but he couldn't get close enough to Somoza to fire.
That same month Nicaragua celebrated the first centennial
of the national war against William Walker. Rigoberto tried
again and failed.

On September 21 Somoza was scheduled to attend two
events: the Liberal convention for the presidential nomination and a party in his honor at the workers' club. Rigoberto
rescheduled his plot for that evening. The plan was that the
men would rent taxicabs which would flick their lights to
signal the other conspirators to cut off the current at the
electrical works. This would create confusion, allowing
Rigoberto to escape. Yes, my chances are slim, Rigoberto
liked to say, but don't forget that I am insured for eight thousand dollars with the Pan American Life Insurance Company
in the name of my mother.

Somoza danced all through the night, first with his wife,
then with the local women. Then he danced with a local
beauty pageant winner. Between eleven-twenty and eleven-
thirty, while he was resting, one of Somoza's cronies approached him with newspapers and asked him to read about
local politics. Somoza picked up the paper and looked
through it. Just then Rigoberto walked up and shot Somoza
five times, through the paper.

A bodyguard hiding beneath the table fired the first of hun-
dreds of shots into Rigoberto's body.

Salvadora Somoza took over immediately. Her husband
was badly wounded. The children, then in their late twenties

and early thirties, were terrified but Salvadora proved stronger than anyone could have suspected, rallying the family behind her and re-establishing calm. President Eisenhower had offered a private doctor and medical care in the Canal Zone. The Somoza children wanted to accompany their father on the plane. Cowards! Salvadora shouted at them. She forced her children to remain behind, sending them to Managua's main military installation, "The Hill." Somoza himself was moved to Managua by helicopter and then flown to the Canal Zone. A rumor quickly spread throughout the country that while Somoza was dying no one dared attend to him, for fear that if he then died, the last man to touch the general would be blamed. Somoza did not receive any serious medical attention until he was transported out of the country.

He remained alive in the Canal Zone until September 28. Or so the country was told. No one knew whether it was true. But the mere fact that the country thought he was still alive allowed for a smooth transition from Somoza to his older son. The Senate appointed Colonel Luís Somoza President, on September 28, to complete his father's term.

Luís' first problem was the issue of Colonel Gaitán, the most popular soldier in the army, a huge, fat mestizo who had fought against Sandino. Gaitán was the logical choice to succeed Somoza. He claimed that he had received a letter from the conspirators, who thought that he would be willing to ally with their scheme. He wasn't, Gaitán said. He showed the letter to Somoza himself, who said, son, they are trying to trick you into being an accomplice. Don't worry, we will put the letter in a safe. The government safes were now ransacked for the letter but it could not be found. Some say Gaitán was involved and his story was a fabrication. Others say he was not involved.

Tachito Somoza, the younger son, wanted Gaitán thrown in jail. But Luís called for a meeting of the supreme command of the army, along with Guillermo Sevilla Sacasa, the ambassador to Washington. It was decided, when no firm evidence could be brought against Gaitán, that he would be relieved of his military command and appointed military attaché to Argentina.

Gaitán was brought before Luís and Tachito in the Presidential Palace to be told the decision. He carried a pistol and when he arrived in the building Tachito's men informed him that Gaitán was armed. But Luis would not let him be disarmed. He simply gave his aides, Morales and Alegrett, permission to shoot Gaitán if he drew his pistol.

Sevilla Sacasa had drafted a letter for Gaitán to sign, a briefly worded announcement of his decision to go to Buenos Aires. As the letter was shown to Gaitán he crossed his legs. But he was so obese that he needed to use his arms to reach down and grab one leg to cross it over the other.

As he did this, it was assumed he was reaching for his gun, and Morales and Alegrett drew their own pistols and aimed. Gaitán calmly continued to cross his legs and agreed to sign the document, protesting his innocence but willing to prove his loyalty to Somoza and his family by going.

Some days later, after many conspirators had been jailed, Tachito Somoza, the new commander of the National Guard, after drinking with Morales and Alegrett, went to The Hill where the men were jailed and shot several of them.

The succession was eased by the knowledge that American doctors were taking care of Somoza, who had been flown to the Canal Zone in an American plane, that the American ambassador was watching over the Somoza children, that the United States supported all of them. For three hundred years the Nicaraguan mind set dwelled beneath the magical, distant crown of Spain and then beneath the American State Department. The one who understood these mysteries ruled, and anyone who didn't lost power, as when the Americans demanded from Washington that Zelaya leave the country in 1909.

The Somozas understood the Americans well and used this

knowledge to act as though they were interpreters of the United States to Central America, translating the secrets of the State Department not only to Nicaragua but to the other generals in the region.

In the first third of the twentieth century the American presence was prodigious. The first American intervention took place on August 15, 1912, when 2,000 soldiers and 125 officers arrived to help put down civil strife. The Americans remained in Nicaragua until November of the same year, when they left a "brigade of firemen"—100 Marines who kept the peace from 1912 to 1925.

The result of the occupation was the Chamorro-Bryan Treaty, signed August 5, 1914. Nicaragua gave the United States all rights to build a transoceanic canal for ninety-nine years, to allay the Americans' fear that a foreign power would build a canal to compete with Panama. The Nicaraguans received three million dollars in return. I remember hearing as a child constant arguments as to whether this three million dollars, which Nicaragua barely saw, was stolen by Emiliano Chamorro, who had been Nicaragua's envoy when the treaty was signed and then became President when it was enacted. The actual truth, I later discovered, was that the Americans used two and a half million of it to pay off Nicaragua's external creditors. (The treaty was abrogated in the era of the last ruling Somoza, at the time of the Nixon administration—our second independence, Somoza called it.) On January 6, 1927, 3900 soldiers, 865 Marines, and sixteen warships appeared at Corinto, on the Pacific. They withdrew finally on January 2, 1933.

The Americans' every action was assumed to be purposeful. Americans did not make mistakes. Americans made money, and sense, and power. Americans built the Panama Canal. Americans forged the highest buildings in the world, they built the cars, they built the highways for the cars, in America and in Nicaragua. Since the 1860s, Nicaragua had felt that the railroad, along with the telegraph, was the symbol of the future. The Americans came and explained that railroads were old, that automobiles were progress. American roads and cars followed.

They brought their culture too, including baseball, which became Nicaragua's national sport (Cuba, the Dominican Republic, Panama, Venezuela, and Puerto Rico were the other Latin countries which adopted the game); the Marines brought it to Nicaragua with their occupation of 1912. When I was growing up the New York Yankees were Nicaragua's favorite team—eventually the Los Angeles Dodgers replaced them.

Our teams could never beat the Americans. We could beat Cuba, which probably fielded better teams, but never the Americans. (By the 1960s the squads were named the Managua Boers, the Granada Orientals, the León Leóns, and the 5 Stars, from Somoza and the army. The 5 Stars had the best team because they could afford the best players, but these men, mostly Americans anxious for a real career in the major leagues, played halfheartedly, fearful of injuries. The Boers, who played harder, usually won.)

Americans also brought money, finance, and banking. The currency under Zelaya had been unstable; under the Marines, it was stable. Americans opened the first modern banking institutions and Americans who were clerks in the United States became very important people in Managua. As Nicaraguans progressed to important positions within the bank they began to be called Mister—the title of respect.

After World War II the country went crazy for America: the best tractors (Caterpillars), the best cigarettes (Camels), the best razor blades (Gillette). When the Japanese bombed Pearl Harbor, Somoza and Dominican Republic dictator Rafael Trujillo raced to be the first to declare war on Japan to prove their loyalty to the Americans. Somoza declared war on Japan even before Roosevelt did. He rounded up Germans and Italians and put them under strict supervision and revoked their right to travel freely. (He also confiscated their land, one of the sources of his fortune.)

The transition from Anastasio Somoza to Luís Somoza was graceful. The country continued on its course, which included recurring ill-planned and ill-fated attempts to kill the Somozas.

In 1959 the Chamorro family once more started plotting to take over National Guard headquarters, inspired by Fidel Castro's 1953 success at the barracks of Moncada in Cuba—a military disaster, a political success. (My brother Alvaro Fidel was one of many in his generation named after the man.)

The Somozas loathed Castro. The Bay of Pigs invasion was launched from Nicaragua, where an expectant Luís Somoza allegedly said, here is an envelope, please bring me back the beard of Castro.

Everyone in the Caribbean paid a visit to Castro in the early 1960s—even the children of the Nicaraguan Conservative Party. Toward the end of the decade Pedro Joaquín Chamorro and Reynaldo Tefel called on Castro, who quickly denounced them as reactionaries. He called them "sellers of the fatherland"—the ones who had subscribed to the 1916 canal treaty. Chamorro told Castro, yes, I am a Chamorro, but I am a Chamorro belonging to another generation; my attitude in *La Prensa* has clearly demonstrated that I am different. But I cannot take the blood of the Chamorros from my veins.

Okay, Castro said, but this Nicaragua thing, it has been delegated to Che Guevara. Whatever he says is okay with me. But talk to him.

Che Guevara, the other great Latin revolutionary, said to the men of the Conservative Party, if Cuba doesn't help you, then it is a crime of Cuba. He promised to lend them weapons somehow.

Chamorro's group returned to Costa Rica to plan an attack, not in a boat, as Castro had done, but by air. The plane landed on May 31, 1959, between 5 and 7 A.M., with sixty-five men and weapons obtained from Costa Rica's Pepe Figueres. The plane returned and then left again under the command of Napoleón Ubilla, who landed with sixty men in Olama. It was never clear whether the Cubans responded with arms but if they did, both Chamorro and Ubilla departed before they arrived. Four hours later the National Guard was mobilized. The revolt lasted eleven days and then languished. Six men died, all of them members of Ubilla's squad.

When the remaining men were taken to see Somoza at The Hill, he asked them to stand in line with their backs to him. He would not speak face to face to men who had surrendered without a struggle.

The Chamorro family, led by "El Negro" Chamorro, and their allies attempted another coup d'état in November 1960. The effort included a plan to carry out simultaneous takeovers of the country's barracks, but only the barracks at Jinotepe and its sister city Diriamba (four miles from Jinotepe) were captured. Two days later they fell back into Somoza's hands. These were mere skirmishes among rival clans—nineteenth-century squabbles over power still being played out in the twentieth century.

The day the rebels took the barracks at Jinotepe my father instructed my sister and me not to go to school. School at the time meant a morning session from eight until eleven and then an afternoon session from two to four. The schoolhouse was only a block and a half from the barracks where every day the flag would be lowered in a ceremony accompanied by a single clarinet playing the national anthem. Drivers would stop their cars and stand quietly while the anthem was played.

But that November day we were excused from the afternoon session. My father told us we were going to visit my uncle in a small neighboring town. The afternoon soon passed and we had not gone anywhere, although the anthem had already been played, the town had stopped, but still we had not gone. Then at five o'clock, while calling on friends, we thought we heard firecrackers in town. By seven the barracks were in the hands of the Chamorros.

My father did not participate in this attempt. My mother told him, if you do, this time I will divorce you. She had put up with my father's political activity long enough, she explained to me, for in the end one should never sacrifice the family for the sake of politics.

From that moment on my father kept away from the rebel forces until the late seventies, when every part of the country underwent a revolution and almost every Nicaraguan played a role. Even those like me who had been raised in a timeless world of village and family now left the past behind. Something new, something alien, was born in Nicaragua.

Bliss to Be Alive:
The Fall of the Dynasty

Throughout the 1950s and 1960s the small houses in the Nicaraguan countryside were decorated with dozens of photographs. The pictures were either pasted or taped to the walls, or set in gilt frames on top of the plastic radios which served as the focal point of most homes.

Photographs were a national fixation. If a Nicaraguan didn't possess any of his own he would clip colored advertisements out of magazines *(Life, Vanidades, Bohemia)* and frame them: well-groomed young men smoking Lucky Strikes, beautiful blond women soaking their hands in Palmolive Dishwashing Liquid, suburban American couples driving Buick station wagons. The people most commonly pictured were the leading Mexican matinee idols of the time —Pedro Infante or Libertad La Marque—and Pope John XXIII, who was an enormous favorite throughout Latin America.

By the beginning of the 1960s another image began to appear on top of the radios: that of John Fitzgerald Kennedy. It took only a year for Kennedy to become the most popular American in the history of Nicaragua. Besides his stature as President of the United States, Kennedy was handsome, he was Catholic, he had an attractive wife, and, above all, he had developed a subtle manner with which to express his discontent with the rule of Luís Somoza.

Most of us received our information from newsreels in the movie theaters. Television hadn't penetrated our lives yet, the radio was entertainment. When we went to see Mexican or American movies we watched the newsreels of Kennedy's trip to Central America. In the films President Kennedy appeared with all the Central American presidents, warmly embracing each one—except Luís Somoza, with whom he simply shook hands. From this gesture came the famous watchword of the anti-Somocistas in the 1960s: An embrace for democrats, a handshake for dictators.

By the time of the Kennedy administration the Somozas had held power for twenty-five years. Luís had maintained a base of support with connections to all the social classes, but the regime was constantly being challenged, usually by the Conservative Party.

Luís Somoza never doubted that both Nicaragua and America could be handled. The policymakers of the Kennedy administration seemed only to want intimations of democracy, fragments of change. They did not press for an actual transfer of power. Luís knew he could suppress Fernando

Aguero and at the same time provide America with one indication that he was loosening his grip on the country.

Luís Somoza was the oldest of three legitimate Somoza children. He was thirty-three when he came to power. Raised by his father to oversee the family businesses, he was sent to study the sugar industry at Louisiana State University.

Luís' younger brother, Anastasio, was known as "Tachito." Within Nicaragua, the three ruling Somozas were most often called, in order, Tacho, Luís, and Tachito. Tachito Somoza was one of only five men from Nicaragua to attend West Point. But the magic of West Point could only belong to a Somoza: the other four cadets were never allowed to serve a single day in the army. Since Tachito's future was in the military, he had a monopoly on the cachet of West Point.

Luís was the most politically sophisticated of the Somoza brothers. He decided he could formally relinquish the presidency, offer the post to someone else, but still maintain his dominance in a different post. After all, he told his children, one must always remember that, to remain in control of the car, one may have to sit in the back seat.

To restructure the government Luís needed to strengthen the Liberal Party. He soon sent Nicaragua's best and brightest functionaries to Mexico City to study the workings of Mexico's Institutional Revolutionary Party. The PRI had effectively dominated Mexican politics since 1929, furnishing a semblance of democracy to a one-party state. Luís wanted to emulate its operation.

Luís believed he needed more than the support of the army and America; he needed an efficient political machinery. Unlike his brother Tachito, he understood that Washington was moody—he knew that Americans could not be reliable allies over a long period of time.

Luís requested that either Julio Quintana or René Schick be selected for the presidency. Both men were from humble backgrounds in the Somozas' favorite city of León, both were the type of Nicaraguan promoted by Tacho in the past:

talented men lacking in any social or familial connections that could challenge the Somozas. After a brief deliberation Luís decided upon Schick, for no other reason except that Schick wasn't nearly as intelligent as Quintana. That little monkey is too damn smart, Luís used to say about Quintana, whom he subsequently offered the ambassadorship to a South American country where, he said, there are a lot of intellectuals and you will feel at home. Quintana's intelligence, however, might have prevented the country's next embarrassing incident.

Like President Argüello before him, Schick used his new office immediately to plot against his patron. And, like Argüello, Schick did not prove to be an adept conspirator. At the time of his appointment to the presidency Schick was having an affair with the wife of his stepson (Schick's wife had been previously married).

In 1966 Schick decided—some say he was motivated as much by a desire to solve his domestic crisis as by any political gain—to escape with his lover to Mexico. From there he intended to denounce the Somoza family. So, during his first meeting in Nicaragua with visiting Mexican President Díaz Ordaz, Schick said to the Mexican, I am a prisoner of Somoza. I need help. He asked if he could use Mexico as a stage from which to denounce the dictatorship.

Díaz Ordaz agreed. His relationships with the Somozas were cool. In recent years the two other powerful dictators of the region, Trujillo in the Dominican Republic and Batista in Cuba, had been deposed. The Mexican found it appropriate to provide sanctuary for a plot against the area's surviving dictatorship.

Schick had always kept a room at the Gran Hotel in Managua where he used to meet his mistress and where he next went carrying approximately $200,000 in a briefcase to use in his flight to Mexico. The money came from the Cuenta del Socorro (the Emergency Relief Account) deposited in the National Bank and available to the President and the Foreign

Minister. It was used to help relatives and friends in times of crisis. Schick cleared out the account.

By doing so he inadvertently alerted the Foreign Minister, who monitored the account closely. And the brother of Schick's mistress, a Somoza loyalist, also uncovered his scheme. Schick, in turn, soon guessed that the Somozas suspected him. The stress became unbearable; he looked for clues, mistrusted everyone, jumped at the slightest provocation. Nervous, anxious, apprehensive, he went to the hotel to retrieve the money hours before his planned departure. While there he was stricken with a heart attack.

The Somozas took immediate control of the patient. They isolated Schick from the rest of the country and refused to allow physicians in to see him. His wife was informed of his love affair at the same time that she was told of the heart attack. She lost interest in attending her husband: she'd already suspected his infidelity anyway. Only an army physician and the military nurse (who was the wife of the man who later became Tachito Somoza's security chief, General Genie) watched over him. Schick didn't die of natural causes, some say, as much as of being asked to die of natural causes. Regardless, he died. The presidency was once again available.

Luís Somoza then decided to install as the next President the reliable Lorenzo Guerrero, who had proven his loyalty to the Somoza family over a period of three decades. Somoza appointed himself head of the Institute for Land Reform, from where he could steer the country. All of this was done to continue the myth of Nicaraguan democracy. Luís wanted to be thought of as a populist, a man of the people. He preferred this post to something such as the head of the National Bank.

Tachito Somoza disagreed; he thought he should be named President. Luís was not inclined to let Tachito accept the position. The difficulty with you will not be getting you elected, he told his younger brother, but getting you out.

Tachito worshiped his older brother and Luís took advantage of this to manipulate him. Acts of violence or suppression which occurred during Luís' reign were blamed on Tachito and his security force. In reality the younger brother was another tool in Luís' political arsenal. Tachito's wife, Hope, and his oldest children recognized this and resented Luís deeply for it.

Despite Luís' misgivings, Tachito's wife and his mistress urged him to demand the presidency. Eventually he prevailed upon his older brother. But on April 13, 1967, eighteen days before Tachito was to be given the job, Luís suffered a heart attack and died. He was forty-four.

A few days later Tachito began his reign by disassembling the political apparatus Luís had been building. Tachito wanted to import the Camelot of John F. Kennedy into Nicaragua—to end what he considered the old-fashioned clan politics of his brother and father and instead create a stylish, modern political atmosphere.

He envisioned himself as Nicaragua's JFK, ruling over a glittering enclave in Central America with his wife, Hope, as the Jacqueline Kennedy of the tropics. Hope spoke American English, she was beautiful and cold, and she adored Mrs. Kennedy.

To build Camelot, Tachito first had to weaken the Liberal Party, the party his older brother had been strengthening in order to emulate Mexico's PRI. Tachito erased Luís' appointments and instead surrounded himself with technocrats trained at American schools like Harvard, Yale, Chicago, and Berkeley, who had studied economics—the career of the future. The task of these advisers was to establish a free enterprise system with Tachito in place as the popular political leader, the *caudillo* of capital gains.

Unlike Luís, Tachito-the-West-Point-graduate trusted the United States. He felt so comfortable with America, he could not see anything outside of it. A product of the new American Empire, he spoke American army slang, he wore American suits and Florsheims, he followed American politics more closely than most Americans. His friends were the American army, congressmen, businessmen. When he eventually suffered his own heart attack, he insisted on flying to Miami for treatment, for he trusted only American doctors. Once, when asked why he didn't bother to upgrade the derelict Nicaraguan air force, Tachito replied, if I need planes, Uncle Sam will send me planes. His oldest son, Anastasio III, also known as Tacho, was sent to Harvard. The daughters went to exclusive American prep schools. His wife traveled frequently to the United States and shopped vigorously in Miami. The Somozas lived in a California-style ranch house designed by Hope, who refused to live in the archaic Nicaraguan presidential residence.

Hope lost her chance to become the first lady of Central America when Tachito's mistress, Dinorah, became his constant consort. Tachito socialized openly with Dinorah, not Hope, in a gross breach of social and political behavior. Mistresses were common in Nicaragua, but they were not supposed to be seen or heard. Tachito's behavior was accepted, however, because Hope was unpopular and Dinorah was clever. Hope dealt only with the oligarchy. Dinorah lived the life of a politician's wife; she talked to everyone equally.

Although Tachito adored the United States, the United States paid little attention to him or to Central America. America was preoccupied with Vietnam and itself. And so any small gesture on the part of the Americans was historically interpreted by the Nicaraguans as a huge event. If a middle-level State Department officer attended to the needs of a Nicaraguan official in Washington, the Nicaraguan official could benefit from that small interaction in his native province for years. The meeting might have been only to talk of the moon. In Nicaragua it was an event of imperial significance.

When President Lyndon Johnson flew down to Central

America in 1968 he stopped in Managua for two hours. One of his advisers may have said, We don't want to spend too much time with this dictator, we'll only stay a couple of hours. But even in that short time Johnson's natural effusiveness came through. It looked to the country as though he thoroughly backed Tachito and Tachito's faith in America was confirmed.

The late 1960s provided few anxieties for Tachito. The economy flourished, the countryside prospered, the revolts of the *caudillo* Chamorros were over. Tachito's only worry was the eye doctor Fernando Agüero, a Conservative Party member with a great gift for oration and a mellifluous voice. Agüero planned to run against Somoza in the 1967 election.

Nicaraguan presidential elections, fair or foul, have always included a trip to each Nicaraguan department by the opposition candidate, ending with a large political rally in Managua. In 1967 Agüero ended his campaign with an unusually impassioned speech. He deplored the electoral process, professed that elections in Nicaragua could never be fair, and urged his followers to march with him to The Hill, the symbolic home of the country's military power. When the *caudillo* Emiliano Chamorro took The Hill for several days in 1926, it was considered tantamount to his taking the country until the American minister persuaded him to let it go.

The crowd reacted dramatically. Agüero's eloquence moved the entire procession, which marched several blocks until it ran into Tachito's army, stationed close by. The two groups of Nicaraguans stared at each other across a narrow path for a time, no one moving, each uncertain what to do. Then a helicopter flew over the crowd. A shot was fired. No one ever knew where it came from—some say from the helicopter, some say from the crowd. But the lieutenant in charge of the army's squad fell dead.

A riot ensued. Dozens of people were killed. The crowd dispersed, shots were fired back and forth, and Agüero,

Pedro Joaquín Chamorro, and Agüero's bodyguard, the future hero Edén Pastora, sought refuge in the Gran Hotel.
Several American hunters had checked into the hotel with
their rifles. The rifles were "borrowed" by Agüero's supporters and it wasn't until the following day, when Tachito sent a
Sherman tank to the hotel under the command of Colonel
Alegrett, that the rebels surrendered.

Many were jailed but the next week Agüero remained a
participant in the election, running as though the incident
had never happened. His supporters were so affected by his
treachery, wondering if he had sold out to Somoza even before the speech, that there are still those in Nicaragua today
who refuse to believe that he stood in the election at all,
erasing Agüero's treason from their political memory.

Tachito assumed the presidency on May 1, 1967. He gave a
speech in the National Stadium soon after. I remember that
day, for although it was 90 degrees outside we ate boiling-hot
soup at noon and my father, while sweating, said that
Tachito had given the best speech of his life. We later learned
it had been written by the technocrats. Nonetheless it was
the high point of his political career.

Agüero succumbed to the age-old Nicaraguan tradition of
losing to an enemy by capitulating to personal power strug-
gles. He dedicated himself to the lesser struggle of settling
the leadership within the Conservative Party. In 1970 he allied with Tachito in a Liberal-Conservative coalition. No
longer did he have to kowtow to his rivals, the Chamorros,
fellow members of the Conservative Party whom, some felt,
Agüero hated much more than Tachito. Agüero was tired of
fighting the Chamorros. By virtue of his pact with Tachito, he
could raise money and distribute political favors without
even talking to his rival Conservatives.

Tachito in turn used Agüero in the creation of what was
called his *Kupia Kumy* (a Miskito Indian phrase meaning to
beat with one heart, as a couple in love soon share the pas-

sions of one heart, or, as politicians in accord follow only the heartbeat of their leader). Tachito wanted to re-elect himself two years before his term expired, an act prohibited by the constitution. So, in the Latin American tradition, he called for a convention to rewrite the constitution according to his taste.

For the sake of appearances he stepped down and appointed a triumvirate to assume the presidency: Agüero, General Roberto Martínez, and Alfonso Lovo Cordero.

These men, as Tachito knew, were irrelevant to the supervision of the country. For example, at a time when rising prices for everyday commodities were of growing concern, General Martínez was asked by journalists what would happen to the price of *La Pana del Mercado*—the basket of staple goods for a normal family. Martínez replied, I certainly wouldn't know the answer to that—after all, my wife does all the family's shopping.

To ensure that this triumvirate remained innocuous, Tachito installed Cornelio Hueck, the most adept of his machine politicians, as its executive secretary.

Meanwhile, in the jungles, the members of the Sandino Front for National Liberation (FSLN), popularly called the Sandinistas, had just begun to organize. They were dying in silence. Few Nicaraguans knew much about their activities, except for isolated acts of urban violence which briefly captured the people's imagination.

The early 1970s saw two swift acts of significance: Howard Hughes' arrival in Managua, followed by the earthquake. The two had set in motion the forces that destroyed Tachito.

The busboys were the first to know that someone had rented the top two floors of the Intercontinental, the best hotel in Managua. They told the waiters, who told the taxi drivers, who told their passengers. It took only an hour for Managua's gossip switchboard to inform the country. The speculation was so wild that Tachito was forced to hold a press conference the next day to confirm the rumors. Howard Hughes had moved the capital of his empire to Managua.

Following a meeting held in the Bahamas, the American ambassador, Turner Shelton, initiated the move in order to allow Hughes to operate in a country run with an iron hand by a friendly dictator. For Hughes, it was a chance to administer his operation safely away from investigators in the United States.

For Tachito, it was his first glimpse of real money. The Somozas' wealth derived from rice production, textiles, airlines, land, cattle, sugar. No one knew how much Tachito was worth but everyone knew he didn't have as much as Hughes. Hughes was rich in American dollars. Tachito only owned a small country. Now he expected to participate in joint ventures with Hughes, although it turned out that Hughes was not so inclined. Only one deal was arranged, whereby Hughes sold four Lockheed 1011s which had belonged to a Peruvian airline; he let Tachito have them in return for fifty per cent of the Nicaraguan national airline. The planes made too much noise for new American requirements and were not allowed to land in Miami, so they had to be abandoned.

Nicaragua is a small country where corruption has limits —there is only so much in the country to corrupt. Tachito had already wrested from it as much as he could. Hughes wasn't as forthcoming as he had anticipated. Having fully exploited Nicaragua, there were no avenues left from which to get more dollars.

Then the earthquake struck.

Nicaragua is said to be a country of poets, lakes, and volcanos. In colonial times volcanic lava was confused with gold —the Spanish called lava fluid gold and thought the mountains were filled with it. The mountains were constantly shaking. In 1648 and 1651 earthquakes made the San Juan River unnavigable for certain ships, protecting the inner cities of Nicaragua from English pirates. The 1834 eruption of

Cosiguina was supposed to have covered all of Central America with ashes. For forty-eight hours the air was pitch-black and Nicaraguans thought they were witnessing the end of the world. Earthquakes and volcanos doomed Nicaragua's chances of a trans-isthmian canal. Panama had not been the first choice, even after the French started construction. Nicaragua lost the project and Panama was chosen only when an American senator, on the French payroll, showed the United States Senate a Nicaraguan postage stamp which featured smoking volcanos.

The quake that struck in December 1972 was the worst in the country's history. Thousands of people died, crushed by rubble, burned in fires. The whole of downtown Managua was destroyed. A small group of American Marines arrived to help keep the peace and Tachito stayed close to them, trying to prove to the people the depth of his American support.

Six hours after the quake, Howard Hughes left the country for good. It was unstable after all. Tachito had seen Hughes only twice—when he arrived and when he left.

Tachito's greed had been whetted by Hughes. He saw limitless opportunities after the quake. Soon he had appointed himself the sole head of the Emergency Reconstruction Committee. The committee managed the international relief aid flowing into the country, an amount estimated somewhere between eighty and a hundred million dollars.

Even Tachito couldn't pocket all the money. Some of the earthquake funds had to be actually allotted for reconstruction, so contracts were assigned to Tachito's own companies. Trucks and tractors, banking and finance, all industries previously belonging to the private sector, were now dominated by Tachito, including the building of Managua's roads.

The flow of aid abated after a year. But Tachito's appetite for money never waned. He began to borrow heavily from international money markets for other development projects, always paying himself a fee as the middleman in every transaction.

The Nicaraguan bourgeoisie—the Pellases, the Chamorros, the Montealegres—were infuriated. Before the earthquake hit, Tachito's free enterprise system had allowed the local bourgeoisie to manage significant elements of the economy while the Somoza clan ran the country. In return they generally refrained from challenging his power.

Another problem was Tachito's son, Anastasio Somoza, who had recently returned from Harvard and Britain's Royal Military Academy at Sandhurst. Spain had offered Nicaragua an eighty-million-dollar line of credit for the purchase of jeeps, tractors, and cars from Spanish manufacturers, and also for spare parts, which was where the real profit could be made. But Spain's ambassador to Managua was a close friend of the Somoza family and he arranged for Anastasio III to become the representative for Spanish products in Nicaragua. The young man took over management of the Spanish government's line of credit for spare parts and further infuriated the private sector.

The salaried middle class had been undergoing a boom in both population and economic well-being. Once their children were all educated as lawyers or physicians. Now business, engineering, and other technocratic careers were the chosen paths to social mobility. Tachito's greed threatened the status quo of access to wealth, and both the bourgeoisie and the middle class were becoming indignant, becoming politicized.

At the same time the children of the bourgeoisie, who attended schools in the United States in the 1960s, found that America was not omnipotent after all. The American officials whom their fathers had considered demigods were regarded by the new generation of Nicaraguan children as social inferiors. Nicaraguans who wore Brooks Brothers suits and enrolled at Stanford and Harvard were not intimidated by the Sears-attired, Oklahoma State-educated men who manned the United States embassies at that time. These children began to develop for the first time a genuine sense of equality with Americans.

Like many, I went overseas to school, attending St. John's High School and then American and Johns Hopkins Universities. Many of my friends and schoolmates in the seventies found new answers in radical politics and education. The University of Chicago went out of fashion. The Universities of Mexico and Chile under President Allende, offering Marxist teachings, were the vogue. We were soon more familiar with the debates of Lenin and Kautsky than with our own history.

Students who didn't matriculate abroad were being radicalized by the Nicaraguan Jesuits. A powerful group of young bourgeois were under the sway of the charismatic Father Uriel Molina, who lived in a poor neighborhood and kept a retreat for spiritual examination. Many of these children, including my cousins the Carrións, Joaquín Cuadra, Alvaro Baltodano, and Oswaldo Lacayo, became powerful Sandinistas.

As the church developed a social consciousness in the late sixties and seventies the Jesuits instructed their students that they had an obligation to the poor in Nicaragua. Before the 1972 earthquake the urban poverty wasn't so obvious, the disparities weren't so clear. But after the earthquake, reconstructed middle-class neighborhoods stood in stark contrast to the ruined hovels of the poor neighborhoods.

Within Managua three high schools educated the upper and middle classes: the Calasanz, the Instituto Pedagógico, and the Centro América. Among the schools a competition had begun to develop over which students spent the most time working with the poor.

Sandino was the name used by the only faction to defeat the Somoza family. Augusto César Sandino himself, however, like the Somozas, meant many things to many people. He had been a rebel generally opposed to the United States Marines, but his myth was open to numerous interpretations.

Sandino was, along with Rubén Darío, the most powerful figure in the Nicaraguan imagination because of the romantic way he chose to defy the United States Marines in 1927. He was known for his ability to surround himself with charismatic people and for his silhouette, composed of his great sombrero, revolver, and huge American boots which were laced up to his knees.

He became a martyr because of his betrayal and assassination by Tacho Somoza. The first Somoza had come from a similar rural town and had belonged to the same Liberal Party as Sandino. We were told that at the end, when asked by his companions, who were also to be killed, why he was crying, Sandino replied, I am not crying because I am afraid. I am crying because I have been betrayed.

Sandino and two of his closest generals were executed at eleven o'clock on the night of February 21, 1934; all Managua heard the cracks of the Thompson submachine guns. My father was in bed but along with his friends he shared the same abrupt instinct that Sandino was dead.

The Marxist-Leninist Carlos Fonseca Amador linked the memory and name of Sandino to the insurrection. Fonseca was the illegitimate son of Fausto Amador, the administrator of Somoza's agricultural properties. He understood how easily Sandino's name and personality could be adapted as a rallying symbol of national unity for an anti-Somoza movement. He also understood the importance to the revolution of keeping Tachito Somoza alive. Unlike many others who wished to assassinate the dictator, Fonseca knew that as long as Tachito lived class struggle could be hidden within democratic, antidictatorial struggle.

Fonseca used to say, "My only authentic brothers are the ones who follow me," referring to the rift between him and his stepbrother, who was also called Fausto Amador. Amador openly disagreed with Fonseca; the two were both Marxists but Fausto was also a Trotskyite. They quarreled bitterly.

Fonseca founded the Sandinista Front for National Liberation (the FSLN) in 1961, after breaking from the old Communist Party of Nicaragua. The Communist Party elders did not believe in armed struggle so much as they believed in verbal debate. They felt it was impossible to defeat the National Guard. Fonseca looked at the Cuban model, where the "Foco"—a small uprising led by guerrillas—had been the catalyst used to launch a national insurrection. The Cuban revolution had succeeded in part because of Castro's charisma, and partly because of the ineptitude of Batista's army. The Sandinistas did not have a figure comparable to Castro but they imitated Castro's methods: they waged guerrilla warfare unsuccessfully through the sixties. These attempts were, militarily, a total failure.

The most vivid incident occurred at Pancasán in 1967, in response to an open letter to Latin American revolutionaries sent by Che Guevera from Bolivia, proclaiming the need to create many Vietnams for the destruction of imperialism. The National Guard crushed the Sandinistas with great ease —after which the Guard staged a victory parade. I was thirteen at the time and I remember watching the parade in downtown Managua. Three trucks of National Guardsmen drove through the streets. They were very clever. Their parade was scheduled just at the moment that work ended for the day. Crowds filed from their offices into the streets in time to watch.

Through its defeats the FSLN developed a reputation for bravery. It lost men but it began to win the country's admiration.

Tachito Somoza tightened his rule over the country. He was not only President now—his *Kupia Kumy* had ended—

but he had also appointed himself the head of the National Guard.

On December 27, 1974, Nicaragua was again shaken. That evening one of Tachito's former ministers, José Maria Castillo (whose daughters eventually became Sandinistas), was hosting a Christmas reception, which was attended by Tachito's brother-in-law, Guillermo Sevilla Sacasa, the ambassador to Washington; Danilo Lacayo, the local head of Exxon. Turner Shelton, the American ambassador, had already left when a dozen Sandinista commandos broke into the house. Castillo moved for his gun and was shot dead; his body was packed in the freezer. The commandos seized the house, which was then surrounded by the National Guard for three days. The FSLN asked for money, the right to read an announcement over the radio, the freeing of jailed Sandinistas, and an escape plane to Cuba.

Their demands were mediated by Archbishop Obando y Bravo, an anti-Somocista although not a member of the FSLN. But the FSLN trusted the archbishop, who had taken progressive positions against the Somozas. The Catholic Church was making its own generational leaps. The old Church hierarchy had been tolerated by the Somozas because they knew they could manipulate bishops like chess pieces. (Once, when the first Somoza inaugurated a harbor, he invited two bishops to bless the installations and also invited a line of conga dancers from Cuba to join the bishops, simply to watch the two holy men squirm with discomfort.)

I had just returned from school to Nicaragua in time to witness the event and the following reprisals. What surprised me most were the names of the young Sandinistas which surfaced in connection with the attack on the house: Cuadra, Carrión, Lacayo, Lang. These were the children of the better families in Nicaragua, the kids with whom I had grown up. The FSLN could no longer be viewed as a band of outcasts or outsiders. Rather they were the children of the country's bourgeoisie.

Tachito Somoza struck back with incredible violence. Besides fortifying his security apparatus he deployed his troops, detained and killed activists, and while doing so, slaughtered large numbers of peasants. It was a slipshod way to suppress a few dozen rebels and it did not translate well in the United States, either in the media or in Washington. Congressmen Edward Koch (NY) and Donald M. Frazier (Minn); and Bill Rogers, the Undersecretary for Latin American Affairs under President Ford, all began to agitate against Tachito. Several Americans supported Tachito vigorously, however, including Congressmen Charles Wilson (Tex) and John Murphy (NY), an old schoolmate of Tachito.

The Vietnam War was over. America was retreating from geopolitics and showing a new concern for human rights violations. Nicaragua proved to be an ideal target for post-Vietnam liberals, a nearby dictatorship with flagrant rights abuse. Americans saw within Nicaragua excessive corruption, excessive violence, and a degree of American responsibility in both.

Tachito still refused to worry. Inside Nicaragua he was as effective as ever. He captured several FSLN members, including Tomás Borge in December 1975, and he had defused their first successes. And the FSLN itself entered into a period of inner turmoil and divisions. The organization split into factions.

The FSLN's new members demanded a revised strategy. These younger men and women, mainly from the upper classes, began questioning the demand of the old line for prolonged rural warfare, as Mao Tse-tung had done in China. The new adherents argued that Nicaragua had changed drastically since the 1960s. With the postwar economic boom had come both a rural and an urban proletariat; a new strategy called for the creation of a workers' party based on this proletariat, especially in the cities. This was called the proletariat tendency. It was the new blood which challenged the old schemes of the FSLN.

The old blood of the FSLN refuted the new. It justified its longtime emphasis on the rural guerrilla war. The old guard didn't deny the importance of urban areas but it relegated the city to a source of recruitment—primarily at the universities—for the rural guerrilla operation. The old blood of the FSLN was concentrated in a faction known as the Prolonged Population War, the GPP. It accused the new of coopting the revolution and consequently expelled many members from the movement.

When Jaime Wheelock, one of the new blood in the FSLN, fled to the Mexican embassy in October 1975, he was fleeing his allies in the FSLN as well as Tachito's continuing reaction to the December 1974 takeover. Wheelock believed that Tomás Borge, the head of the GPP faction, and an enemy of Wheelock's, had sent a follower to execute Wheelock, who only escaped by calling his friend Carlos Coronel, who helped him flee to Granada. While in Granada he stayed at the house of a friend whose father was a close associate of Tachito. No one in the town even thought of entering the house to search for Wheelock. He was taken to the town of San Carlos, across the lake, where the National Guard commander was a friend of Carlos Coronel's. From there they both escaped to Costa Rica.

As new and old-line Marxists fought within the FSLN, a third tendency began to flourish under the guidance of the two Ortega brothers, Humberto and Daniel, who were in Costa Rica at that time. This new group claimed they could mediate the conflict between old and new. They were called the Terceristas—the third way—by Jaime Wheelock and the name struck.

While the three factions fought one another, Tachito Somoza seemed momentarily invulnerable. And on November 8, 1976, the FSLN's founder, Carlos Fonseca, was shot to death in Zinica, in the Central Zone of Nicaragua.

Fonseca had entered the country from Cuba, through Honduras, to unite with Henry Ruíz' FSLN guerrilla column known as the "Pablo Ubeda." Before he could find Ruíz, Fonseca was surrounded by the National Guard and killed. His death marked the end of the most dogmatic and powerful figure in the FSLN.

In the mid 1970s Tachito was more irritated by the Americans than by the FSLN. Pedro Joaquín Chamorro, editor of the opposition newspaper *La Prensa,* and Tachito's most vocal critic, had traveled to Columbia University to speak at the School of Journalism. His personal interpretation of the United States convinced him that Tachito's days were numbered, that the Carter administration would eventually have no choice but to distance itself from Tachito. He was also confident that the Americans would not allow the Sandinistas to take over the government.

As Tachito's support eroded Chamorro strengthened his own antigovernment coalition, known as UDEL, to provide an alternative to both Tachito and the Sandinistas. UDEL was specifically designed to become the democratic alternative to both Somoza and the Sandinistas.

My best friend at the time was Pedro Chamorro's son, Carlos Fernando Chamorro, currently the editor of *Barricada,* the official newspaper of the FSLN. Carlos' older brother, Pedro Joaquín Chamorro, Jr., eventually became a prominent figure within the contras. I always preferred the more intelligent Carlos to his brother.

Carlos was studying at McGill University in Montreal while I was at Johns Hopkins and we often traveled together. Once, just before the American presidential elections in 1976, the two of us returned home and spent a weekend at the Chamorros' house at the beach.

Pedro Joaquín, Sr., suggested that if Carter were elected he would support the ouster of Tachito. Carlos and I disagreed strongly, arguing from a Marxist perspective that we could see no substantive difference between the Republicans and the Democrats. There would be no policy changes.

The two of us whipped ourselves into a frenzy. We decided to write an impassioned article for *La Prensa*, denouncing Carter's human rights policy, charging that Carter opposed Tachito only because Nicaragua had no value to the United States. He could afford to attack such a useless country. Otherwise his policy was just bluff.

We thought the article might bring us trouble. But Pedro Joaquín Chamorro told us that Tachito's censors had no problems with it. We then realized that our hot-blooded Marxist attack on the United States coincided with Tachito's unhappiness at the human rights pressure from Carter.

The new messenger for this pressure was a young American named Bob Pastor, who had been appointed national adviser on Latin American affairs under Zbigniew Brzezinski. The United States hoped to depose Tachito but never did much more than hope to achieve its policy. Pastor, we were told, was eventually assigned the task of planning Tachito's departure and preventing the Sandinistas from replacing him. The transition was supposed to pressure the National Guard, which was, in America's eyes, the last guarantor of stability in the country.

Pedro Joaquín Chamorro became Pastor's choice to succeed Tachito. Chamorro also allied himself with Venezuela's President Carlos Andrés Pérez, who had been Chamorro's friend when they met, in exile, in Costa Rica years before. Chamorro left Pérez one of his few prized possessions, his refrigerator, when he left the country.

With the United States caught between its rhetoric and its refusal to act, and the FSLN's energy being expended in political quarrels outside Nicaragua, 1977 was relatively quiet for Tachito Somoza. But in July of that year he suffered a heart attack and flew to Miami for treatment. While he was recuperating the Torrijos-Carter Panama Canal Agreement was signed and all the Latin American presidents were invited to attend the ceremony.

Tachito's health didn't permit him to travel. In his stead he sent his trusted crony Cornelio Hueck, the man who had been in charge of the ruling Liberal Party machine. While in Washington Hueck, who for years had been quietly nursing his own ambitions, started to plot against Tachito.

Give me a green light, Hueck told the Americans. I can end the Somoza rule.

The moment he heard of Hueck's machinations, Tachito, whose spies were omnipresent, moved back to Managua in spite of his health.

He asked Hueck to meet him at the airport in Managua and Hueck agreed. He showed up at the gate and crumpled as soon as he and Tachito met face to face. If there was one thing Tachito knew, it was how to command. Tachito was six feet six. Once, when he asked a friend to light his cigarette, the much shorter man lit a match and extended it to Tachito at his own height. Tachito grabbed the man's entire arm and raised it and the match to his mouth. A Somoza, he said, does not bow.

Now more than ever, Tachito decided to trust only his family. One of his uncles was nicknamed Tío Luz (Uncle Light) as he was in charge of the electrical company of Nicaragua. It was rumored that during Tachito's administration a Japanese company arrived to sell transmitters. In order to reach Tío Luz they had to pass through a maze of nine different functionaries. Each one of these bureaucrats asked for ten percent of the Japanese profits. When the Japanese finally reached Tío Luz, he too asked for ten percent of the profits. The Japanese moaned; this would be impossible. If they handed over yet another ten percent, they said, they would have sold their transmitters without having made a single yen. At that Tío Luz looked shocked. But, he said to the Japanese, we only want the profit on the deal. You can keep your transmitters.

Tacho Somoza, the first dictator, always told his sons Luís and Tachito that if one plans on eating the chicken one has to hide the feathers. Luís agreed but Tachito, growing more and more arrogant, kept Tío Luz in his government.

The more tranquil history of neighboring Costa Rica, Nicaraguans believe, arises from various influences. The cooler climate, we say, has calmed the Costa Ricans' national spirit. In Nicaragua, if you start a discussion at eleven-thirty, by twelve-thirty the heat will have boiled it to a fight. Others contend that the Spanish who settled the territory that became Nicaragua were more bellicose than those Spanish who conquered Costa Rica. Still others claim that Nicaragua was always richer than its neighbor and so it could afford hostilities, whereas Costa Rica's economy couldn't weather a war without suffering famine.

Regardless, the Ortegas understood that the Americans found an FSLN alliance with the democratic and tranquil Costa Rica far preferable to an alliance with Marxist Cuba. A successful insurgency also required sanctuaries in other countries. Costa Rica was the first to provide shelter for the Sandinistas' rear guard; more and more the Terceristas dropped their Marxist-Leninist rhetoric in order to curry the Nicaraguan people's support. Concurrently, the Terceristas were able to recruit more and more disaffected members of Nicaragua's upper and middle classes.

The apex of that recruitment was the declaration of the "Group of Twelve": a dozen respected lawyers, bankers, and businessmen, including my father. All were prominent Nicaraguans; most of them now had relatives involved in the FSLN. They affirmed, on October 18, 1977, that there could be no solution to the Nicaraguan crisis unless the Sandinistas became part of that solution.

Prior to the declaration the Sandinistas had made their presence more pronounced in an outburst of activity. On October 12, thirty-two Terceristas ambushed a column of the

National Guard, killing six and wounding six others, 143 miles north of Managua. On the morning of October 13, at 4:17 A.M., the Terceristas also attacked the port of San Carlos, killing six more guardsmen. On Monday, October 17, they hit the barracks at Masaya and skirmishes broke out across the country.

In my opinion the other major event of 1977 was less notable but eventually proved more significant. It was the emergence within the FSLN of Edén Pastora, the man who had been Agüero's bodyguard and who, in time, became the face and the personality of the revolution.

Pastora was born to conservative parents in the village of Darío, named after the poet, thirty-seven miles from Managua. His grandfather had been a follower of Emiliano Chamorro, the great twentieth-century Conservative *caudillo*. Pastora's mother, Elsie, had been educated in New Orleans. During the American occupation she served as a translator to the Marines, charging $1.50 a day, at a time when a pregnant cow cost only $4.50.

Pastora's father was shot to death over a land problem; his older brother Félix avenged the death by killing one of the murderers.

Being anti-Somocista was effortless for Pastora, who had already been fighting Somoza for decades. He had even invented a myth that his father had been killed by the Somozas for political reasons. Though a member of the FSLN, he was not a full-time militant and never penetrated the FSLN's inner circle because he had married often and had several families to tend. He had also doubted their ability to win. But now he craved military action against the dictator.

Pastora's decision to join the Sandinistas calmed most Nicaraguans and allowed Daniel Ortega to say, we are a nationalistic faction, not a Marxist one. We are supported by Nicaraguans from the entire political spectrum. The American media emphasized the same point. A year later, when Dan Rather filmed a "Sixty Minutes" report on Nicaragua, Pastora was highlighted in a suit and tie in church as his daughter received her first communion while they were staying in Costa Rica. His image as a man of the family rather than of the revolution was always emphasized.

On the morning of January 10, 1978, the anti-Somoza opposition lost its central representative when Pedro Joaquín Chamorro was assassinated while driving to work in his Saab. No one ever claimed responsibility. Somoza dispatched immediate word to the Chamorro family that he had had absolutely nothing to do with it but most Nicaraguans assumed that Tachito was responsible. There was also some suspicion that Miami-based Cubans, involved in a blood donor scam that sent cheap Nicaraguan blood to America to be resold at a much higher cost, had ordered the assassination, because Chamorro had been publishing a series of articles about them.

The assassination sparked a massive anti-Somoza demonstration. Following that, from January 22 to February 4, came the first national strike, including shopowners and mid-level industrialists. Next, in the Indian neighborhood of Monimbó, in Masaya, a separate uprising took place on February 23.

Edén Pastora was responsible for the conclusive piece of drama. He always clamored for the theatrical because he possessed an inherent understanding of the Nicaraguan mind and its love of flamboyant romantic gestures. He realized that the symbolic reverberation of any action, rather than its actual outcome, would determine the future of the country.

In the National Palace on the Plaza de la República in downtown Managua was a massive monument to architectural ugliness, where Congress held sessions from the last week of April to the middle of December. Pastora's idea was to take the Congress while it was in session. To accomplish this, the Terceristas selected a group of around twenty-five young men from the Indian neighborhood of Monimbó, which had been simmering with small insurrections, and from Solentiname, a utopian island community on the lake. The plan was not to kill Tachito, an idea now long out of date. Instead the goal was to create as much domestic turmoil and as many international headlines as possible.

On the day of the takeover the Sandinista commandos approached the Congress in three vehicles, two cars and a truck. They were disguised as members of an elite National Guard unit. If the Guard interfered, the two cars were to stay and fight in order to allow the truck to reach the Congress.

But no incidents occurred along the way. The guerrillas got out of the truck, walked into the Congress, and simply announced to the Guard that they were Tachito's special soldiers and that Tachito was on his way. The Guard let them pass.

The Somocistas had suspected that there might be trouble that day and Congress was supposed to have called in a police detail of sixty men. In charge was Luís Pallais, the man who had almost saved my Uncle Adolfo's life years earlier. Pallais called José Somoza, an illegitimate son of Anastasio Somoza who was a general in the National Guard; he inquired as to the whereabouts of the sixty-man police unit, which had not appeared for duty. José Somoza assured Pallais they would arrive. They didn't. Perhaps someone inside the Congress had helped the FSLN. No one ever knew.

Once inside the building, the Sandinista commandos were able to march through the corridors directly into the legislative chamber before any of the small National Guard contingent there suspected something was awry. By the time they did suspect it was too late. A guardsman was shot. Then Pastora and his team strode into the room and fired at the ceiling. We are the FSLN, Pastora said, and you are my prisoners.

A tumultuous clackety-clack-clack immediately rang

through the hall—the sound of the congressmen throwing their pistols on the floor in front of their seats.

The Terceristas read their list of demands: they insisted on ransom money, the release of prisoners, a plane in which to escape, and that an FSLN communiqué must be broadcast on radio. Humberto Ortega had prepared the speech from San José, Costa Rica. Unfortunately for the Ortega brothers, the message read over the radio was amended by members of the Sandinista internal front, who were the most radical of the Terceristas. They came close to declaring the FSLN a Marxist-Leninist movement, unnerving rather than uniting much of the populace.

Once again Archbishop Obando y Bravo mediated the dialogue and once again Tachito surrendered on all counts. The strong sentiment among Tachito's men for storming the Congress was rejected. Tachito feared five hundred people might die and he did not wish to appear to the world as a barbarian. He had recently received a letter from President Carter commending the perceived improvement in human rights and congratulations for allowing the Group of Twelve supporting the Sandinistas to re-enter Nicaragua from Costa Rica. Tachito did not want to see Carter's letter rescinded.

This time, when they left Nicaragua, the Sandinistas flew to Panama rather than Cuba as part of the continuing strategy to differentiate themselves from Marxist Cubans. Panama's Torrijos, once a Tachito protégé, had become anti-Somocista. He counseled the Sandinistas in their relations with the United States. You can play with the chain, he said to the Sandinistas, but not the monkey. In other words, the Sandinistas' anti-American rhetoric was moderately tolerable but the United States would not understand if the FSLN imported Soviet advisers and equipment.

Just as the Sandinistas boarded their exit plane, Pastora allowed the mask covering his face to fall. A photographer captured the image and the picture of the heroic fighter, rifle in hand, became a *Newsweek* cover and the most famous photo in Nicaragua. The government tried to suppress it but it circulated rapidly. For the first time Nicaraguans could see a noble face next to the cries of revolution.

When the Sandinista plane arrived in Panama, General Omar Torrijos asked for a private meeting with Pastora. The two soon became close personal friends and through this association Torrijos began to compete with Castro as the godfather of the revolution. He provided weapons to the Terceristas and he allowed Cuban weapons to flow through Panama.

Torrijos supported the Terceristas over the competing Marxist factions of the FSLN. The Terceristas had the loyalty of the people, the military fronts, international connections. They were the ones who had created the Group of Twelve. They suppressed their Marxist-Leninist sympathies. Torrijos also realized that Pastora's power would be greatly weakened by unity with the other FSLN factions. But Castro had his own reasons for insisting on unity.

The various Sandinista factions were now cooperating. In early 1978 one of the Tercerista commanders, "Zorro," had surrounded the army barracks in Estelí, in northern Nicaragua. He created some havoc but not much else, since the rival GPP faction, stationed nearby, did not lend support. So the operation failed.

With some effort the three groups then met in mid-1978 and signed a tentative document called "Unity Through Action," the first sign of unity. In early 1979 Castro summoned three leaders of each Sandinista faction to Havana: the Ortegas and Victor Tirado for the Terceristas; Tomás Borge, Bayardo Arce, and Henry Ruíz for the old-line GPP; and for the newer Marxists of the proletariat tendency, Luís Carrión Cruz, Jaime Wheelock, and Carlos Nuñez.

Pastora was excluded. Not only did Castro consider Pastora less reliable from an ideological standpoint, the Cuban *caudillo* simply did not like the man. He referred to Pastora as "The Peasant."

Pastora was upset. I am so loved by my people, he moaned. Why am I not included? But he had no recourse except to complain.

On March 7, 1979, after forty-eight hours of meetings in Havana, it was announced that the Sandinistas had reached a unity agreement and established a National Directorate of nine *Comandantes.*

Torrijos couldn't truly compete with Castro. Castro's name itself was a drug to Latin revolutionaries and nationalists. He was the hero, the guardian of ideological purity, the father, the great orator, the one who gave weapons, asylum, support. Even those who disliked what Cuba had become couldn't dislike Castro—he had the magic of a *caudillo.* Personality precedes politics.

Nicaragua was Castro's special project, especially since he knew Torrijos was in the race for patron of the revolution. In September 1978, 181 men were sent from the FSLN to be trained in Cuba, all but one of them from the radical GPP and the newer proletariat tendency faction. A much smaller group of Terceristas, perhaps a dozen, had already been trained in Cuba. At about the same time Cuban advisers arrived on the mainland; the majority of them, although they came from Cuba, were Brazilians and Chileans.

The United States monitored these moves carefully but the Carter administration still hoped Tachito would simply wake up and go. In October 1978 Carter dispatched special envoy William Bowdler to negotiate a diplomatic settlement. Bowdler, who had already been involved in Nicaragua, met with those anti-Somocistas acceptable to the United States—this included the Group of Twelve, but not the leaders of the FSLN. A group called the Mediating Commission—consisting of the United States, Guatemala, and the Dominican Republic—had already been formed by the OAS to see if a replacement for Tachito could be found. But it was unfairly rumored that Bowdler spent all of his time in Nicaragua buying primitive art.

He did try to tell Tachito that he had to leave the country but he was overly polite, which was not entirely his choice. Tachito agreed to talk with Bowdler if he could tape the conversations using a tape recorder given to him by the CIA. The point man of the Carter administration did not dare give unilateral orders to Tachito. The Administration avoided such one-sided action.

America's best hope at this point was to find someone in the army to stage a coup d'état against Tachito. But the United States refused to initiate the process. Policy notwithstanding, Carter's people were terrified that Tachito wouldn't leave and they were equally terrified that the Sandinistas would take power, so they did nothing.

By mid-1978 I was working for the FSLN. There was never any question that I wouldn't someday support and join the Sandinistas—I believed in the concept of the revolution. I was at the height of my Marxist phase. I joined the new blood, the group which did not, we said, support "putschist attacks" of military adventurers. We provided the intellectual justification for our refusal to fight, arguing the need to organize and disseminate propaganda. We felt deception was more pragmatic than fighting. It also gave some of us an excuse not to die. I had no intention of either firing a gun or being a target for someone else's.

To build up a show of popular support, our group decided it had to emulate the strategy of the broad opposition front to Tachito formed by the non-FSLN antagonists. The FSLN needed a similar front, to boost its credibility and its contention that it was the only legitimate opposition to Tachito. Our contention was that any other group was basically the same thing as Somocismo without Somoza.

And so the United People's Movement (MPU) was formed to simulate a large base of popular support. The MPU was supposedly made of thousands of intellectuals, professionals, and workers. And, through the intercession of Carlos Fernando Chamorro, I became an MPU spokesperson.

My job was to win over the Americans. Throughout 1979 I talked with federal, state, and local governments and toured American colleges. I proved excellent at convincing my audience that the FSLN did not represent a Marxist-Leninist revolution. I pointed always to the face of the folkloric Edén Pastora, even though at the time we all disliked him. We were afraid of Pastora. We thought he could take our nominal goals away from us. He wasn't ideological enough. We used to complain bitterly that not only did no one on the Southern Front study Marxism, but that they were even rumored to have *burned* books by Marx.

Several new faces were emerging alongside Pastora's as revolutionary leaders. The most important among them may have been Carlos Coronel.

He was the son of the most influential Nicaraguan thinker of the twentieth century, José Coronel Urtecho. A protofascist in the 1930s, Urtecho later became a prominent Sandinista intellectual. Coronel's mother, Maria Kautz, was the daughter of a Prussian military officer who had arrived in Nicaragua at the beginning of the twentieth century to help General Zelaya create a military academy. As a reward for his work the Prussian was granted a large piece of land near the San Juan River in southern Nicaragua. The land was primarily settled by Scottish, German, and Spanish settlers who intermarried and created a white enclave surrounded by the jungle and the mestizos.

When the Prussian Kautz died, his daughter Maria inherited some of the land. She was a local legend, called the "Amazon Lady"—a blue-eyed, red-haired, pale white woman who wore pants, carried a pistol, and drank like a man. For years the Coronel family controlled the San Juan area.

Carlos Coronel had already become Fidel Castro's protégé.

After the Terceristas' trip to Cuba, Coronel was befriended by Castro and he was soon deployed to the Southern Front of Costa Rica, an area he knew better than anyone, where the peasants were loyal to his family. Castro understood immediately that Coronel, more than anyone else, was the key to handling Pastora. They had known each other for many years, since their time together in the Conservative Youth when both adventurers opposed the leadership of Emiliano Chamorro. Both were quick-witted and undisciplined, both given to scheming and plotting. Pastora always trusted Coronel, who could control his friend's frequent emotional outbursts.

The Sandinistas allowed the country to enjoy a calm during the Holy Week holidays in 1979. The final insurrection began just after, starting slowly in May with a defeat in Nueva Guinea, becoming powerful and decisive in June. The Americans watched but did not intervene. Until the very end Nicaraguans fully expected them to do so and were continually surprised when they didn't.

Armed attacks racked the country. Rumors flew: that Pastora was coming back to the Southern Front; that he was dead; that he had been seen in the countryside dressed as a nun. Alfonso Robelo, a successful Managua businessman, tried to fill the vacuum left by Pedro Joaquín Chamorro by organizing the National Democratic Movement (MDN). But it was too little democracy too late. The MDN was also heavily infiltrated by the FSLN.

The National Guard was still supporting Tachito; they continued to do so until he finally fled. Tachito, playing politics to the end, toyed with his men. He told several of his most trusted confidants that they alone would become President if he had to abdicate. He felt if he could outlast the FSLN, if he could survive the one year left in the Carter presidency, if he could handle his own men, prevent betrayal, keep them happy with his unlikely promises—the country was still his and he could pass it on to his sons.

But after January 1979 the American embassy sent out word that no transactions with Tachito were to be permitted. The Somoza past was littered with too many agreements by too many compromisers. And so the formal opposition refused to play by the old rules of cutting a deal with the dictator.

Tachito tried new options. He had intercepted a letter from Humberto Ortega in Costa Rica to the head of the Sandinista military staff in the Northern Front. The letter was printed verbatim in *La Prensa;* it stated that if the FSLN would dispense with left-wing terminology the people would rally around the FSLN, even while the purity of the real Marxist-Leninist intentions of the Sandinistas could be secretly preserved. The letter was an answer to complaints within the FSLN that Humberto had compromised the Marxist left to win the support of the rest of the country. The letter frightened many Nicaraguans. But hatred for the Somozas was too intense to be deflected by one piece of paper.

Managua was a city in revolt. The workers and the peasants were not involved. The FSLN found its followers among the youth of the barrios and the universities. By 1978 over sixty percent of the country's population was under the age of twenty-one. Many of them had no jobs, no future. The FSLN gave these kids the opportunity for a heroic death. They responded by taking up arms and fighting, committing wonderful acts of valor, often dying as they did. The moral indignation of the country rose as the number of slaughtered young men and women rose. Every day the names of newly dead, many of them children in their teens, appalled and frightened the populace.

Humberto Ortega designated the Southern Front and the internal front within Managua as the two most important fronts in the war. Tachito concentrated his best troops and field commander in the south, to prevent an invasion from Costa Rica. Humberto placed the bulk of his forces there too. This stopped Tachito from adequately defending Managua, which was spinning out of control.

Cities throughout the country were taken by Sandinistas. Tachito realized the difficulty of recapturing the poor barrios of Managua. Instead he bombarded them. The American press went wild. When an ABC correspondent was killed by a National Guardsman, the American press itself tried to remove Tachito from power. The country was paralyzed. By mid-July the city of León was completely controlled by the FSLN.

On June 16 the FSLN created what it called the Government Junta of National Reconstruction in Costa Rica. Other Latin American governments initiated contacts. On June 21 the United States requested the formal resignation of Somoza. He was to be replaced by a "government of national reconciliation." The United States accused Cuba and "other nations" of grave interference in the civil war. Washington warned that foreign intervention could transform the conflict into an international dispute and requested the formation of a hemispheric military force to support the new Nicaraguan government.

Discussion of this force took place in the seventeenth meeting of the foreign ministers of the Organization of American States, at the request of the United States. Both sides in the Nicaraguan conflict believed that Zbigniew Brzezinski, the American national security adviser tried one last time to intervene in Nicaragua. Arguing against him in the Administration was Secretary of State Cyrus Vance, who definitely opposed any American intervention whatsoever.

The hemispheric security force was Brzezinski's idea. He assumed that the OAS would rubber-stamp his request. But the great geopolitician had been too occupied with global concerns to understand his own hemisphere. Nicaraguans speculated that Vance was smarter and allowed Brzezinski to make the proposal, knowing it would be soundly defeated by an OAS no longer obedient to the United States.

I was present at the OAS debate and remember hearing Nicaragua's Foreign Minister Quintana, the man Luís Somoza had called the little monkey, defending Tachito while Father Miguel d'Escoto, allowed by the Panamanian delegation to join their ranks, spoke against Quintana. D'Escoto later became Foreign Minister for the new regime.

The session lasted three days, from June 21 to 24. When it ended the OAS, instead of suggesting a Dominican Republic type of police action, demanded Tachito resign and that elections be held immediately thereafter. I had been speaking to a group of Nicaraguans and radical Americans, expecting the OAS to follow the American lead, and was ready to denounce their action. Their refusal to accommodate Brzezinski astounded me.

Tachito Somoza, when informed of the OAS's action, demanded an oath of loyalty from the National Guard in each principal department of the country. Angry, frustrated, and exhausted, he compared his struggle to that of a donkey tied to a tree while being attacked by a tiger.

By July 17 Tachito's game was over and he began to make discreet preparations for his departure. In an effort to spite the country he left behind a buffoon as his successor: Chico Urcuyo. Tachito quietly assured Urcuyo that after his departure the United States would come to Urcuyo's aid.

Now, with the country split apart, with the cities in revolt, Tachito insisted on due constitutional process to select a new President. The Americans had expected the new President to rule for no more than forty-eight hours in order to dissolve Congress and then, in the name of peace, to call for a government of national salvation in which the armies of the opposition were to merge with what was left of the National Guard.

According to a former Somoza aide, Brzezinski and Bob Pastor went to Carter and argued that the National Guard should receive some American military support, to show, after Tachito left, that the Americans were still behind them. Carter refused. U. S. Ambassador Lawrence Pezzullo informed Urcuyo that no military help was available.

No one had told Urcuyo that he was to rule for only two days. The Ortegas were informed and agreed. They knew that the Guard would collapse without support. But for the only time in his life Urcuyo played his own game. He announced that he would fulfill his duties as the constitutional President of Nicaragua until the term of Tachito expired in 1981.

He never explained how he dreamed up this antic. Some thought Tachito, hoping to see the country torn apart after his departure, told Urcuyo he had worked out a high-level deal that would bring American support. Others said that the National Guard persuaded Urcuyo to act in such a manner. And some say that Urcuyo, the joker himself, never got Tachito's last joke. He truly thought he had been given power. In any case, he then called an emergency session of Congress, a relatively easy chore as most of the congressmen were staying at the nearby Intercontinental Hotel next to the presidential bunker. Congress met and approved Urcuyo's succession.

Part of Tachito's agreement with the United States was that if he abandoned the country he could fly to Miami, as a temporary move. When he left Nicaragua, only a handful of associates accompanied him to Florida: Pablo Rener, who sat on a bagful of money in the plane; Julio Quintana, the one known as the little monkey; Tachito's son Anastasio; and the military officers Porras and Corrales.

The plane took off in the early hours of July 17. A few moments later the National Guard collapsed. Without the chief there was no more will left to fight. Whole units of soldiers abandoned their posts in battle and ditched their uniforms to avoid being identified as members of the Guard.

Meanwhile Urcuyo was distributing cabinet positions just

as though full power rested in his hands. He wore the presidential sash around his chest and informed a bewildered United States that he was the President of Nicaragua, telling them his plans to govern as the country was falling around him.

Ambassador Pezzullo was furious. A United States Air Force C-130 arrived in Managua in the middle of the afternoon at an airport packed with National Guard members trying to hitchhike plane rides out of the country and picked up Pezzullo. The symbolism was powerful. America did not support Urcuyo.

Instead the United States, studying those selected by the FSLN to govern—Moisés Hassan, Sergio Ramírez, Violeta Chamorro, Alfonso Robelo, Daniel Ortega—decided incorrectly that a non-Marxist majority controlled the new revolutionary junta. They didn't realize that Ramírez was a Marxist. An envoy from Washington was sent to Tachito's Miami home to have him instruct Urcuyo that there had been no deal after all, that he was not the President, and that he should go away. Tachito called his old friend and said, "Chico, get out, it's over." Tachito was nervous that the United States might rescind its Miami welcome if he did not behave.

Urcuyo finally understood. He called his friends in Guatemala, who sent an army plane to pick him up. He flew to Guatemala with the presidential sash around his waist and refused to remove it until the end of his three-year constitutional term.

Urcuyo never attended any gathering unless the Nicaraguan national anthem was played upon his arrival. But things grew worse and worse for him in Guatemala. When Christmas of 1979 came, he had nowhere to go to celebrate. And so a friend asked him to join her that day. He refused. Why? the friend asked him. He just couldn't, he said. The friend badgered him until he explained. He had lost the presidential sash and so he couldn't be seen in public. The friend was kind and sewed him a new sash.

When the revolution came, one of my first tasks was to help reclaim the residence of the Nicaraguan ambassador in Washington. A beautiful mansion in one of Washington's best neighborhoods, it had been bought by the first Somoza and given to his daughter (Tachito's sister). In order not to pay property taxes, the house was in the name of the Nicaraguan government. It was now ours. A group of us from the Sandinista Solidarity Committee went over to liberate it.

When we arrived the ambassador, Tachito's brother-in-law, Guillermo Sevilla Sacasa, looked out the window and panicked. We were told he could not reach anyone in the Carter administration, so he phoned Henry Kissinger, who to his amazement took the call; supposedly it was Kissinger who managed to send the diplomatic police over to the house to safeguard Sevilla Sacasa. Negotiations then commenced between the government of Nicaragua and the State Department for a peaceful recovery of the house. We agreed that for the next two days we would take the first floor and the Sevilla Sacasa family could live on the second floor while they packed all their personal possessions.

But we had to inventory the house at the same time as the family was moving out, so occasionally we were forced to climb to the second floor where the entire family was now encamped. Somoza's eighty-five-year-old mother, Yoya, was there, mentally unwinding. The maids constantly removed us from her sight. We'd go into one room and the maids would rush in and stash the woman in the adjoining room. We'd go in the next room and the maids would race her back into the first. Throughout all the movement Yoya kept screaming, I told you, Tacho! I told you that the Conservatives would come back! I said you couldn't trust the Granadans!

In an odd way she was right. Many scions of the conservative Granada families were now Sandinistas. Yoya was simply off by fifty years, which in political terms meant she had missed the birth of a new order in Nicaragua. But the birth was to be more painful than I ever imagined.

4

The People in Power

In 1983, long after leaving his less than influential position with the Sandinista government, contra leader Edén Pastora lived in a large house with an empty swimming pool on a hill in San José, Costa Rica. The swimming pool he purposely left unfilled to distinguish his surroundings from what he considered the Mercedes-Benz-type excesses of the new ruling Sandinistas in Managua.

The house was encircled by bodyguards and machine

guns. Pastora's fear of assassination was legitimate—"El Gordo" Clachard, a quiet, pudgy associate of Pastora's, had recently exploded in a parking lot near the American embassy. An ostensible defector from the FSLN, Clachard had just finished calling Pastora's house to announce his imminent arrival when the bomb wired to his body, a bomb intended to kill Pastora, accidentally detonated as Clachard entered his car.

Pastora would regularly invite a group of us to his house for lunch. Those in attendance included Carlos Coronel, who sat at the other end of the table from Pastora; "Pichichín" Jérez, aide to Alfonso Robelo; one of Costa Rican ex-President Figueres' children; Pastora's deputy, Harold Martínez; his cousin, Orión Pastora; his brother-in-law, Emiliano; and several others including myself.

Pastora's wife, Doña Yolanda, served the lunch. Pastora called her his "Indian," arguing that she had Indian blood in her veins just like Sandino's wife, Blanca. Pastora's old wet nurse, more than eighty years old, also sat in attendance, as did the "Little Doctor," Pastora's male nurse, who had also been Tachito Somoza's nurse and who was Doña Yolanda's brother.

Playing nearby were Pastora's children, Edén Atanacio (which supposedly was spelled thus to represent the reverse of Anastasio Somoza; to Pastora, *Anastasio* meant darkness and *Atanacio* meant light). Pastora's young daughter Yaosca and his other daughters, who were fat, were also near the table. He called the girls his "Shermans," after the tanks. All in all, Pastora claimed responsibility for between twenty and twenty-two children.

Sometimes Doña Yolanda would cook the food herself. Other times Pastora ordered Kentucky Fried Chicken and, as he pretended he did not drink, he dispensed only fancy liqueurs, especially Cointreau, which infuriated Carlos Coronel, who was a legendary drinker.

When the meal ended Pastora would reminisce over the

glorious days of the old Sandinista Southern Front. The story he repeated endlessly was how he could have had it all: the army, the government, the whole country. Command of the Southern Front had provided Pastora with between two and three thousand men, good artillery, and relatively controllable Cuban advisers. But he never made it to Managua before the city fell—the charismatic Somocista Commander Bravo had kept Pastora at bay. When the city did fall Pastora had advanced only as far as Masaya, twelve miles from the capital, into an area called Piedras Quemadas.

At this point Pastora would pause for effect and say that some of his comrades had suggested he should ask Managua to meet him halfway: i.e., he should share power with those already in the capital. But others—and here he would turn and face Carlos Coronel, never accusing Coronel of any misdeeds but nonetheless speaking with enormous bitterness— had advised him that such a demand might mean continued civil war. It was time to show the Pastora sense of discipline. The people were tired of war.

The initial wave of Sandinistas, including Tomás Borge, Violeta Chamorro, and Daniel Ortega, flew to León, the first FSLN-liberated city in Nicaragua, from Costa Rica. They entered Managua on July 18. The next wave of rebels, including Humberto Ortega, followed shortly thereafter. The moment Humberto reached Managua he called upon the man responsible for the internal insurrection, Joaquín Cuadra, and the two of them drove to the country's most important military complex, The Hill. They took it. The symbolism of this conquest was enormous. Humberto now held The Hill and, historically, whoever held The Hill held the country.

Pastora didn't appear in Managua until July 20, with about two thousand men travelling slowly in trucks. As they drove Pastora sat at the head of the truck convoy, passing through town after town dressed in his filthy uniform, which he thought symbolized his hard work.

When his truck drove by, the people shouted his name out loud. They went crazy for him. Pastora's face was still the best known throughout the country.

The moment Pastora arrived, minus five hundred men left behind to keep order in the countryside, the FSLN Directorate moved him to El Retiro, Hope Somoza's old house. The unreliable Southern Front was now lodged and disarmed—with the excuse that the revolution had to register every weapon—until something could be done with the men. By the time Pastora finally managed to make it to the military installation on The Hill—already renamed Chipote, after the northern Nicaraguan hill from where Sandino had operated—he found that Cuban advisers were in place, giving directions as to who would enter and who would exit. The number of Cubans was increasing to the point of domination. Even Humberto's bodyguard was a Cuban. Before Pastora had any chance to consolidate power it had slipped out of his reach.

On July 26 Pastora received his first official orders from Humberto Ortega. He was chosen to lead a two-thousand-man militia into northern Nicaragua and fight what was already turning into a small counterrevolution. The nucleus was not the two thousand members of the National Guard who had sought refuge in Honduras but members of the Northern Front of the Sandinista Terceristas. Commander "El Danto," in the last days of the insurrection, had fallen in combat. Some of his people refused to surrender their weapons as Pastora had done. They didn't trust the FSLN National Directorate and they retreated to the mountains where they had once hidden in their struggle against Somoza.

Pastora was chosen to fight these people for the symbolism: to show that the most popular commander was toeing the line. Two days after he left he received a quiet order to return to Managua, which didn't really want a fully armed Pastora roaming freely through the countryside.

The two principal beneficiaries of Pastora's inability to seize the government were Humberto Ortega and Tomás Borge.

No single natural leader had emerged among the FSLN since Carlos Fonseca's death. The likelihood of a power struggle loomed behind all decisions. The FSLN Directorate were forced to balance their forces like jugglers, throwing each other off center, engaging in continuous small skirmishes. For the next few years the sovereignty in the country tipped between the Ortegas and Borge and their supporting factions. Humberto's first act was to take control of the army, while Borge established the Sandinista security apparatus and a police squad which mutated into a formidable paramilitary force.

None of the Sandinistas had ever previously governed a country and their talents, or lack thereof, began to surface. Humberto proved the most politic of all. His premier talent was his ability to fashion a loyal cadre of dedicated followers. He did this by appointing the children of the aristocracy as some of his closest commanders. True to Nicaraguan political history, Humberto chose men who were loyal to his personality rather than to any ideology. The gamble was that his field commanders would never conspire against him because they had a distinct ideological inferiority complex. These men were descendants of the upper classes. They had to work harder than the others, to evidence more zeal, to prove their revolutionary fervor and to emerge from the shadow of their privilege. They were not likely to stray from Humberto's line.

The CIA advised that these field commanders would someday rebel against the Sandinista leadership, that their inherent class instincts would ultimately surface. But Humberto has proved accurate so far.

Once it was established that Borge and Humberto would command two distinct armed forces, the two battled over power bases: who would control the customs—and therefore the quasi-military force proximate to it—the helicopters, etc. The struggle was decided in part over the Lenín Cerna connection. Cerna had always remained faithful to the party of the old Marxist line. Tomás Borge interpreted this as an expression of personal commitment and he selected Cerna to head the security apparatus. Old ties eventually proved stronger. Under the table Cerna was close to the Ortegas, who had been his companions in the San Antonio neighborhood in old Managua. Cerna, in fact, had recruited the Ortega brothers into the FSLN in the early 1960s.

Cerna's role in the Ortega/Borge seesaw became pivotal as Borge's security apparatus increasingly evolved into an ugly, brutal force. Its sins and its excesses were consequently blamed on Borge. In reality the Ortegas were responsible, employing a strategy similar to the way Luís Somoza had used his brother Tachito to carry out the unpleasant parts of his agenda. The Ortegas dispatched their orders through Cerna but, as Borge was ultimately responsible for the actions of the apparatus, he was seen as culpable for the brutality. His reputation as a hard-liner widened.

To help create a government palatable for international consumption, cabinet posts were distributed to the nonideological bourgeoisie, to the praise of America and Europe. It was soon evident inside the government that behind every minister was a member of the FSLN, one who usually disagreed with the policies of the ministers. As a result policies were seldom carried out. The conflicts which rapidly developed between the ministers of the facade and the ministers of the Sandinista Party created government paralysis.

The government junta was supposed to represent other forces outside the FSLN but the real organ of power was the FSLN's National Directorate, in which each of the three tendencies was represented by its three top men: the nine *commandantes*. The party was still in the hands of Borge's hard-line GPP faction. Borge believed that the party would overpower the government, as it had done in the Soviet Union.

Jaime Wheelock, the leader of the proletariat faction, was awarded the Ministry of Land Reform. An able theoretician, Wheelock believed that the peasants in the cooperatives would develop a social conscience and give him their allegiance. But the ultimate failure of land reform left Wheelock without a power base.

Humberto Ortega controlled the army, Borge the security apparatus. Daniel Ortega, as a member of the junta, was preparing to undertake an international role, looking for a higher profile overseas. Three people immediately understood the likelihood of Daniel's success and gathered their forces behind him: Rosario Murillo, Daniel's common-law wife; the Maryknoll priest Miguel d'Escoto, who was the Foreign Minister; and Sergio Ramírez, a writer and member of the junta.

The Ortega brothers, like the Somozas, were classical products of the rural petite bourgeoisie. Their family came from the province of Chontales; their mother, Doña Lidia Saavedra, was a descendant of a devoted Catholic, very conservative family. The Saavedras were followers of the *caudillo* Emiliano Chamorro.

Don Camilo, the Ortegas' father, was the illegitimate child of a well-known member of the Liberal Party, a schoolteacher at the public school in Granada. He was also the representative of various German commercial products in Nicaragua—Don Camilo was fixated on Germany and its culture and became a great admirer of Adolf Hitler. He named his daughter Germania.

Don Camilo was also an admirer of the economic vitality of the United States. Once, when some Americans came through town operating a land-purchasing scam in Florida, he bought some theoretical property, paying ten dollars each month to the scam for years. When Humberto came to power, one of his first questions was whether he could go and collect his father's land in Florida.

The three Ortega brothers—the youngest, Camilo, died in the February 1978 Monimbó uprising—first attended school at the Instituto Pedagógico in Managua and in the school yearbook they are pictured with their classmates, the sons of Luís Somoza. They later quit the Instituto when Don Camilo suffered financial difficulty. The brothers were transferred to El Maestro Gabriel, a poorer school where they were politicized.

Humberto, two years younger than Daniel, was the stronger personality—he was considered smarter, more pragmatic. Humberto never trained to be an ideological cadre. While in Cuba he was instructed in radio operation and explosives. Daniel had undergone much more serious Marxist training. He was more ideological, more serious, and he combined the two traits with the sense of bitterness developed by seven years spent in jail. As the two began to cultivate their power base in the government, Humberto's more visible role disappeared and Daniel emerged from his shadow.

The Murillo/d'Escoto/Ramírez troika sensed that Daniel was pliable. Father Miguel d'Escoto, a man with whom I quarreled endlessly, was the first to support Daniel, as he believed he could eventually influence him.

Father d'Escoto was another Nicaraguan contradiction, an ardent Sandinista raised by a fervent Somocista. His father, Miguel, had had a close relationship with all the Somozas, especially Tachito, and was the godfather of one of his daughters—Tachito was godfather to many but he had only five children himself and they had only five godfathers. Miguel, who was widely nicknamed "Count d'Escoto," regarded himself as a man of nobility. He bought the title of a genuine Italian count and changed his family name, Escoto, by adding the "d" and the apostrophe. He served as Tachito

Somoza's ambassador to Paris and was famous for his collection of cars and watches.

He was also renowned for his wit and daring, a small sense of limits, and a great instinct for nobility. You see these hands, he used to say, holding out his perfect white fingers. These hands have never worked a day in their lives.

When his son, Father Miguel d'Escoto, correctly foresaw the future, he switched sides and accommodated his past to the present regime. When Ambassador d'Escoto died, Father d'Escoto rehabilitated him in one sentence. At the funeral, in front of a large government audience, d'Escoto declared that his father had been the country's first real Marxist.

Father d'Escoto became the interpreter of the world to Daniel Ortega. He taught the boy from the provinces how to eat, how to talk, how to conduct himself with propriety. Call Miguel, Daniel said when he traveled abroad, whenever he met customs that were strange or perplexing. Let him explain these matters to us.

Sergio Ramírez joined forces with d'Escoto to work with and influence Daniel Ortega. A member of the petite bourgeoisie, during the revolution Ramírez had been one of the members of the Group of Twelve. He was very confident of his intellectual ability, always a very clear, very focused man.

His hometown was Masatepe, where both his parents were minor Somocista officials. Ramírez' marriage was similar to that of the first Somoza: studying law in León, Ramírez fell in love with his present wife, Tulita Guerrero, while exchanging glances in church. Ramírez' provincial background wasn't acceptable to the Guerreros. But, as in Somoza's life, the potent Leónese family of Sánchez interceded. They knew Ramírez' parents and sympathized with his plight of love. They also wanted to help the son of a Liberal Party family.

The third member of the troika behind Daniel Ortega was his common-law wife, Rosario Murillo. Her father owned land near Tipitapa and an urban bus company. Murillo herself was educated in Switzerland, where she learned French, before she returned to Nicaragua to work as a secretary for Pedro Joaquín Chamorro at *La Prensa*. She had met Daniel Ortega while they were living in Costa Rica. There she was known by her code name "Aura." Her expensive taste and mannered deportment made her a good partner for the more provincial Daniel.

Humberto's wife, Marcela Trejos, was much less ostentatious than Rosario Murillo, although she came from a very distinguished Costa Rican family. She disliked Rosario Murillo probably as much as Murillo disliked Marcela Ortega. Marcela did not take an active role in the government, although she had a powerful revolutionary past—she had participated in a plot with Carlos Agüero, a distinguished Sandinista commander and a nephew of the famed peasant orator and eye doctor Fernando Agüero, to hijack a plane in Costa Rica. As ransom, they obtained the freedom of Carlos Fonseca and Humberto Ortega, who was in jail himself for a failed attempt in December 1970 to liberate Fonseca from a Costa Rican jail.

The formation of the new government marked the first profound tension between the Ortega brothers, whose wives were already antagonistic and whose advisers conspired against one another. The brothers learned to spend their time alone, in each other's houses or in the home of Doña Lidia, their mother, who tried to help her sons maintain some semblance of a typical life.

Most often, to avoid the friction of others, they met at Daniel's bungalow in Tipitapa, under a mango tree, where they could talk in peace.

The Nicaraguan bourgeoisie never developed a fully integrated class consciousness. The Somozas had not allowed them to cultivate such an awareness as they dealt with the families individually, inhibiting the formation of a cohesive social class. After the revolution many in the bourgeoisie felt reassured because they had relatives within the FSLN.

But not all families were so represented. To help guarantee a sense of status quo they resorted to a historically Nicaraguan means. The daughters of the bourgeoisie were offered in marriage to the Sandinista commanders, allowing the bourgeoisie the opportunity to forge compromises similar to those it had made with the Somozas. These women ordinarily might never have been interested in the men. Now they found themselves in powerful liaisons with them. And family land, which might otherwise have been confiscated in the name of the revolution, was protected in the names of their owners by the revolutionary marriages.

The cleverest families of the bourgeoisie were the first to recognize in the Sandinistas the image of the Somozas. I remember a visit by Carlos Pellas, the elder son of the most financially powerful families in Nicaragua, to Humberto Ortega, one year after the revolution. Accompanying Pellas were members of the Chamorro clan from Granada. Humberto had agreed to see them, more out of curiosity than anything else.

The men's first words were: this was the office of Somoza, no? In other words, I have been here before, I know how to do this.

The visitors were not curious about democracy or the country's new economic model or the recently formed government. They had questions about visas. They wished to enter and exit the country freely. They wanted permits for their yachts at the port of San Juan del Sur. They felt that harassment by the local authorities could be avoided. Perhaps in twenty years all these families will be banished to Miami. But they will have accumulated a fortune in the meantime.

After the Pellases and the Chamorros had left, Humberto turned around and asked his close aide, Mario Castillo, this is the bourgeoisie? These are the people we hate? The

Sandinistas had regarded these families as the giants of the country. Finally standing close to them, they appeared to be pygmies.

I was, at this time, twenty-six years old and the counselor at the Nicaraguan embassy in Washington, D.C. I was very close to the ambassador, Rafael Solís. He was twenty-seven. We had been friends from childhood.

I had received several offers from the Sandinistas; above all, d'Escoto wanted me to work with him in Managua at the Ministry of Foreign Affairs. He proposed I work at the Central American desk in the Foreign Ministry. He flattered me exhaustively with praise of my diplomatic skills and my inestimable intelligence. There was a problem, however. The other counselor at the Nicaraguan embassy was d'Escoto's younger brother Francisco, who had always ridden on his father's coattails. D'Escoto knew that Solís would rely much more heavily on me than on Francisco d'Escoto, because of our long friendship, and he wanted me out of his brother's way. The best means of getting me out of Washington was to keep me in Managua.

Solís was aware that it would be wise for his personal interests to retain my services. When Daniel Ortega flew to Washington in 1979 to meet with President Carter, Solís appealed to Daniel directly for permission for me to stay at the embassy. Daniel agreed. Father d'Escoto never forgave me.

Carter's Washington was absorbed by the dilemma of confronting or coopting the revolution. The rationale for assimilation was that if America hadn't alienated Fidel Castro he wouldn't have turned to the Soviet Union for aid. The hostility between Cuba and the United States was a product of American instigation as much as of Cuban ideology. The Carter administration could learn from history and avoid another Cuba. This view prevailed for a short time.

One reason was the efforts of Ambassador Lawrence Pezzullo, one of the most diligent Americans I ever met. We should work with these people, he said to Carter. We can help the revolution. Pezzullo brought with him to Managua Larry Harrison, one of the ablest bureaucrats in AID. The two worked in unison to solidify U.S. ties with the revolution.

It was due to the force of Pezzullo's personality and the strength of his convictions that, early in the junta's history, the United States developed a special relationship toward Nicaragua in several ways. It played a positive role in all multilateral lending institutions, such as the World Bank and the Inter-American Development Bank, helping the Nicaraguan government to obtain the loans necessary for its survival. The Americans were also key players with regard to the commercial banks in New York and the International Monetary Fund, asking them to be flexible in renegotiating commercial debt with Nicaragua. When Nicaragua renegotiated its debt with the steering committees of the banks to which it owed money, the deal was accomplished without having to enter into a standby agreement with the IMF.

Pezzullo also guaranteed that government bilateral programs such as AID would be generous, and he made sure that the Nicaraguan government of national reconstruction could benefit from Public Law 480, which allowed purchase of food in the United States market. And a high percentage of the aid from the United States was special support funds, at low interest rates, money normally loaned only to friends of the United States such as Israel, Egypt, or Jordan.

By accomplishing all this, Pezzullo provided an example for the rest of the world to follow.

The American Democratic Congress, however, was uneasy over Managua's increasingly visible manifestation of radicalism, perhaps most exemplified by the PLO leader Yasir Arafat's arrival in Managua. Congress heard for the first time the anthem of the FSLN, which contained an articulate statement of belief that America was both Nicaragua's enemy and "the enemy of humanity." Congress in turn demanded that a good percentage of the aid should be given to the private sector. Pezzullo supervised the money's direction as much as he could. He firmly believed that the revolution would take time to mature and tolerance was the proper attitude.

In the junta's first two years, the government of Nicaragua received $1.6 billion of net capital—eighty percent of it from the West. Instead of being strangled in the cradle, the revolution was overfed with milk.

The CIA couldn't contain its misgivings. Their operatives sent cable after cable to Langley, reporting how the Sandinistas were sending pilots off for training in Bulgaria, the Soviet Union, East Germany, and Cuba; how the Vietnamese, North Koreans, Palestinians, and Libyans were coming to Managua. The CIA was also tracking the increasing dissatisfaction of Panama's Torrijos, who was not being allowed to participate in the new government as fully as he had hoped. Torrijos' offer to help train the Sandinista police and air forces was rejected, demonstrating that Managua was willing to accept money or advisers from the West, but for tourism and tax collection. As far as the army, security apparatus, or the party was concerned, the advisers were all from Communist regimes or from the PLO. Only these outsiders were allowed inside Managua.

The CIA station chief warned, We are paying for the eventual establishment of a Soviet base in Nicaragua.

Pezzullo counterargued: what other choice did America have? Particularly in a noninterventionist Carter administration? Besides, Pezzullo added, as long as men such as Arturo Cruz, Sr., and Edén Pastora were moderating forces within the government, how far left could the country possibly drift? Pezzullo firmly believed that Nicaragua's geographic position made it inevitable that the country would have to swing, if not directly under the American orbit, at least within its gravity.

And, he argued, Nicaragua was basically a traditional

country. The power of the Church and the peasants would combine to moderate the government. Pezzullo recommended that the Americans buy the Sandinistas' good will and cautioned them to remain patient. The animosity between Pezzullo and the CIA widened. But for the time being Pezzullo prevailed.

Other complications arose. Foremost was the shipment of Soviet T-55 tanks to the Sandinistas in May/June 1981. Pezzullo quickly sought an audience with Jaime Wheelock (Humberto could not be reached) and told him to throw the tanks in the lake. Wheelock declined.

The tanks were a controversial issue for some time. Their arrival helped delineate the growing discord within the government. Humberto Ortega had requested the tanks to help him establish power. Borge did not support the request because he did not want Humberto's power to grow. But when the Americans heard Borge caution against accepting major Soviet weaponry, they wondered if Borge was the hard-liner they had previously assumed. Perhaps a deal could be worked out with him?

When Pastora heard about the tanks he said, the GPP tendency of Tomás Borge will never unite with the rest of us. Let's just surround the Ministry of the Interior with the tanks and let's get the dwarf Borge to come out with his hands on his ass. Borge is very short. For that matter, so is Pastora.

My diplomatic work was comprised of three major tasks. I was to interpret the mood of the United States and report my findings back to Managua. I was to convince the Americans to ignore our fiery rhetoric; that we were indeed sending men and women to East Germany and Bulgaria, but these were minor details. If you were truly clever, I said, you would always remember that the United States is the sun, and we are just the moon, only a pale reflection of the huge country above us. And I was also engaged in what we called "father management." My father was beginning to suffer severe reservations about the revolution. Every time he endured a bout of these doubts my role was to fly to Managua and appease him.

He attached continuing strong symbolic importance to the Managua regime. He had an international reputation as a democratic moderate who nonetheless supported the ruling junta. He was the Valium of the revolution. At any time, when a sense of uneasiness pervaded the Nicaraguan middle class, the commanders would trot out my father and ask him to talk openly about the economy.

Politics made the relationship between my father and me, always complicated, even more so. My father was fully aware of and skeptical about what I was doing.

Even if he hadn't been, the CIA cautioned him in 1982, after I had left Nicaragua, not to trust me because I was a Marxist. My father never told me this. I found out from my mother long afterward. She despaired of the Americans by this time. She accused them of trying to separate my father from me.

I honestly believed that reading my father's moods for the Sandinistas was proper and pragmatic. The revolution relied on him, and when I talked to my father I tried to make him believe this. We were, after all, on the same side.

Another key part of my job was to meet with Manuel a Cuban intelligence officer operating in New York, at the United Nations. Manuel was on a constant information quest. The two of us would meet at Washington bookstores where we would stand and read every kind of publication available, analyzing American society, tracking who was powerful, who had lost power, comparing and analyzing daily trends, formulating the lines we felt it necessary to take and how we could defend ourselves in the American debate.

Our major obsession was the prospect of an incoming Reagan team, should Reagan win. Before the 1980 elections I visited Managua to talk with Jacinto Suárez, the Deputy Minister for Foreign Affairs, d'Escoto's number two. When we told him we had to make these contacts, he responded that the revolution was not a prostitute. I said, from my knowledge of Manuel's work, the Cubans are the biggest whores in town—they've already made their contacts.

I was also, throughout the late 1970s into the '80s, spending time with "Valentin," a KGB officer attached to the Soviet embassy in Washington. I had originally met Valentin while studying at Johns Hopkins University, at a conference I was attending on Latin American affairs. Approaching me carefully, he simply said, my name is Valentin, I'm from the Soviet embassy and I would like to talk to you.

I had guessed. Valentin looked like an undercover parody —he wore the standard 1950s Russian hat, a pathetic white raincoat; his skin was pale and his hair greasy black. Even in conspiratorial Nicaragua I had never known anyone to look so furtive. Maintaining eye-to-eye contact with Valentin was formidable. The man was endlessly glancing over his shoulder to check for a tail. We met at unpleasant restaurants which took us hours to locate in order to beat the feared tail. It never occurred to him that he might not have a tail. I never spotted it.

Valentin usually picked me up at the corner of 17th and Corcoran streets in Washington, at a McDonald's. Other times we'd meet at monuments, where he'd open the car door and I'd jump inside.

Unlike the smooth, facile Cubans, Valentin was brutally direct. His questions could be embarrassing, explicit to the point of alarm. The Soviets often displayed this maladroit bent. Once Manuel and I were at the United Nations to meet his Soviet counterpart after a meeting of the nonaligned nations. The Soviet was waiting at the door, in full view of the public, to be instantly briefed by his subordinate, the supposedly nonaligned, impartial Cuban.

Valentin tried interminably to recruit me into his service. He was very pessimistic about my relationship with the Cubans, whom he did not trust—nor did most Russians, which was why the Bulgarians were assuming an increasingly important role in Nicaraguan affairs. The Cubans were too complicated; the Bulgarians, the one country in the socialist world always loyal to the Soviet Union, were easier to comprehend.

The new Soviet attitude was that the communist world could not afford any more Cubas that take but never return money. Nicaragua was receiving a great deal of foreign exchange, and the Bulgarians wanted some of it.

When I first met Valentin the U.S.S.R.'s policy toward Nicaragua was one of interested distance. They had accumulated a prodigious sense of geographical fatalism about Central America. How could an area directly within the American Empire ever truly break free? The Cuban revolution was deemed anomalous.

Valentin explained how surprised the U.S.S.R. had been to discover how rabidly pro-Soviet the Sandinistas were. The early Cuban years were different; Castro had proved an annoyance to the U.S.S.R. when he accepted an enormous amount of Soviet aid and then behaved as he wished on the global scene. At that time—the 1960s—the Sino-Soviet rift was at its peak. Castro spoke out against both countries in an effort to establish a position for himself, and his ego, between the two giants. The Soviets were furious. But Nicaragua was a windfall profit. The Sandinistas were more doctrinaire, more pro-Soviet than Castro's Cuba. As if to prove this, the FSLN refused to establish relations with the People's Republic of China and retained, for a while, the diplomatic relations that Somoza had established with Taiwan. And at the sixth meeting of the nonaligned countries in Havana, Daniel Ortega took the classic pro-Soviet line on issues from Kampuchea to disarmament. We are with you, we said to the U.S.S.R.

I would always say to Valentin, I can't tell you everything I know. He'd insist: comrade, my friend, you are a promising young diplomat. Since a promising young diplomat such as yourself shouldn't walk, you must have a car. The mission can get you a lovely car.

Whereupon he would retrieve a plain envelope from inside his coat and place it on the table.

I could never touch it. To pick it up, to count it, was tantamount to admitting you were for sale. I nearly died of curiosity; I never knew how much I was worth to them.

Valentin maintained a profound respect for the Soviet system which, as he said, allowed his mother to put butter on her bread. He was from the generation still grateful. The Sandinistas aroused his cynicism. He told me it took the Soviets decades to ride in a limousine. In Nicaragua, he said, it took them days.

Valentin was also cynical about his own superiors in the Soviet Union, how ignorant they remained of the American political system. After a few drinks he would complain about the arduous task of explaining American politics to his bosses—that the American Congress had a mind different than the President, that the Washington *Post* and the New York *Times* did not operate like *Pravda*.

As his tenure ended Valentin became less Slav and more elegant. Soviet yuppies were moving up into his intelligence area. This new generation was more confident. They dressed fashionably, they understood the American mind better, they were more facile at bribing American office boys to steal reports. Instead of meeting at obscure Chinese cafés they dined at trendy restaurants such as Clyde's. Valentin knew that if he didn't adjust he'd disappear into the bureaucracy, a casualty of the rising young professional class below.

The first anniversary of the revolution in July 1980 was marked by several curious phenomena.

Among them was the spooking of General Chinchilla. Chinchilla was the head of the Honduran air force, the most powerful armed service of his country. He had come to Managua with other world dignitaries to participate in the celebration. At one point Humberto took Chinchilla aside and told him of his blueprint to build a great army, the largest in Central America. Chinchilla returned to Honduras obsessed with possible Nicaraguan aggression. When the time came to find sanctuary for the counterrevolution, the Hondurans, anticipating an invasion from Nicaragua, provided the land.

Another phenomenon was Fidel Castro's visit. Castro proved he had learned a lesson by staying only five days. During the time of Salvador Allende's leftist government in Chile, Castro had visited the country for three weeks—much too long a time to spend in a land suffering from a nervous right and an apprehensive center. He caused some considerable trouble for the Allende regime.

But Castro's short visit to Managua further clarified Humberto Ortega's status as Castro's personal favorite among the nine commanders. Tomás Borge had prepared a place for Castro but Castro stayed where Humberto asked him to stay. Castro could not tolerate any sounds whatsoever at night, so Humberto provided not only for security but also for noise. Castro rode in Humberto's car. Castro only met with the Ortega faction. All these were powerful symbols. The revolutionary father was blessing Humberto.

Humberto was younger than Castro and, like his Cuban mentor, he had been the great strategist. Borge felt himself almost an equal to Castro, in both age and experience. He found it difficult to accept the role of Castro as father and of himself as the child. Castro could neither dominate Borge nor trust him.

Castro spent most of his time in Managua but at one point Edén Pastora accompanied him on a trip to the southern border of Nicaragua near Costa Rica. Pastora later told me that he could never forget the look of hunger on Castro's face while he looked at Costa Rica.

I always thought that, more than anyone else, Carlos Coronel was truly Fidel Castro's favorite in Managua. Unfortunately the favoritism didn't pay when it came time to apportion the favors of the Sandinista government. Either Castro didn't have enough power to push Coronel or, more likely, Castro's agenda lay elsewhere. Whatever the reason, Coronel felt ignored by the revolutionary government and, when nothing was offered commensurate with his expectations, he withdrew to his father's plantation in the south.

The Sandinistas essentially distrusted Coronel. He maintained equable relationships with both Pastora and Castro. He was too shrewd. He could juggle more conflicting conspiracies at one time than any other Nicaraguan—than any other human being—I have ever met. Tomás Borge hated Coronel and wanted him removed.

Humberto agreed. If there was anyone with whom Ortega had to share credit for the revolution it was Coronel. Carlos Coronel was the one who had first conceived of Costa Rica as the rear guard. He was the one who had insisted on moderating the political rhetoric to increase international aid, who helped invent a "Tercerismo" alliance with the bourgeoisie. He introduced the Ortegas to former Costa Rican President Figueres, who provided them with weapons. Coronel was also the one who most clearly understood that, without money, revolution was only theory. He was the one who recruited the nucleus of the Southern Front. He was so talented, he was too dangerous.

But the Cubans possessed enormous power in Managua. Their ambassador, Julian López, affected the government as much as, if not more than, any American ambassador ever had. (López was popular with the National Directorate but he was recalled to Cuba in 1987 when he made the fatal blunder of criticizing Raoul Castro, Fidel's brother.) López pressured the Sandinistas into providing Coronel a position of power and Coronel was named Minister of Fisheries. The Cubans prided themselves on their first-class fishing; they considered the post a potential power base.

Coronel was thus reintegrated into the game, whereupon,

according to Carlos, Castro flew Coronel and his family to
Cuba in his private plane.

You're going to screw me, Coronel told Castro after the
plane ride.

How could that be? Castro asked him.

By giving me favors, you are creating too much jealousy
on the part of the others in Managua, Coronel responded.
Still, Coronel never rejected the attention from his political
godfather.

As soon as Coronel was back in a position of influence the
Soviets began to court him as a potential ally. Coronel
promptly persuaded Humberto Ortega that Fidel Castro had
accrued too much influence over the Sandinistas, that Alex-
ander Haig in Washington worked on the assumption that all
Nicaraguan questions could be handled through Castro, not
through the FSLN. To the Americans, to the Soviets, to the
world, Castro had fashioned himself as the father of the nine
unruly commanders. If you have a problem with the
Sandinistas, he said, fix it with me.

My father's experience validated Coronel's perception.
When he once asked Connecticut's Senator Chris Dodd to tell
him how he would remedy American policy on Managua if
given a chance, Dodd replied that he would take Castro fishing and in a few days the two would resolve the whole thing.

Humberto accepted Coronel's advice and embarked on a
campaign to forge his own relationships with Moscow. The
first accomplishment of Coronel, the man rescued by the
Cubans, was to convince Humberto to appeal directly to
Moscow over the heads of his Cuban advisers.

The final phenomenon of that first anniversary was the
momentary resuscitation of Edén Pastora. He was given an
appointment to serve as the leader of the military parade. It
was not a position of any power but the concept of the job
pleased Pastora immensely.

Nicaraguan processions are imbued with symbolic power.

Pastora was not the only one to succumb. After the revolution the conductor of the National Guard band was allowed to remain in the country as the leader of the new band. No one else had the requisite skills. The man was a very clever survivor. On his first ceremonial occasion he had to perform with members of the governing junta standing on one side of his band and the National Directorate of the FSLN on the other. According to custom, the bandleader required permission from the executive to start. In Somoza's era he knew where to look: to Somoza. Now he was in a quandary. Who was more powerful, the Sandinista party or the government? Who was the executive? He had no idea. Nobody did. So, raising his left hand to the left side of his head, and his right hand to the right side of his head, he saluted both factions at once.

Pastora enjoyed the parade. When it ended he went back to his role as a powerless vice-minister at the Ministry of Interior. There was never any paper on his desk. Anyone who wished to see him simply walked into his office and said hello. Unhappy, bored, and restless, Pastora, the warrior without a war, spent most of his time visiting the Indian neighborhood of Monimbó, where he was revered as the hero of the revolution.

The last Sandinista party apparatus meetings in which Pastora was asked to participate concerned the Salvadoran guerrillas. By January 1981 the Salvadoran rebels had decided, along with the Cubans, to launch their final offensive against the government. If successful, they could present the incoming Reagan administration with a fait accompli.

And so, in Managua, a final offensive in El Salvador was planned. The Cubans sent the man known as Ramiro Abreu, an official from the Department of the Americas, which was headed by Commander Manuel Piñeiro. Piñeiro was known as "Red Beard" for the unusual color of his hair. I always considered his looks more Viking than Cuban.

Pastora disagreed with the consensus. There was no ugly

ruler to depose in El Salvador, he said, no equivalent of a Somoza to facilitate a national insurrection. The situation was too confused. But he held great sympathy for the Organización Revolucionaria del Pueblo en Armas (ORPA) guerrillas in Guatemala who he thought worked with the political flexibility of the Terceristas in Nicaragua. And the ORPA understood the primacy of the Indian struggle in the primarily Indian nation of Guatemala, which had a reputation, at that time, almost as bad as South Africa's.

Aiding a guerrilla force in Guatemala with a reputation as noncommunist, in a battle against an army already loathed in the world community, Pastora argued, made much more sense than aiding the Salvadoran guerrillas. Furthermore, if ORPA were victorious, Honduras and El Salvador would be caught in a geopolitical squeeze between Nicaragua and Guatemala.

The assumptions of the Salvadoran guerrillas also were awry, Pastora argued. They believed the army's principal barracks would turn against the government. This was dubious, Pastora said. And the ratio of bullets per man in guerrilla units was less than 50:1; this would allow maybe twenty minutes of combat. Finally, he contended that the guerrillas' tremendous setbacks inside the cities meant that urban insurrection, and therefore the revolution, was hopeless.

But Sandinista military commander Joaquín Cuadra accused Pastora of being overly technical, saying that he lacked the necessary trust of the revolutionary potential of the masses. The Cuban Abreu sided with Cuadra and said to Carlos Coronel, while waiting at the airport to leave for Panama, We will soon celebrate with champagne in El Salvador.

The Salvadoran offensive was launched days before Reagan's inauguration. It turned into just the debacle Pastora had predicted.

Pastora knew his peers did not take him seriously. Top commanders mocked him to his face. Bayardo Arce used to salute Pastora and laugh out loud. Both Borge and Arce understood Pastora—most people did. They knew he could be humiliated, broken down. And if he were to leave, his defection would hurt Humberto Ortega worse than it would hurt them.

Pastora did leave Nicaragua. Before he did, his friend Carlos Coronel attempted to create one last conspiracy to detain him. Coronel knew that a mild rapprochement between Wheelock and Pastora would strengthen the anti-Borge faction. The problem was that Wheelock and Pastora hated each other. Pastora acted upon impulse, Wheelock was an intellectual. Pastora imagined himself a soldier. He accused the blond, handsome Wheelock of being effeminate. "The Virgin Carbine," Pastora used to call Wheelock. The only pistol Wheelock has, Pastora would say, is the pistol of his hair dryer.

Wheelock owed his life to Carlos Coronel; Coronel had helped save him from Tomás Borge's execution attempt years earlier. The men were close friends. Wheelock allowed Coronel to talk him into meeting with Pastora.

Coronel planned an excursion to Corn Island on the east coast. The island once catered to the Somocistas but now is a Sandinista resort. It is a lovely island in the Caribbean, surrounded by clear turquoise water and the untouched wrecks of colonial ships lying beneath the sea. Coronel invited Wheelock and his wife, Pastora and his wife, and their children. He also invited Luís Carrión Cruz and his wife, and Dora Maria Tellez and her friend, my cousin Gloria Carrión Cruz.

The expedition was a catastrophe. Instead of Wheelock and Pastora becoming friends, sharing their mutual misgivings over Arce and Borge, Pastora spent his time trying to seduce my cousin Gloria. But his considerable charm floundered on the wall of Gloria Maria's indifference.

At the end of the trip Coronel said of Pastora, I will never deal with this man again. It was only wishful thinking on Coronel's part.

By mid-June, Pastora was restless. He felt pushed aside and decided to leave the country. He had always admired Che Guevara. When Che left Cuba to launch his Bolivian adventures in the mid-1960s—and Pastora had always predicted that there wasn't enough room in Cuba for both Castro and Che—he left behind a fiery letter explaining that he intended to fight for revolutionary justice and liberty in oppressed lands.

Pastora too wrote a letter. He entrusted it to Humberto's aide, Mario Castillo, who was to pass it along to Humberto the morning after he had left.

Humberto Ortega knew the letter could damage his political standing. This will be expensive for us, he told Mario Castillo. Humberto tried to lessen the potential political fallout by letting others know that, like Che, Pastora had written a letter and that revolution still lived inside Pastora. The fact is, and everyone knew it, Pastora was simply unhappy.

During Holy Week of 1981, Pastora left the country. He took his bodyguards, and two Mercedeses, a Fiat, and a Toyota jeep with him, but left his family behind.

He first went to Costa Rica, where he spent only a few hours, and then continued to Panama to see Omar Torrijos. A few days after Torrijos had deposited him safely in a protocol house, Mario Castillo arrived and requested an audience with Pastora and Torrijos. Torrijos agreed but not before complaining bitterly to Castillo about how ungrateful Humberto had been to him. In the war against Somoza, Humberto had gladly accepted Torrijos' military aid, along with Panama's diplomatic recognition, but now Humberto ignored Torrijos' offers of military training and turned instead to the Cubans and the Soviets. Moreover, the Sandinistas were disregarding his ambassador to Managua.

Mario Castillo left for Nicaragua but soon reappeared with Tomás Borge, who arrived accompanied by a crew of Sandinista commanders. Borge immediately met with Pastora.

Upon seeing him, Borge burst into tears; he embraced Pastora and called him his "lost sheep." They conversed for hours until reaching an agreement whereby Pastora could return to Managua. Pastora was willing to accept, he later told Castillo, as long as he knew he was in the hands of Humberto Ortega's people and not Borge's.

Pastora returned to Nicaragua briefly, after visiting Panama. His former comrades-in-arms came to visit him one by one, except for his antagonist in the army, Joaquín Cuadra. Pastora was pleased with the reception and hopeful for his future.

He then lost the game for good. The FSLN offered him exactly the position he had requested in his letter—the bridge between the Guatemalan guerrillas and Managua. He hadn't really wanted this job; the request had been purely for the sake of posturing. He wanted a post in the Directorate. Now he had no choice but to accept the position, or leave for good. He left.

What next followed were the global travels of Edén Pastora. He went first to Panama and then took off for Cuba, to see if he really could work with the Cubans to aid the Guatemalan guerrillas. While in Cuba he asked the Cubans to give his bodyguards military training so that his men could do something while they waited. Pastora then flew to Madrid, from where he crossed to North Africa to visit the Polisario guerrillas fighting against the Moroccans. Then he went to visit Qaddafi in Libya. Qaddafi agreed to provide five million dollars for Pastora to operate a revolutionary program in Guatemala.

When the FSLN discovered the amount, they sent a delegate to Qaddafi to request that the money be given to them instead of Pastora. Pastora, on his return to Panama, discovered the FSLN maneuver and became further upset. He felt he alone had possessed the means to provide the Guatemalan guerrillas with military supplies, which according to his people he had already done by purchasing 150 M-1 semiautomatic rifles (for ninety dollars each) in Hialeah, Florida and introducing them into Guatemalan territory through Belize. Pastora flew to Cuba to complain to Castro that the FSLN was interfering with his success. When Humberto Ortega heard Pastora was in Havana, he pleaded with Castro to keep Pastora in Cuba until he knew what to do with him.

Pastora's final departure from Managua destroyed the equilibrium of the true FSLN vanguard. The forces which actually defeated Somoza, I have always thought, were not the FSLN, composed of the new revolutionary set, the old-line Marxists, and the Terceristas in the middle. The Terceristas alone won the war. They too were composed of three forces: the military hero Pastora, Joaquín Cuadra and the other young Terceristas in the internal military front, and between them the Ortegas. The symmetry among these three had forced them to become flexible enough to adapt to changing external pressures.

At the same time, the Ortegas felt they had to reinforce their radical rhetoric. Humberto may have been the least ideological of the Directorate, but the need to assert himself within the new equilibrium forced him to address issues in which he did not really believe. Likewise, Daniel Ortega, who would have favored a mixed economy as a tactical tool in the transition to socialism, felt pressured by the hard-line GPP and the proletariat tendency to create a "revolutionary" economy right away. The difference was not of direction but of pace. The Ortegas, in order not to lose the battle for revolutionary posture, were being pushed further and further left, with no Pastora on the other side to balance them. Torrijos was probably correct. Pastora did leave too soon.

A few months later, in August, the month of rain in Panama, Torrijos died in an airplane crash. No one ever knew who or what was responsible but many Panamanians claimed that Torrijos himself was to blame. He had demanded his pilot take off in rough weather—and it is hard for a pilot to say no to the leader. When the plane went down the force most likely to moderate Managua was lost.

Just after the Sandinistas' first anniversary the Washington diplomatic corps was invited to witness Ronald Reagan accept the Republican nomination in Detroit. I attended the ceremonies in place of my friend Ambassador Solís, who could not leave Washington. The corps was flown to Detroit by the American government on a plane crowded with diplomats from around the world.

The agenda of activities resembled an American high school field trip. We were herded from function to function and in the process were able to talk freely to one another in the company of our enemies. I remember one reception when an East German diplomat approached me while I was standing next to the Soviets. He said, Arturo, Russia is too far from you, don't count on them for help.

At the mayor's residence Nancy Reagan put in a brief appearance in a helicopter and all the diplomats ran toward her and snapped her picture as though she were a Hollywood star. We were escorted through the Detroit Art Museum, and all the while the East Germans followed me, warning me about the Soviets.

I did spend much of my time in Detroit with the Soviets, especially the younger ones, who, when we discussed Lenin, were embarrassed that they had not read *The Development of Capitalism in Russia*—required reading for the young Marxists of Latin America. The older ones were simply cynical. They looked at me, their expressions saying, I'd like to see you in twenty years; you tropical revolutionaries are such a pain in the ass. We pay for you, we give you money, but who knows what will happen?

As for myself, I was looking in the mirror and in my vanity I was seeing a young George Kennan. His *Russia and the West* influenced me more than any book I had read. In time I learned to respect the anti-Stalinists, such as Bukharin, even

Trotsky. They allowed one to be a Marxist without being pro-Soviet. And just as Kennan the young diplomat explained the first year of the Soviet experience to America, I was trying to educate the Sandinistas about the United States. As I envisioned it, my role was not only to advise my ambassador but, through my dispatches and trips, to explain the mysteries of Washington to Managua.

Over and over I had to correct the Nicaraguan notion that every piece of legislation enacted by the American Congress which hurt Nicaragua was enacted for that and only that reason. I would have to explain repeatedly that, for foreign aid bills, the budgetary process of all nations, not just ours, was affected; that legislation had to pass through a complicated procedure, little or none of which related to Managua.

The Soviets were even more of a conundrum to Ambassador Solís and the Sandinistas, who were too preoccupied trying to understand the Americans to pay proper attention to the Soviets. According to the diplomatic code in Washington, D.C., a new delegation of diplomats must present its credentials to the President of the United States; after that, a courtesy visit to the dean of the diplomatic corps is required. The dean is chosen by seniority. Until 1979 that dean had been Somoza's ambassador, Guillermo Sevilla Sacasa, the brother-in-law of Anastasio Somoza. Number two in the hierarchy was the Soviet ambassador, Anatoly Dobrynin, who was now first.

As the new Nicaraguan embassy staff, we made our perfunctory call on Dobrynin at the end of 1979. Solís was terribly excited at the prospect of meeting the Soviets and looked forward to a full discussion of socialist brotherhood. In fact, Dobrynin couldn't wait to get rid of us. He had called in his Latin American specialist, who trembled throughout the meeting. Given the limited Soviet historical involvement in Latin America, it was highly possible the man had never before been called to a meeting with Dobrynin. The two welcomed us as briefly and politely as possible.

At the time of the Republican convention, angry discussions between Father d'Escoto and me concluded with d'Escoto canceling my diplomatic passport. My Washington career over, I went to Managua to begin work for Julio López in the international relations department of the FSLN party. The Cubans immediately invited me to Havana, which indicated their degree of support, something I could draw upon if needed. I believed highly in Cuba's political analysis, and in the skills of the analysts themselves. Unlike America, Cuba employs its best and brightest people in intelligence work. The country was a disaster at the management level and the economy was in chaos. But in the realm of international intelligence, the world beyond the island, the Cubans were exceptional.

Above all the Cubans always understood that talking, intimate social interactions, and getting drunk are the means to invite intimacy and cajole confidences. Such contact reveals the inner soul of a country. A person's loves and hates reveal his tribe. The CIA agent meets socially only to delegate his instructions from above. He doesn't have the time to drink. He doesn't drink on the job. He is a manager, not an analyst of the soul. The Cuban intelligence officer can be a man of enormous charm and he pretends to be your friend. The CIA operative acts like your boss.

CIA agents believe in management. Their heroes are management gurus such as Lee Iacocca or Tom Peters. The United States has the capacity to buy a country. The Cubans buy only the government ministers.

The advent of the Reagan administration was cause for extensive anxiety in the Sandinista regime. But the apprehension abated when it appeared that the difference between the new Reagan and the old Carter administrations was only one of rhetoric. A huge chasm between words and action soon appeared. We will go to the source, Haig announced ominously, implying that the Administration blamed Cuba for Central American turmoil and that it would construct a policy to deter Castro's activism in the area. Or that they would topple Castro himself. The truth is, they didn't seem to have any clear idea of what to do.

The Sandinistas increasingly believed that the Reagan administration was a paper tiger. More and more they followed the internal complications of American policy and planned how to exploit those considerations. To speak to the Americans they hired Paul Reichler, a perceptive Washington lobbyist from Torrijos' old law firm of Arnold and Porter. Reichler was now working on his own and he was very effective in opposing Reagan's policy. He became a central part of the Sandinista regime.

When Julio López and I met with Reichler, López was impressed by how the only word Reichler could speak in Spanish was *compañero*. This guy, said López, calls us comrade, but he charges us like a capitalist.

American foreign policy was caught in a crisis of power and will. The conservatives argued that America's failures had nothing to do with power. We have all the power, they said. When are we willing to use it? Then they would point to Nicaragua and say, We have the power to remedy the situation. Do we have the will?

The answer was no. The Administration retained Ambassador Pezzullo in Managua because they didn't have any other ready options. Pezzullo still argued that the Administration should explore the possibilities of dealing with the Sandinistas. The argument prevailed because the Administration was much more concerned with El Salvador than with Nicaragua. Reagan could successfully argue that Carter and the Democrats lost Nicaragua, but not El Salvador. The Administration directed its primary attention to the disaster next door, where the early hopes for an easy victory were already waning.

Reagan's point man for these efforts was Thomas O. Enders, Undersecretary of State for Latin American Affairs. Enders initiated what was called the "two track" approach: America would use force on the Sandinistas if necessary but they would revert to negotiations if the Sandinistas remained within their borders.

Working with Enders to reach a solution was my father, who had been appointed the Sandinistas' ambassador to Washington. It was his third job in less than two years. In May 1980 Violeta Chamorro, feigning illness, had left the ruling junta. The truth was that she didn't agree with the Sandinista politics and could no longer pretend she did. Soon after she left, Alfonso Robelo quit the junta also. This further heightened the sense of political urgency. The Sandinistas asked my father if in the interests of stability he would replace Robelo. He wasn't disposed to serve at first, but Archbishop Obando y Bravo helped convince him, arguing that moderation was still possible.

But my father also became disenchanted with the Sandinista radicalization. He realized he was at best only a nominal force. He refused, however, to embarrass the Sandinistas by leaving them openly. After delicate negotiations the FSLN commanders arranged his departure from the junta into the ambassadorship, explaining to the world that this was in accordance with his own wishes.

By 1981 Washington was sensing the beginnings of a natural base of opposition within Nicaragua. The depressed economies of El Salvador and Guatemala had kept the guardsmen who had left the country jobless. A return to Nicaragua meant certain imprisonment, so many of them gathered on the Honduran border where small towns offered relative sanctuary and the men were able to operate inside a growing black market for cattle.

In Nicaragua the business community was upset over the FSLN's fiery rhetoric on the subject of private property. The actual Sandinista confiscations appeared arbitrary, aimed not at the most powerful members of the bourgeoisie but at the rank-and-file middle class.

The Church, too, was tense, displeased by the repudiation of what they considered to be the original plan of the revolution. *La Prensa*, now run by ex-junta member Violeta Chamorro, was openly critical of Sandinista repression. Ex-junta member Alfonso Robelo's political party, the MDN, once allied to the Sandinistas, was attempting to establish itself as an alternative party.

In the countryside, the peasants were feeling victimized by the government's price policy. Food prices were being kept artificially low to benefit urban consumers, whose wages had been depressed. The peasants were farming at a loss. Workers were upset that their wages couldn't match the country's growing inflation.

The question of land was never as vital in Nicaragua as it was in Guatemala or El Salvador. Historically, land was abundant and labor expensive because the ratio of people to land was low. When the Spanish first arrived in Nicaragua, the Indian population was estimated at between 600,000 and 1,200,000. From 1528 to 1540 around 200,000 of these Indians were sent to Panama or Peru as slaves; others died from disease or slaughter. By 1867, Nicaragua was a country of only 167,000 people. Long after the country received its independence, it remained a simple economy, isolated from the world, a place where the cattle ranch was the principal economic unit. The Somozas' full integration of Nicaragua into the world economy was accomplished by increasing commodity production for exports (cotton, sugar, meat, coffee) but without sacrificing the food-producing sector of the peasant families.

In their first two years the Sandinistas were able to manage the economy with the huge influx of foreign aid, which was used among other things to import and to subsidize the price of food. By early 1982 it was apparent that the international bonanza could not last forever. The Nicaraguan economy had to be put in order. Consumption had to give way to investment; the external debt had to be paid.

At the same time as dissent grew inside Nicaragua, the exile community in Miami and Tegucigalpa, some of them admirers of the past regime, began to fantasize that the new regime was crumbling and that American forces would back them. In February 1981 the United States suspended the balance of fifteen million dollars of aid still in the pipeline to Nicaragua and in March they stupidly suspended PL 480, canceling a purchase of wheat. The American people take the bread from the Nicaraguans, they said, while they then sent a symbolic shipment of wheat.

The Nicaraguan exiles began to organize for a return. Armed with their expectation that a Reagan presidency meant it was only a matter of time before the Americans would intervene in Nicaragua, the exiles celebrated the 1981 New Year by packing their bags to prepare for a new government in Managua. They even started an embryonic military movement, training on weekends in the Florida keys, under the aegis of Cuban exiles.

But President Reagan's early attempts to galvanize the American public against the Sandinistas were poorly received. In February the Administration distributed "The White Book," which contained documents captured from the Salvadoran guerrillas showing the involvement of the Sandinistas. Julio López and Commander Bayardo Arce were most concerned—their code names were mentioned in the documents released in the book's text. But the American press, rather than accepting the largely true report, questioned its authenticity, in part to protest the Administration's policy. In the end, the release of the study damaged Washington more than Managua, and the Sandinistas understood that, in a curious manner, Reagan could prove to be their best ally because the mainstream American press opposed

Reagan's foreign policy and did not appear eager to attack Managua.

The Nicaraguans were impressed that Enders, a six-foot-eight, silver-haired American patrician, would venture down to their country at all. Here was a man of the Empire bending down to meet the Sandinistas on their own turf. The Sandinistas were delighted. There could be no incipient military threat—just a bunch of cowboys on the border and the weekend clowns in Miami—if Washington was being so conciliatory.

Enders' agenda was simple: you keep out of El Salvador, and we'll keep out of Nicaragua.

Shortly after the talks with Enders the Sandinistas jailed four members of the private sector who had issued a communiqué accusing the FSLN of Marxism. The FSLN resented the openness of the attack, not the attack itself—they later jailed members of the Communist Party also for having defied their authority.

My father became furious over the incident. I was with him at the Nicaraguan embassy in Washington when he heard the news. He immediately called Henry Ruíz, for whom he held a deep affection, going back to Jinotepe. Ruíz defended the action. He knew that the behavior was arbitrary and capricious but said he found it necessary. My father argued back; he compared the incarceration to killing a fly on a window with a baseball bat.

This incident, along with the assassination of Jorge Salazar, a prominent member of the private sector, by the Sandinistas; the growing anger of congressional leader Jim Wright with the Sandinistas; the various government shutdowns of *La Prensa;* Ambassador Pezzullo's departure, and his discouragement because no possibility for compromise between the two sides had developed; and Archbishop Obando y Bravo's clashes with the FSLN—all led my father to quit for good.

I did not want him to leave. I still hoped that the revolution would relinquish ideology in the face of practical need. There might never be a democracy but a rational and honest government was the essence of what I thought we had all fought for. I wanted my father to wait longer but he couldn't.

When I told Managua that he was quitting for good the Sandinistas sent Mundo Jarquín and me to accompany him from Washington to Managua where, at the airport, two Mercedes-Benzes were waiting for us. The one with Father d'Escoto took my father to see Daniel Ortega, and by the middle of the same day a carefully planned resignation was announced. It was all incredibly efficient. My father could exit either publicly or privately. He chose the private exit. He left the country to work at the Inter-American Development Bank in Washington.

He was replaced by a man chosen by Father d'Escoto, who along with Sergio Ramírez was delighted to see my father leave the government (my father's replacement as ambassador defected to the United States shortly thereafter).

At the same time, Ambassador Pezzullo was replaced in Managua by Anthony Quainton. Quainton soon agreed with the CIA that Tomás Borge was most likely to become the country's new strongman. Borge exploited this theory beautifully. He initiated an alliance with Quainton, and Quainton, like most American ambassadors in Latin America, was seduced by the native rulers. This was one of the rare times that the State Department and the CIA were both in agreement, although both were wrong.

Confusion was endemic in Managua. The rivalry within the Sandinista Directorate was unbridled and American intentions ambiguous. Two assassinations, one in 1979 and one in 1980, helped clarify the country's fate for the rest of the decade.

Just after they came to power the Sandinistas began to plot the death of Pablo Emilio Salazar, also known as Commander Bravo. Bravo had been the most daring and skillful young member of the National Guard, a natural leader, a charismatic speaker, and a remarkable strategist. His people would follow him to their deaths. In their fantasy Bravo was the one Somocista who had never lost. The Sandinistas had never defeated him—as the commander of Somoza's elite troop of five hundred, Bravo had halted Pastora's march into Managua. After Somoza crumbled, Bravo had withdrawn to the port of San Juan del Sur, placed his troops on rafts, and sailed to El Salvador and Honduras.

More than anyone else opposed to the Sandinista regime, Bravo had the potential to become the leader of a strong military opposition.

The rumor in Managua was that Edén Pastora discovered the access to Bravo. Pastora was having an affair with a woman whose closets, one night, he happened to be idly searching—he seldom hid either his curiosity or his paranoia. While rummaging through the woman's clothes he discovered a National Guardsman's uniform. The uniform had the name of the owner attached to the shirt pocket—Salazar.

Why do you have this? Pastora asked the woman.

He was my lover, she replied.

The woman became the crux of the plan. She was asked to call Bravo in Tegucigalpa, Honduras, to let him know that she still thought of him longingly. He said he was thinking of her too and arranged to fly her in from Managua. When she arrived in Honduras they met near the Hotel Maya in downtown Tegucigalpa. On October 10, 1979, they took a taxi to the Hotel Reno across the street from the airport. Bravo's companions warned him not to go; he ignored them.

At the hotel the Sandinistas captured and tortured Bravo, slowly protracting his death. In the process, Bravo's face was ripped off. The intention was not only to kill him but to send a clear message to anyone so disposed to challenge the regime. Daniel Ortega's old friend and recruiter, Lenín Cerna was in charge of the operation that culminated in Bravo's death, although he did not participate in the torture. The operation was such a success and so exalted Cerna's reputation in Sandinista circles that it led to his eventual appointment as chief of the secret police.

The counterrevolution lost its natural leader with Bravo's assassination. Upon news of his death, Tomás Borge announced: The head of that sector of the counterrevolution has been cut off. So when the time came for the United States to organize the contra forces in northern Nicaragua they were forced to look for another leader.

On September 17, 1980, Tachito Somoza was assassinated while living in exile in Asunción, Paraguay. Tachito was having a fight with his mistress Dinorah, and angrily ran out of his house and climbed into his unarmored Mercedes. Tachito disliked armored cars as much as his father did because he couldn't drive with the windows open. They both claimed it made them feel claustrophobic. Tachito's bodyguards scrambled to follow him but they were too late. Somoza drove to his bank to attend to his financial work and along the way a bazooka attack killed him.

His death was welcomed by the Americans. As long as Somoza lived there was little possibility for a counterrevolution which wasn't under his direct control. It would always have been said, even if it weren't true, that Somoza was controlling the movement. And no one in America would have supported it.

The Sandinistas were never stupid. If they planned this assassination they were betraying an inherent ignorance of the world, as the event helped launch the contra movement. So the word was that the Americans must have killed Somoza.

It was a false conclusion. What was certain was that, with this death, the contra (that is, the counterrevolution) was ready to begin.

5

The Birth
of the Contra

By mid-1981 it was clear that official United States policy
in Nicaragua was one of containment rather than rollback.
The CIA did not yet dare dream of overturning the Managua
regime. Instead they made their intentions clear through the
neighboring country of Honduras. The Americans solicited
Honduras' blessing to establish a military base in the Gulf of
Fonseca—a body of water shared by El Salvador, Nicaragua,
and Honduras—in August 1981.

A month after the base was installed, Honduras and the United States engaged in joint military maneuvers. The Honduran government construed these maneuvers as forceful assurance that the United States would reinforce Honduras' position in Central America—that the United States would aid their country just as the Soviet Union was supporting Nicaragua.

These measures were enacted while Enders' two-track State Department initiative was still under way. My experience with the Sandinistas indicated that, like Reagan's hardliners, they had no desire for the Enders initiative to succeed either. At this point the concept of the counterrevolution was not a threat to Managua. The government was actually able to use it as an excuse to move in a more radical direction while blaming the Reagan administration.

The Nicaraguan economy, buoyed by foreign aid, was still growing. World opinion remained positive. El Salvador appeared ready to collapse at any minute. Why should Managua negotiate when it could win?

While Pastora was in Havana in transit to Europe, Daniel Ortega stopped in after a meeting with Enders in Nicaragua. What did the American say? Castro asked Ortega while Pastora was still in the room. Ortega explained that Enders' goal was to keep Nicaragua out of El Salvador, and in return the United States would leave Nicaragua alone.

Oh, no, no, no, Castro said. Don't deal with the Americans yet. Not on El Salvador. You must hesitate. You must stall. You will probably win.

Events in Central America mutate rapidly. The failure of the Salvadoran guerrillas' offensive had created the illusion inside the Reagan administration that Central America might be handled easily. A few months later it became clear that this would not be the case. The Salvadoran situation soon worsened. The army was in disarray and its motivation was suspect—it was an army that the American press began to call the army that worked from nine to five and then took off for the weekend. The presence of Salvadoran guerrillas in the urban areas continued to increase. Suddenly Washington was overcome with the fear that the Administration which had a policy of standing up to communism might now lose a country—El Salvador—to the communists.

It became increasingly obvious that not just El Salvador but all of Central America was going to cost the Americans dearly. Throughout the decades of the 1950s, 1960s, and 1970s the United States had invested relatively little money in the forgotten frontier. One of the most significant findings of the bipartisan Kissinger Commission, established by Reagan in July 1983, was that Central America was to become an expensive proposition. Keeping it within the American sphere of influence might cost billions, not millions.

The United States no longer held a monopoly in the area. With the large military presence of the Soviet Union in Nicaragua, the United States was being forced to upgrade the quantity and quality of military hardware provided to the other countries in the region. Moreover, in terms of financial support, the demands of the urban societies had grown while the economies of the region had not.

Within Nicaragua the social base of a genuine contra movement was emerging. Remnants of the old Somoza National Guard—sergeants who had never known any life but battle—were joined by members of the old Sandinista Northern Front and entire clans of peasants chafing under the Sandinista policies. Aligning with those groups were the "Milpas": young students who had fought as allies, not subordinates, of the Sandinistas and who now refused to give up their arms. And on the Atlantic coast, in the city of Bluefields, the blacks too were instigating revolt, although they were easily suppressed by Managua.

The Miskito Indians were also restless. The Sandinistas perceived the ethnic Indian issue as one of national security and thus they resorted to repression rather than dialogue to resolve the problem. As early as December 1981 Humberto Ortega decided to depopulate vast tracts of the Atlantic Zone in order to deprive the growing counterrevolution of a base. From the Coco River to Waspan, the area was "cleansed." The Sandinistas forcibly removed the Miskitos from their Coco River homes to resettlement villages elsewhere in the country. Coercing the Miskitos to leave the Coco had repercussions on the Indians not dissimilar to moving the Egyptians from the Nile. But the Miskitos were unable to develop any effective form of protest, nor were they able to find anyone outside Nicaragua to listen to their plight. Barely two months later, Humberto's personal envoy to the Atlantic Zone told him that the program was turning into a nightmare. It was Humberto who decided to recall the army and pass the problem to Tomás Borge and State Security. Said Tomás Borge in 1981, the Indians will have to recognize the inevitability of history. If not they will be crushed.

The Argentines were the first foreign force to try to organize all these disparate Nicaraguan dissidents. Engaged in their "dirty war"—the battle against the Argentine internal radical left, the Montoneros—the Argentine government entered the operation in 1980. An Argentine intelligence officer in Tegucigalpa, Honduras, met with a member of the Chamorro clan, "El Negro" Chamorro, and the other anti-Somocista civilians, along with ex-officers of the National Guard. The Argentine offered to organize the men in return for their commitment to combat the leftist Montoneros believed to be inside Nicaragua. This was, for the contra rebels, the first mark of international recognition.

The Argentine intelligence captain returned to Buenos Aires to explain the significance of the Nicaraguan rebels to his superiors. On his second trip to Honduras he offered a new proposal. Buenos Aires was willing to provide training to the men—two to three weeks in Argentina—and also financial support. In return the men would help the Argentines fight against any Montoneros in the region, but especially inside Nicaragua. The Argentines' military training would help the Nicaraguan exiles in their battle with Managua.

Three groups of fifteen to thirty Nicaraguan exiles flew down to Argentina for training. Then an Argentinian colonel, Santiago Villegas, arrived in Guatemala with a new proposal. Disband the 15th of September Legion (an early confederation of Nicaraguan exiles which had provided temporary organization), he said, and create a new political organization, to be called the FDN: the Nicaraguan Democratic Force. The Argentine asked that Colonel Enrique Bermúdez be included within the military part of the FDN.

The solemn, poker-faced Bermúdez had been trained in the Panama Canal Zone and the United States. He was the man chosen by Somoza to lead the Nicaraguan platoon dispatched to the Dominican Republic in 1965 in support of the United States intervention. Bermúdez was the son of a domestic servant, a man who used the National Guard for social mobility and who married above his class while stationed in the Dominican Republic. When the Somoza regime collapsed, Bermúdez was serving as a military attaché in Washington. The Argentinians thought he was reliable. And so the contras were formally organized.

I was in Managua as these forces began to align under the direction of the Argentines. It seemed, at the time, as though a bunch of politicians had now been added to some unhappy northern ex-National Guardsmen. The forces of darkness were uniting. My recollection of one of the men chosen to lead the political wing of the FDN—a prominent anti-Somocista and an ex-Sandinista—was of a rotund, convivial drinker. Once at a party for Nicaraguan businessmen in Washington to lobby for aid, this man became so inebriated that, when he wished to urinate, he asked me if I would help him. I pushed him up a flight of steps to the third floor, and then, after asking me to hold him at the urinal, he missed.

Instead, he urinated on me. This was my image of the men of the north: men who pissed on other people's pants.

Among those joining him were Justiniano Pérez, who had served as a deputy of the magnetic Commander Bravo. And there was Aristides Sánchez, a former member of the Liberal Party whose grandfather had been the Foreign Minister for the great modernizer, Zelaya. In other words, it seemed as if the past, the defeated remnants of Somocisma, were being recreated in the north, trying to confront the wave of the future in Managua. Tactically, it all appeared more useful than threatening to the Sandinistas.

Then, at the end of 1981, a meeting took place in Buenos Aires, attended by a representative of the United States (although at the time it was not clear to the Nicaraguans whether this man represented the CIA or the Pentagon). General Mario Davico, the chief of Argentinian President Leopoldo Galtieri's military intelligence; Colonel Torres-Arias, chief of security in Honduras; and another Argentinian named General Balin were also there. They agreed on the need for a more effective counterrevolutionary operation. They also agreed on how to divide the shapeless movement: the Argentinians would provide the advisers; the Hondurans the territory; the Americans the money; and the Nicaraguans the bodies.

Close to the same time as the Buenos Aires meeting President Reagan requested and received from Congress for the first time nineteen million dollars for covert operations against the Sandinistas. The approval supposedly was for the contras to intercept weapons going to El Salvador. So the policy continued to be about El Salvador rather than Managua, even when the first American monies were approved.

As a result of the Argentine meeting and the American money, for the first time the contras began to receive weapons, in January 1982. Five hundred FAL rifles were distributed among three groups, organized under the old National Guard code names: Sagittarius, Libra, and Ariel. It was not long before they were active inside the country: by March 1982 the bridge over the Río Negro was sabotaged, providing the Sandinistas an excuse to declare a state of emergency.

The Argentinians were not long for the contra coalition, however, owing to the outbreak of the Falklands War. Argentina fully expected their new partner in Central America, the United States—the author of the Monroe Doctrine—to cooperate and support them against the British. The Americans explained repeatedly that they had no intention of declaring war on Britain. The Argentines could not believe the Americans would desert them. They also never really believed that the British would steam all the way down to the Falklands. But events dispelled their beliefs. The Americans didn't help, the British did arrive, and Galtieri's government fell. The Argentine advisers in Honduras disappeared back to Argentina. The only offer of help the Argentines received was from Managua, which publicly volunteered to send troops to help Argentina fight British imperialism, a shrewd gesture which truly touched the hearts of the Argentine military. Also, the Nicaraguan ambassador in Quito, Ecuador, showed up on the doorstep of the Argentine embassy, volunteering to fight.

In March 1982 El Salvador held successful civilian elections, initiating a process which eventually placed Napoleón Duarte in the presidency. The Sandinistas were stung by what they considered a major blow to the guerrilla movement when the American Congress, encouraged by the elections, voted to provide aid to fight the Managua-backed Salvadoran guerrillas. Both the American press and House Majority Leader Jim Wright seemed to be genuinely touched by the elections in which civilians, under constant threat of gunfire by the guerrilla forces, went to the polls and voted.

With the elections, the FSLN realized that the Reagan administration now had a bipartisan consensus and with that legitimacy. El Salvadora's breakdown was no longer inevitable. Managua now developed an interest in negotiations with the United States. The Administration, however, impressed with the number of peasants appearing at the Northern Front to fight Managua, was stepping up its war. It now recommended that the United States did not have an urgent need for direct talks with Nicaragua.

The CIA's new man—code-named "Maroni"—was a well-liked figure within the CIA offices, a man of great energy and charm. At six foot six he was almost Enders' height, although not as patrician as the Yankee Enders. A huge man with a great appetite, Maroni became known to us as the "Man of the Cigar," since he always had one in his mouth.

Maroni realized that the war was to continue with a Northern Front and the Southern Front. The Southern Front was the wild and undisciplined force, largely made up of anti-Somocista members, while the Northern Front would become a conventional army composed of people with whom he was familiar—Bermúdez, for instance. Bermúdez was not an inspired soldier, but he was reliable. He had known the American Empire at its height; and he trusted that when the Americans said they wanted to destroy Managua they would do so. With Bermúdez' talents, Maroni began to dream of possible victory.

To engineer the triumph, the CIA set in motion a plan which resembled the successful Sandinista operation against Somoza: a Northern Front, a Southern Front, and an internal front to promote urban insurrection within the cities. Who better to provide legitimacy to the Southern Front than the ex-leader of the Sandinistas' own Southern Front, Edén Pastora?

Further, Maroni reasoned, if Pastora were to join the contra, wouldn't many members of the Sandinista militia desert to join his ranks? This assumption had some basis in reality. Written on walls throughout Nicaragua were words such as *"Edén, Regresa Que Tus Milicias Te Esperan* [Edén, return, your militia is waiting for you]."

Enlisting Pastora became the center of the CIA's Pygmalion-like strategy to mold a man into the Che Guavera of the right.

The next question was: how to get Pastora out of Cuba to assume his new stature?

The answer, I believe, was Panama's Manuel Antonio Noriega, with the assistance of Carlos Coronel. The Sandinista National Directorate had suspended Coronel's party status because—they said—Coronel had not warned them of Pastora's departure. Coronel replied, "But you were the ones who drove him out." The actual reason for his trouble was that Coronel, like Pastora, was much too loose a cannon for the increasingly controlled Managua regime to stifle. No one —Managua, Moscow, Washington—could control Coronel's loyalty, or his mouth, with the possible exception of Fidel Castro.

Coronel left Nicaragua in September 1981 and traveled to Panama, then, for reasons never revealed, to Cuba. He next appeared suddenly in a house in Cuernavaca, Mexico, the home of a Nicaraguan dentist who had served as the Sandinista ambassador in Mexico City before quitting his post.

Carlos Coronel already had established CIA connections. I have been told that, sixty days before the fall of Somoza, the CIA asked to see Pastora. The Ortega brothers did not allow Pastora to go and instead sent Carlos Coronel. In the meeting that ensued the Americans indicated that they were aware the Sandinistas were likely to form a government. As the CIA often regards politics as though the process were similar to portfolio investment, they thought they might buy some stock in the Sandinistas. The rumored amount of money involved ranged from as little as thirty thousand dollars to a high of thirty million.

Pastora's people suggested to the United States that the best means of taking Pastora from Cuba was through the offices of Noriega. Noriega complied; he sent Martín Torrijos, the son of Omar Torrijos, to ask Castro to release Pastora. The Cubans were delighted to throw him into the waiting hands of Coronel, trusting Coronel's ability to Pastora-sit —and do the Cubans' bidding when necessary.

Those close to Castro say he has always felt he erred when he crushed all opposition to the Cuban revolution, and that a dissident Church and a controllable opposition would have served him well. He now contended that the Sandinistas should not repeat his lapse. He also had faith that the Sandinistas could manage their own counterrevolution. And so Pastora, one of the potential leaders of that movement, was released to the opposition camp.

Pastora was not overly conscious of any of these motives. But it never mattered in what ways Pastora was conscious. Someone simply had to handle him. Coronel was the one chosen. Along with Torrijos' son, Pastora arrived in Mexico from Cuba in early 1982. Maroni knew that Coronel was close to Castro and Pastora. The fact that he still wanted Pastora as a CIA asset was revolutionary in itself. The CIA deals with known quantities: businessmen and professional soldiers—Pastora was the apotheosis of the unknown, an adventurer, a man who had been with Fidel, a revolutionary who had petitioned Qaddafi for money for the Guatemalan guerrilla force ORPA. The CIA was taking a definite risk.

While in Mexico, Pastora and Maroni agreed on a basic exchange. Maroni would provide Pastora with weapons and monies to raise an army of seven thousand men. In return, Pastora would declare his enmity to his old comrades-in-arms. Pastora then returned to Costa Rica and received his first air drop of weapons, at El Tortugero.

According to those on the receiving end of the air drop, over half of the arms were destroyed when they hit the ground. The weapons were hurled from the plane on parachutes at such a low altitude that they didn't survive the bounce.

While meeting with the Americans in Mexico City, Pastora also met with a man called Rapel. Rapel was a representative of the Guatemalan guerrilla group ORPA. He and Pastora traveled together to Panama. Back in Costa Rica, Pastora decided to appoint one of his most trusted men to meet regularly with Rapel, so that Pastora would not be seen with the Guatemalan guerrillas publicly but they could continue to talk—just as Pastora also met with a representative of the Sandinistas.

Pastora also was making an affiliation with Alfonso Robelo, who had recently left Managua for exile in Costa Rica, taking his MDN—the opposition party that never quite became the opposition—with him.

Alfonso Robelo was an engineer, the preeminent businessman in his field. A member of a good family from a town near León, he thought of himself as a man of order. He was never seen with a hair out of place, his beard was always trimmed. He gave the constant impression that he had just gotten out of the shower. Robelo had been a prominent anti-Somocista. He then founded the MDN after Pedro Joaquín Chamorro's assassination. He was now poised to become a player in the contra rebellion for years to come.

Pastora brought Robelo into his movement. Robelo claimed not to have been aware, when he joined with Pastora, that Pastora was colluding with the CIA. And so Robelo, the democratic ex-Sandinista civilian, was introduced to the CIA by Pastora, the great revolutionary hero.

One year after his mysterious departure, Pastora gave a press conference in San José, Costa Rica, designed to make his opposition to Managua public. The document had been written by two people: one was Don Edelberto Torres, an old man of the left whose revolutionary credentials had been permanently sealed when FSLN founder and martyr Carlos Fonseca called him the patron saint of the Sandinistas. His cooperation was a symbolic and powerful gesture of Pastora's intact revolutionary credentials.

Pastora's statement was notably conciliatory toward the Sandinista regime. He called upon the National Directorate to reflect on the mistakes it had committed and asked if there wasn't still time to return to the promises of the original revolution.

Pastora read the release with unexpected polish. He was well received and all was calm. Then Chris Dickey, the reporter for the Washington *Post,* posed a series of questions which touched Pastora's most intimate fibers. No longer working with a prepared text, Pastora erupted in acrimony against Tomás Borge, Bayardo Arce, and Jaime Wheelock. The more he blustered, the more he referred to himself in the third person. Pastora is the most beloved commander of the revolution! he shouted. Pastora has been vulgarized by his old comrades! Pastora will bring them fire and fury! The tranquillity of his performance was shattered.

He also offered several moral judgments on the Sandinistas' life style, the luxurious habits of the *Comandantes* at a time when the Nicaraguan people were lacking basic means. The next day in the *Post* Chris Dickey commented on how ironic it was that Pastora mentioned all this while he himself was wearing a gold Rolex—a gift to Pastora from Humberto Ortega which he "sold" repeatedly whenever he needed to raise cash. No one who "bought" the watch, however, ever had the heart to actually remove it from his wrist.

The day of Pastora's press conference I was working with Julio López in the office of the Foreign Ministry in Managua. Father d'Escoto, the Foreign Minister, was not present. He seldom was. He traveled around the world so frequently that he was known among my friends as "The Flying Nun." The more d'Escoto traveled, the less power he accrued, but soon he seemed content with the perks of the job while permitting López to perform the office's primary work; d'Escoto still had Daniel Ortega's confidence and his ear. Julio López had taken over the ministry, literally, moving all his people from the international relations department of the FSLN into d'Escoto's office at the ministry.

While Pastora was speaking someone rushed into our office to say he was on the radio and that everyone was listening. López calmly walked outside, where we saw the entire Foreign Ministry staff holding radios in the garden, dozens of antennas extended. Turn off those radios now, López demanded. Go back to work. Everyone marched back inside, and no open discussion of Pastora's broadcast was permitted. But no one questioned that Pastora had touched an open wound of dissent.

The government was silent the day of the conference. The next day Pastora's old comrades of the Southern Front denounced him on Managua television. One even accused him of being the "Trotsky of our revolution." Sandinista army Chief of Staff Joaquín Cuadra—who was not only a brave warrior in his own right but who vigorously disliked Pastora —then delivered a furious speech, denouncing the revolutionary traitor Pastora and vowing that the long arm of revolutionary justice knew no boundaries. Everyone knew that Cuadra spoke for Humberto Ortega. Those who had militia identity cards issued under Pastora, who had been a nominal commander, burned their cards in public.

Most effectively, the Sandinistas sent a cadre of double agents to saturate Pastora's camp. His key advisers and even his mistress were Sandinista agents. The panorama of intrigue was such that the Southern Front's movements in Costa Rica were soon more carefully monitored by Managua than by Pastora's financiers in Washington.

Pastora's declaration had an enormous impact on me. Most importantly, I felt liberated from the revolutionary myth. He made me believe that one could be a dissident without being a Somocista or a National Guardsman. As long as I adhered to the new line defined by Pastora's text, I decided I could be critical of the Sandinistas but faithful to Nicaragua.

Property confiscations were now being levied against the middle class, rather than just against the rich. I was tired of the rhetoric, the lack of rational behavior. I was tired of my dual life—praising the Sandinista commanders during the day, getting drunk at night with friends and blasting the junta. I was unhappy with the overwhelming Soviet and Cuban intervention; that we were so pro-Soviet in everything we did. Ours is often a copycat culture. For the bourgeoisie everything that was American was perfect; then, for the Sandinistas, everything Cuban or Soviet was also perfect.

The economy was suffering, yet Ortega, who had gone to Moscow expecting help, returned with little in hand. But the party refused to adapt its attitude toward capitalist countries. In 1985, everyone kept saying, in 1985 the Soviets will come through. No one really knew why 1985 would be a magical year.

In early 1982, Orlando Nuñez, a young economic adviser to the FSLN, showed me an internal party document which I was told I could not copy or keep, but which I was to analyze. I read it through and told Nuñez the economy was a disaster. Investment had to increase but Managua at the time was increasing consumption instead. Through the sixties and seventies Nicaragua had developed a diversified export structure unlike Cuba's, made of sugar, beef, coffee, rice, seafood, and with a list of buyers other than the United States. That export base was now gone and was being replaced with nothing but wishful thinking.

A few months later I was asked by more experienced bureaucrats to take the economic statistics to Commander Henry Ruíz. The statistics were bad news. I said that the only way to compensate for the economy's decay would be either to export more, in cooperation with a private sector, or to make the Soviets provide more aid. Aid was a possibility. But Ruíz was adamantly opposed to cooperation. He gave me a lecture based on his years as a guerrilla leader in the hills, and said that if Nicaraguans had to go to the hills again, they would. The revolution, he said, is not for sale.

I left the meeting knowing that I had been used as the

messenger of bad news. But Ruíz' primary reaction was to fulminate against Jaime Wheelock, who, Ruíz said, did not know the meaning of sacrifice. His concern was the other commanders and not the statistics.

Some of us did not believe Nicaragua could become another Cuba. Nicaragua could not imitate the Cuban road to socialism, because we could never receive as much aid as they had. The Soviets could only afford so many Cubas, just as the Americans could only afford so many Puerto Ricos.

I was also offended by the growing cult of personality. None of us could leave a house or an office unless a superior commander departed first. We couldn't criticize. When Commander Bayardo Arce tried to justify the blunt transition of North Korea's government from Kim Il Sung to his son as something consistent with Asian Marxism, we were powerless to criticize such stupidity. We were turning our leaders into gods. There is nothing worse than to stand too close to the gods. The more you see of them, the worse you feel about them. The mystery is gone, and with the mystery, the respect.

Only Comandante Henry Ruíz seemed to be living with apparent humility—although some were less than impressed by his revolutionary code name, "Modesto." After the revolution he moved into a modern house. But he never bothered to furnish it as the others did, instead leaving it ghostlike—although he did have a pool table brought in. Living with him in the emptiness were his two elderly aunts—women who spent their entire day glued to an old black and white television.

The Moscow-educated Ruíz recognized the increasing materialism of others, and he decided to combat their habits of conspicuous consumption. Arnoldo Martínez was, at the time, the Subcomptroller of the Republic. Nicknamed "The Bald One," Martínez was remarkably honest and appalled by the corruption of many top Sandinista officials. One day I went to the beach with Henry Ruíz' subordinate, Mundo Jarquín, and my old friend Carlos Fernando Chamorro, editor of *Barricada,* the official party newspaper.

At the beach we spoke ardently about reform. Jarquín had already told me that the greatest enemy of the revolution was not counterrevolution but corruption in the Sandinista family. The three of us developed the notion that Carlos Chamorro could interview Martínez about the excesses and publicize them, embarrassing the revolution's leaders so that they would reform their ways.

Carlos Chamorro talked to Martínez and Martínez then checked with Daniel Ortega to see if he could talk to the party paper. Instead Ortega ordered Chamorro to terminate the scheme. Henry Ruíz, it seemed, was being encouraged by his GPP partners—Arce and Borge—to get at Ortega by pinpointing corrupt Terceristas. Jarquín had been taking advantage of our zeal for reform to involve Carlos Chamorro in a newspaper campaign against the *dolce vita* of the corrupt Sandinista officials. Daniel Ortega understood this, so he killed the article. Eventually the disillusioned Martínez left Managua.

Another problem in Managua was the growing Cuban presence. Formerly the Cubans were limited to a small group of high-quality advisers. Their number now multiplied and the quality of those sent decreased. The Cubans taught what they already knew. But Nicaragua's economy was not theirs. Our level of technocracy was higher, our computers were more up to date. Oddly, the Cubans were aliens in Nicaragua, despite their geographical proximity, because for years they had been politically isolated from the region. Their experts—at the general, not the intelligence, level—knew more about Africa than about Central America.

My job at this point was to prepare position papers for Julio López at the Department of International Relations. Among the issues I studied was the case of Soviet MiG fighters. During the first months of 1982 the portended arrival of MiGs in Managua overshadowed all other events. At the beginning of the revolution the FSLN had dispatched seventy young Nicaraguans to Bulgaria to study aviation mechanics and be trained as pilots for various MiG models. Speculation that Managua was about to receive MiGs was always rampant, especially after the Cubans received two squadrons of MiG-23s, the most advanced Soviet jet fighters, indicating that perhaps Nicaragua would now receive a lesser model from the Cubans.

But in Bulgaria the Nicaraguan student pilots failed their courses. Bulgaria was a closed, racist society, and the young dark-skinned Nicaraguans were mistreated and unhappy. The training was challenging but the students had been chosen for their potential capacity as fighters rather than their academic skill. Most of them had not finished high school and could not complete the pilot course. So the question was now, who would fly the MiGs? The speculation was, of course, that the Cubans would. Or worse, the Bulgarians themselves.

I drafted various scenarios to defend the MiGs' arrival to the Americans. But my conclusion was that it was almost impossible to do so because an absolute air-shield defense for Nicaragua was as provocative as an offensive capacity. Honduras was already using the justification of the MiGs to upgrade its own air force, which it felt was its only card in the balance of military power vis-à-vis Nicaragua. This already proved how expensive it was becoming to maintain a status quo in Central America.

The other part of my job was to draft papers on negotiations with the United States, based on three principles: that the negotiation process was a tool to buy time for the revolution; that the negotiators we chose had to be weak, so they could not make any decisions; that our negotiating strategy had to be based on the dynamic of American fears and anxieties so that we could take advantage of American dissension over Central America.

We grew more and more to understand the American psychology and were amazed. Julio López once told me that he could never understand the American reaction to the Iranian hostage crisis. Only fifty-six people were in jeopardy. The situation has proven that American life has become so valuable, López told me, that the troubles of only a few citizens can paralyze the entire country.

Another issue was whether or not we should negotiate with an agenda. The United States favored one. We refused. It was all an exercise in futility. Negotiating was a means, not an end. But many of us felt negotiations with the Americans were imperative. We felt we needed their financial collaboration—without it, the economy would die. We also felt that geopolitics demanded we not ignore the Empire. But our superiors were not excited by the idea.

More and more competent people were leaving the government, including Alfredo César, the young technocrat from Stanford, the economic star of the Tercerista faction, who had been close to the Ortegas. César had recently begun a program to provide incentives to the private sector to increase exports. Our balance-of-payments situation was impossible. But Soviet-trained Henry Ruíz opposed the plan on the ground that it gave a windfall profit back to the bourgeoisie. Ruíz also felt strongly that the Nicaraguan masses would willingly endure suffering for the revolutionary cause and that César did not understand the people. The Ortegas had first defended César, but not against ideological attacks. Now they retreated from his economic program and César decided to leave the country.

As a member of the party, he could not leave Nicaragua, however, without a special permit—no party member could. So he asked permission to leave the country for his honeymoon. He received permission on his wedding day, and he left with his wife. I found out on the Sunday following because a friend at the Central Bank told me that César's MasterCard had been revoked—the surest means of detecting that a defection had occurred.

César went to Costa Rica to stand on the sidelines and wait for an opportunity to return. With his departure, the economic situation became more hopeless than before.

For those with access to the statistics, the country seemed to be collapsing. We would mention this to our superiors. They would answer by accusing us of being too technocratic. They pointed out the success of the security apparatus, the police, the army. But life was becoming repressive. I ran into a friend who had been jailed for helping the Miskitos and he told me he had been tortured. I fled from him, frightened that the security police would see me with him and that my loyalty would be suspect. Then I hated myself for what I had done, for the life I was leading.

I decided to leave the revolution.

The excuse I used was that I would fly to America and persuade my father to refrain from becoming involved in the contra revolution. Since this was considered part of my job of father management, I received permission to leave, three weeks after I had already decided to go into exile. I told no one of my plans and left all my books behind me, pretending I was taking a four-day trip. I flew to Washington.

During the period just before I departed, I became totally uncritical, for the first time, of my commanders. This was, I realized, the worst disservice I could perform, to rubber-stamp everything without thought or dialogue. Yet I noticed that those who were doing the same thing alongside me were becoming the most successful bureaucrats, the rising stars of Managua.

The day I was supposed to return to Nicaragua from the United States I handed a letter to Manolo Cordero, who had taken my old job at the Nicaraguan embassy in Washington. It stated in no uncertain terms that I could never come back. I was already in graduate school at Johns Hopkins and it was my intention at that moment to stay in school and lose myself in my books. But I actually felt too emotionally destroyed just then to see any future, anywhere, at all.

6

The Warrior
and the Intriguer

In the four months since I had left Nicaragua I hadn't spent a single hour without thinking or dreaming of the revolution. My intention to stay away from the affairs of my country was, I realized, not possible. I was totally, irrevocably involved. My studies in history simply did not engross me in quite the same way as the revolution. I looked everywhere for an excuse to rejoin. So when the chance to meet the great Edén Pastora arose I jumped. He sent me a ticket to Costa Rica and I accepted.

While in Washington I had discovered that the cowriter of the speech Pastora broadcast from his press conference, whose words had affected me so deeply, was my father. Despite our complicated personal relationship, once again it looked as though we were playing on the same side of the game.

I did not yet wish to fight against the Sandinistas. I was disappointed in them but not ready to see anyone else take the country. As a professor of mine at Johns Hopkins used to say, The tiger is always on the loose, we have to be careful: i.e., even if the Sandinistas are faltering badly the far greater threat is the constant one of American imperialism.

In early November I flew to Costa Rica. Pastora met me at the airport. He was surrounded by his bodyguards—young boys whose energy and devotion reminded me of the Sandinista kids in Managua. I approached Pastora anticipating that he would have to try hard to convince me that his politics were coherent. It took him no more than a few hours to seduce me. We spent a day and night talking and I was his.

Pastora is like the gypsy whom, on your first night together, you cannot help but love more than anything on earth. The second night you notice she is blind. The third she smiles and she has no teeth. The fourth night you notice she has no legs. But my first night with Pastora lasted a full year. I met few others who did not fall for his seduction.

Pastora drove a station wagon. In front of him and to the rear were Cherokee jeeps filled with three bodyguards each. We rode five hours through the drenching rain (does it ever stop raining in this country? Pastora grumbled) to the Costa Rica-Panama border, where we met many Nicaraguans, peasant families who had found work in the banana fields, people who had come looking to fight against the Sandinistas, for Pastora. Among them I met for the first time peasants from the Atlantic coast who showed me their scars, received when they confronted the Sandinistas and were tortured for their efforts.

A friend once told me, that revolution is a hard dream to kill. Even when faced with evidence of Sandinista abuse, I could not condemn the Managua regime.

The day after we arrived we went to a party at the house of Octaviano César. There I finally met with Carlos Coronel, who felt so ill at ease with the upper-class members of Nicaraguan exile society at Octaviano's party that he refused to join the gathering indoors. We sat outside, glad to talk.

As much as by Pastora, I was entranced by Carlos Coronel, who made me believe we were going to become the salvation of the revolution. He was a convincing polemicist. His own rationale for *Pastorism'* was that the Cubans were unhappy with the Sandinistas. Our task was to create the potential for a strong Southern Front opposition to pressure the FSLN hard-liners—Borge and Arce—to compromise.

Coronel and I agreed that we would never join forces with the Northern Front of the contra in Honduras, a front dominated by former National Guardsmen and mediocre politicians. Such a union would destroy whatever legitimacy Pastora's Southern Front would carry inside Nicaragua. We felt that Havana, not Washington, would solve our problems in the end. We declared ourselves not anti-Sandinista but anti-GPP. We said we had no problems with the Ortegas but only with Bayardo Arce and Tomás Borge.

After I left Coronel, Pastora drove me throughout the region. While we were together I saw weapons carried from safe house to safe house. I did not yet know the money to buy the weapons came from the CIA. I assumed Pastora was the man of the Social Democrats. I did not want to deal with the reality of the CIA and no one talked to me about it. Coronel had decided one had to be a more mature man than I was to handle it. And so when *Newsweek* assigned a journalist to write a cover story on the contras at the end of 1982, I became furious when relentlessly questioned about the possible CIA presence. If the people of Pastora thought this were true, I said, they would kill him. I was, in a word, naive.

By the end of 1982 the CIA saw that Pastora was going to be a liability and that the Northern Front could not depend on him for its legitimacy. That is why they organized a meeting and put together a political directorate including Edgar Chamorro, Lucía Salazar (the widow of slain businessman Jorge Salazar), Benjamin Zeledón (a descendant of a general in the anti-American forces of 1912), Alfonso Callejas (a former Vice-President of Somoza's and a cousin of Robelo's), and Indalecio Rodríguez. The Nicaraguan Democratic Force —the FDN—was thus refined by its sponsors.

Then the CIA transported Adolfo Calero to Miami, to bring him into the same rebel directorate. They also, quietly, left the military figure of National Guard Colonel Enrique Bermúdez. In January 1983 Calero was appointed the coordinator of the FDN.

Adolfo Calero grew to become perhaps the most prominent figure in the contra movement. He was the quintessential product of Nicaragua's middle class of the fifties, a first cousin of Somoza's wife Hope—and an occasional guest at her tennis parties. Calero believed in management, not in philosophy. His father was a well-liked poet and intellectual who rode a bicycle; Calero became an anti-intellectual in an American car. He was the consummate managerial personality—he operated the local Coca-Cola plant, where he proved to be an enormous success. He was suspected, in Somoza's time, of being a CIA asset, although a minor one, as everyone always assumed the more intelligent, gracious Danilo Lacayo, head of the Exxon refinery, was the real CIA asset. Only years later was it evident that Lacayo wasn't.

Calero had been jailed just prior to Somoza's end. The incarceration proved to be the greatest gift Somoza could have granted the former conservative businessman.

To their own amazement, the contras were recruiting massively in the north and the south. It is my belief that, by 1982, this led the Americans to shift their policy from "containing" the Sandinistas to a goal of "rollback"—overthrowing the FSLN. This shift benefited from the newfound coordination of Maroni at the CIA with the man in the White House, Oliver North. I had not yet met North but I was beginning to hear that this man operating quietly "in the basement of the White House" (actually the third floor of the Executive Office Building) was more powerful than the many Americans we had already met.

The Americans' first concern was unification of all the anti-Sandinistas. Their second concern was the creation in the north of a conventional army and in the south a guerrilla force. Then two other fronts were to emerge: one on the Atlantic coast, where the Miskito Indians were active, and one an urban internal front.

To stress the unity of the two contra fronts in Costa Rica and Honduras, the Americans suggested meetings between the north and the south, to be held in Honduras and to be mediated by Colonel Gustavo Alvarez, to implement a joint military strategy. They started to supply Pastora with aid, eventually providing between $400,000 and $600,000 a month to the southern alliance—Pastora and Robelo—along with approximately eight thousand weapons of war over a period of a year and a half.

The American scheme demanded the purchase of geopolitical space in Central America, just as the Sandinistas had bought off Costa Rica during their insurgency. The Americans opted for Honduras, a country with an army of colonels that had never developed a single strongman mentality— Honduras had, for years, a military regime of strongmen. The only developed institution within Honduras was its armed forces. The Superior Council of the armed forces makes the decisions for the country. The colonels on the council, to sustain the institutionality of the army, have never allowed any one strongman to ascend over all the others.

Americans historically prefer to work with one man rather than many, and they insisted upon, and subsidized, the promotion of Colonel Alvarez to general, to lead the army of colonels. The word throughout Central America was that the American ambassador, John D. Negroponte, had leaned heavily on the civilian President, Roberto Suazo Córdova, to promote Alvarez.

Alvarez was the first head of the armed forces in Honduras who had graduated from a military academy. He was a genuine leader with a clear sense of ideology and of the power of the state. He also maintained good relations with the former Somoza Guard. He seemed a sensible choice for the CIA at the time.

What actually ensued was that the United States, by promoting Alvarez, created friction within the institution of the Honduran army by sponsoring a new cult of the individual commander. The United States has always complained bitterly that the problem with Latin America is its endemic inability to create reliable political institutions. Instead, Latin America conjures up dominant personalities. But time after time the Americans themselves chose to create and exploit these personalities, an Alvarez or a Somoza, to facilitate their own management of the peripheral empire. In Honduras the United States undermined the institution of the military and the weak political structure of the country in order to promote Alvarez to do America's bidding.

Honduras is, historically, a country that responds to the needs of Washington, whatever they may be. The Hondurans were afraid that if they did not help the CIA they would be squeezed between the Salvadoran guerrillas and the Sandinistas. They collaborated, expecting that the Americans, as promised, would shortly depose the Sandinistas. The Americans didn't. So the Honduran colonels eventually deposed the Americans' general, Alvarez.

The American strategy of several key fronts was derived from the similar success of the Sandinista fronts. Still, a qualitative difference existed between the two experiences of war. The social control exercised by the Sandinistas was much greater than that of Somoza. During the tenure of the last Somoza in the 1970s the Sandinistas went to town, bought supplies, and drank at the cantina. Now, however, the mechanism for the distribution of basic goods in Nicaragua, from toilet paper to food, had become an instrument of social control wielded by the Sandinistas.

The Americans were also seeking victory even before the war had truly commenced. A revolution needs both internal and international support to succeed. It took considerable time for the international community to isolate the Somoza regime. To go to war, Pastora's people told the Americans, one must also speak of peace—to establish that the ultimate goal is a negotiated settlement for the country, not a tactical victory for just one side. One uses negotiations to weaken the enemy and win advantages.

The Sandinistas understood this and the Americans didn't. They felt time was working against them; they were reluctant to draft a long-term strategy. They suspected the American political system could not sustain such a commitment. This led to their urgency for victory—and to their obsession with keeping their strategies secret. It was a policy which later exploded in their faces. Further, the American belief that victory was possible within a year was a self-defeating notion. The real strengths of the contras were lost in these unrealistic objectives. The confidence of the Americans' allies was eroded as the year passed and still the Sandinistas showed no sign of relinquishing power.

The Sandinistas' multi-front strategy succeeded in part because the fronts cooperated. No such cooperation existed in the contra. Pastora proved this conclusively at the CIA-sponsored conference with the Northern Front in Tegucigalpa. Arriving with his bodyguards, Pastora greeted Honduras'

General Alvarez with a rambling diatribe on how he really didn't want anything to do with Somoza's old National Guard. He then demanded that all contras should now wear the red and black handkerchief of the Sandinistas. Alvarez was not pleased. Because the Americans hoped that Alvarez and Pastora would get along, Alvarez was willing to give the meeting a try. He had not anticipated an easy alliance—but now he realized he faced an impossible one.

Alvarez had decided to permit Pastora to use some Honduran territory. Pastora did not want some territory. He wanted to control the whole Northern Front. He began to condemn every uniform that wasn't a revolutionary uniform. And there were many nonrevolutionary uniforms in Honduras.

Pastora spouted his revolutionary discourse until Alvarez could take no more. Enough, he snapped, and he ordered Pastora temporarily removed to a safe house.

Pastora, now isolated from his men and unsure of his circumstances, flew into a rage. He assumed he had fallen into a trap, that he had been captured, although he wasn't sure by whom. He always carried a Russian pistol, a gift from Tomás Borge years earlier when the two had still been comrades. When Alvarez finally came to visit Pastora in the Tegucigalpa safe house, Pastora grabbed the opportunity. He whipped out his pistol, pointed to his own head, and threatened Alvarez: if you don't release me, I will blow my brains out. And the world will never forgive you for having killed the great revolutionary Edén Pastora.

At which point Alvarez said, please take this insane man with the pistol pointed to his head out of my country for good.

It was already 1983, and at the CIA Maroni was baffled, bothered. The Southern Front under Pastora's leadership just wouldn't start. Maroni was fully committed to Pastora but the man was a debacle. He was not spurring desertions within the Nicaraguan army—which was, in fairness to Pastora, no longer the old Somocista army but a new army with political cadres in each unit and East German, Cuban, Bulgarian, and other East Bloc advisers who were unlikely to be swayed by Pastora's claims of legitimacy.

Pastora was reluctant to go to war. But unity with the contras was impossible to achieve while he railed against his own allies. His organization was rife with double agents. He hated any kind of organizational structure and defeated all efforts to build them. I always believed that Pastora, a classic charismatic leader, saw a potential conspiracy in all organizations and therefore refused to let them develop.

While Pastora sat out the war, official Washington came down to meet with him. People wanted to know this man who seemed to be of such importance to the Americans and who had been a revolutionary Sandinista hero. They visited him and inspected him and observed him as scientists might study another species. I remember a dinner with Congressman Stephen Solarz (D, NY). He digested everything Pastora said and was delighted when Pastora absolved Castro from Nicaragua's mistakes: the arrival of Soviet tanks, the failure of the economy. Pastora related the story of how Castro, as the Soviet tanks arrived in Managua, became furious with Humberto Ortega. Castro asked, Chico, how can you bring these tanks into the country? You are bringing the symbolism of the Russian army into the heartland of the American Empire. Humberto replied childishly, no, no, no, no, no, I want the tanks, they're mine.

To which Castro replied, okay, Chico, go fuck yourself. Take your tanks and get killed.

Castro truly didn't want a Soviet presence in Nicaragua, Pastora told the congressman. Not Castro, he said, Castro is too smart for that.

When Pastora was trying to appeal to the Miami Cuban community and the American conservatives, he talked to North Carolina's Senator Jesse Helms and told him Chile's military leader, Augusto Pinochet, was his personal hero. Pastora had convinced himself that talking to Americans was not unlike being the disc jockey of a radio station. You play for your audience whatever song they most enjoy hearing. Pastora would joke about it before meetings. Which tape do I play now? he used to ask, depending upon which American official was about to enter the room.

By spring of 1983 it was time to travel once again. Pastora, who had felt a sense of welcome in his first trip to Europe, wanted to relive the experience. He asked four of us to accompany him—the Miskito leader Brooklyn Rivera; Donald Castillo, a prominent Nicaraguan Social Democrat; Robelo's deputy, Alvaro Jérez (the architect of Robelo's MDN Party); and myself.

We flew on Iberia Airlines, which meant we had an overnight stopover in the Dominican Republic. Once we arrived in the capital, Santo Domingo, we checked into a hotel. Pastora stepped into his room, pulled out his huge short-wave radio, stuck the antenna out the window, and started communicating with his troops in the field back in Costa Rica and Nicaragua. All through his travels, he played with the radio, shouting alpha, alpha, alpha, all night long to nonresponding troops.

The trip was a huge disappointment, hastily organized, lacking a clear agenda. European ministers were not as captivated by Pastora as they had been previously. They suspected he was headed for war and they did not know, or want to know, the details. Pastora was convinced his lack of success was due to his lack of a military uniform, that he no longer resembled a real commander. He had to go back into military action, he said. His instinct was that strength—or a show of strength—could compensate for everything. He also realized something I didn't: that the Europeans were only giving him rhetoric. Only the Americans might give him aid.

In the middle of the trip he announced he was returning to Costa Rica.

The one European leader who did see Pastora may have regretted it. Portugal's perennial head of state Mario Soares coincidentally was visiting Spain at the same time as Pastora. Soares had always cared for Pastora and agreed to receive him for a breakfast meeting. Unfortunately, Brooklyn Rivera, the Miskito Indian leader traveling with Pastora, had not yet mastered the art of European table manners. He was an excitable, charismatic man for whom the exigencies of the Miskito Indians outweighed the demands of European manners. While discussing the politics of the Indians' forced displacement with the patrician Soares, Rivera, speaking with his mouth full, periodically showered the Portuguese statesman with scrambled eggs. Soares was forced to constantly remove his glasses to clean his lenses.

Once back in Costa Rica, Pastora decided that his men—and everyone else—were laughing at him behind his back. The old lady had become too soft, he imagined they were saying of him. Robelo was still among those pressuring him to go to war; so were the Americans, and so, he imagined, was the world. Despite Carlos Coronel's and my insistence that he stay put, Pastora decided it was time to cross the river into Nicaragua.

The Americans were delighted.

Pastora's cousin Orión was asked to coordinate the American press coverage. Orión wanted as sensational a crossing as possible, so he urged Pastora to bring along all his young *comandantes*. In front of the whirring television cameras the men crossed the San Juan River on May 1, 1983. Pastora, the ultimate showman, was at his most magnificent during the staged event. Traveling in small red and green motorboats across an eight-hundred-yard stretch of river, his men sailed as slowly as possible to allow American cameras to record it all for the evening news.

Accompanying the men was the NBC newswoman Bonnie

Anderson. She became such a story herself that when she returned to Miami, NBC covered her in greater depth than Pastora's crossing. Anderson behaved admirably throughout her stay at the front. Pastora's young men had never seen a blond American career woman before and they wanted her badly but she was, of course, unapproachable, and so every night Pastora's bodyguards masturbated in Anderson's honor.

After the commotion faded, Pastora, all alone in the jungle, suddenly aware of the immensity of the battle, became depressed. He drove back to San José.

Historically, when events take a turn for the worse, Nicaraguan leaders have a habit of finding refuge at their haciendas or in their bedrooms. Pastora took to his bed and stayed there. A long line of sympathizers arrived to urge him to return to the jungle. He refused to listen to them until, his ego slowly rebuilding, he regained his enthusiasm. Finally, convinced again of his calling and his popularity, he returned once more to the front.

He spent the bulk of the summer of 1983 inside Nicaragua, in an area, he said, that even the peasants couldn't stand. But the peasant discontent with the Sandinistas was strong and Pastora's troops grew in number. Hugo Spadafora, the Panamanian opposition figure who was brutally beheaded by General Noriega's henchmen on September 13, 1985, had been the leader of a brigade of Panamanians who fought against Somoza in the Southern Front with Pastora in 1979; he now joined Pastora again, penetrating with a group of Miskito Indians deep into northern Zelaya Department on the Atlantic coast. He came back to report that support from the peasants was strong throughout the region. The war was dormant inside the cities but could be expanded in the countryside.

The possibility of a peace agreement with the Sandinistas was slipping further and further away. But it was hard for me to accept that our front was going to spill the first blood in a civil war. Pastora was now openly critical of the Cubans, blasting Castro, telling his troops he had changed his mind about Castro. Cubans, he concluded, are like the neighbors who help you build your house. After it is built, they stay for dinner. Then they want to sleep with your daughters, then with your wife. You have to get rid of them, he said, or they will take everything.

Back in Washington I had dinner with the head of the Cuban Interest Section to discuss the contra. My point was that the Cubans could no longer believe that the situation could be resolved militarily. They had to think about compromise, to consider jettisoning the GPP faction from Managua and adding Pastora to the National Directorate. Cuba had to moderate the hard-liners in Managua. We talked for four hours. As he left, Sánchez-Parodi simply said he would look into it. I never heard from him again.

Around that time Carlos Coronel was invited to Havana to discuss the issue. He told me he had met with Manuel Piñeiro, "Barbarosa," who headed Cuba's Department of the Americas, which, among other key responsibilities, coordinated Cuban support for guerrillas in Latin America. Coronel also implied he had met with Castro.

When he left Cuba, Coronel was placed on a plane going through Mexico, not Panama. Sending him out via Mexico was a conscious Cuban gesture since the CIA and the Mexicans monitor Cuban flights via Mexico. A Mexican departure meant Cuba wanted the visit to be publicized. Secret visits to Cuba were handled through Panama, where General Noriega concealed private itineraries.

According to Coronel, his agenda in Havana didn't matter in the slightest. What was important was that he had been invited. The FSLN refused to meet Pastora's people, but the Cubans were willing to talk. When Tomás Borge found out about the trip on a visit to Spain, he blasted the Cubans for meddling in Nicaraguan affairs.

Both Coronel and Robelo's deputy Alvaro Jérez were in direct contact with Jaime Wheelock. And they also had met in Panama with the same Cuban Abreu who had appeared when the guerrillas were planning the final offensive in El Salvador. While in Panama, Coronel complained that in Managua the power was too diffused, and that was why he was appealing to the Cubans.

At this same time the Americans asked Pastora to visit. Pastora was still highly acceptable to most of Washington in 1983; his presence was likely to build support for his cause. I scheduled meetings with members of Congress, the Council on Foreign Relations, Johns Hopkins, Columbia, and the Nicaraguan community in California. In New York City, *New York* magazine arranged a dinner which included Mike Wallace, *The Wall Street Journal,* and the New York *Times*.

The trip was a success. The Americans did not seem to care that Pastora's answers were wildly inconsistent. Answering questions on how many troops he had, Pastora sometimes claimed five thousand, then a minute later he would claim six. But no one questioned him too rigorously. He was damning the Reagan administration and the liberals loved him. He assumed that in exchange for criticizing Reagan the liberals would support him. He thought that the Democrats could not support the contras in Honduras on account of the presence of Colonel Enrique Bermúdez and other ex–National Guardsmen. Pastora wanted the liberals to tell the Administration, "We will support you if you put Pastora in charge."

The liberals didn't do this and the Administration wouldn't have listened anyway. The liberals simply liked to hear Pastora blast the Reaganites. Still, Pastora went back to the jungle happy.

But soon he became depressed again. Here he was, in league with the most powerful country on earth, one that could do whatever it wished. But the Americans weren't serious partners, he said. He began to complain more. Then he became furious, threatening to quit for good. "Commander

Kodak," as Pastora was now called by his men, wanted more press attention. He was convinced that Colonel Bermúdez was receiving better support because the Americans liked Bermúdez better. He had seen in the war against Somoza how the Southern Front was outmaneuvered by the North. History was repeating itself. He was not going to be the first to get to Managua.

Then there was the great rice and bean problem. Since Americans never make mistakes, Pastora reasoned, they must have had their reasons to drop beans and rice to his men packed in the same bags—when it was obviously preferable to separate the two. What did this signify? Now what had he done?

And the boots sent by the Americans: they were sizes too large. Pastora's men were stomping about the camp with huge American boots flapping around their small Nicaraguan feet like flippers. And why drop Tampax on his men? The Americans may have meant the air-dropped supply for the handful of women in his outfit. But Pastora interpreted the Tampax as a not so subtle hint that the CIA thought he and his men were homosexuals, a band of do-nothing sissies.

So here he was, Commander Kodak, languishing in the jungle with Tampaxcs. It was a long way from glory, and it was the worst part of the jungle, the densest part, where the temperature was always over 100 degrees. The daytime heat was relentless and the brush impenetrable. Pastora's men could barely create a clearing in the tough undergrowth; momentary clearings sprang back into jungle. When the agony of the day ended, the night turned so black that the palms of the hand weren't visible unless held right to the eye. The strongest moonlight couldn't penetrate the rank vegetation and the thick cloud cover. In order to shit, the soldiers had to wander down overgrown paths to the river. And without one of the rare flashlights, the men were as likely to get lost as they were to fall into the water or to step on snakes. The men had no tents. They slept in hammocks. Only two women,

Pastora's mistress Nancy and the cook, Rosita, lived in a cabin at the camp.

When the newest package of the CIA-delivered goods arrived Pastora turned livid. He called the Americans. "It is over!" he yelled. He was leaving for good. And so Maroni was dispatched from CIA headquarters at Langley, to travel down to Costa Rica and then navigate a boat to the jungle to find Pastora. And as Maroni neared his destination, a fuming Pastora picked up his entire camp and moved his men farther inside the jungle to make Maroni walk farther.

Finally Maroni found Pastora. You have everything you want, he consoled the unhappy man. Why are you so angry now?

Pastora listened for only a minute before interrupting angrily. You are humiliating me, he said.

How? Maroni asked. How is that possible?

The clothes you sent us. They are too large, Pastora retorted.

They are standard size, Maroni objected. That's the problem? That's reason to call off the war?

Pastora glared at the tall man from the CIA, as best he could from his lesser height, a full foot shorter than Maroni, and then the guerrilla commander abruptly pulled off his American-made pants to reveal his American-made undershorts—huge shorts tailored for the American body, shorts so large that they billowed down to Pastora's knees. Pastora stood in front of his men, underwear flapping at his knees. See, he ranted. See? This is the worst humiliation of all. Underwear that makes me look like a fool.

But the patient Maroni, a genius at what the CIA referred to as "handling the natives," finally convinced Pastora to return to the war. He knew that Pastora, no matter how angry his mood, responded well to toys. The CIA Santa Claus showered the man with watches, radios, and other mechanical gadgets. He also persuaded Pastora that military cooperation between the north and the south was essential and, if it didn't become a truly organic unity, couldn't it at least become something more cooperative?

Pastora, now anxious to prove himself after his last tantrum, eventually agreed to try. It was a qualitative step forward for the Americans. Military attacks in the south were timed to take place with military actions in the north.

What Pastora actually meant by "coordination" with the north was coordination between his soldiers and their soldiers. He decided to differentiate between the northern contra foot soldiers, who were peasants like his own, and the northern leaders, who were his rivals. He refused, inwardly, to cooperate with the leaders. He was finally ready to compromise.

But now Carlos Coronel wasn't.

Work for us was usually carried out at the drinking table, where the drinking started as early as one in the afternoon. The excuse was always something such as: well, it's already 8 P.M. in Egypt. Why shouldn't we start now? The drinking continued until past 11 P.M. (except for Carlos Coronel, who usually retired early, for he grew up in and had acquired the habits of Río San Juan, where the peasants rise at four and retire by six). Rum and Coke, whiskey, tequila. From the glasses and bottles flowed the most serious decisions and military assignments.

The drinking table was also the scene of conspiracy and intrigue, where the goal was to shift alliances and remain sober, a traditional Nicaraguan political pastime.

Just after Pastora agreed to coordinate activities with the northern contras, Coronel and I were having drinks at the sole restaurant where we still had credit. It was owned by a Spaniard who had been a Loyalist in the Spanish war and who liked Pastora. We'd been there for about three or four hours when Coronel received a phone call. He excused himself, left, and then returned, visibly nervous. He then excused himself once more and left the restaurant.

We later discovered he had been talking with Nancy, Pastora's mistress.

Nancy was a short, small-boned woman from Granada, formerly married to a Chamorro who was a martyr of the anti-Somocista Southern Front. She was fearless. She was not considered a great beauty but she was popular with men —although Pastora's guards disliked her because they claimed they were forced to carry her shampoo and other toiletries everywhere they went.

Nancy was also a capable spy, assigned by the Sandinistas to penetrate Pastora's inner circle. Pastora had known her since the last war when her husband, a combatant in the old Southern Front had died fighting the Somoza Guard. Pastora liked to impress her by telling her everything: the location of safe houses, the amounts of money being dropped by the CIA. He believed Nancy was in love with him.

That afternoon, after leaving the drinking table, Coronel found Nancy and the couple drove off to Pastora's house on a hill in San José, the house with the empty swimming pool. The command operation was run from the second floor. On the first floor were the radio operators and bodyguards. Coronel and Nancy arrived at the house as though they were drunk, creating an unnecessary amount of chaos: laughing, joking, causing everyone in the house to become aware of their presence and their presence in each other's arms. The couple then went upstairs, as no one would dare stop the master's mistress and his best friend from doing whatever they wished. Closing the door to the bedroom, Coronel and Nancy proceeded, as noisily as possible, to sound as though they were making love. Perhaps they were, perhaps they weren't.

But one of Pastora's bodyguards assumed they were and when Pastora heard the story traveled to the river to find Pastora. He told Pastora the story.

At which point Pastora said, stop the war! My best friend has betrayed me! I cannot fight!

He left the front.

He was never angry at Nancy but he was deeply upset that his best friend would betray him.

Pastora never truly believed that Nancy was a double agent. It wasn't until all the details of her activities were published in the Sandinista newspaper *Barricada* that he heard the full story, and still he continued to call her in Nicaragua to tell her how he loved her.

Nancy's treasonous activities convinced the CIA that Carlos Coronel was a double agent. Coronel replied by taking a low-profile home for his family in the village of Los Chiles, Costa Rica. It was a town sympathetic to the contra, but Coronel spent his time with his family: his mother was the Sandinista consul and his father was a Sandinista intellectual, and despite the town's general anti-Sandinista sympathies, the family was popular. Coronel brothers, twins, were both already living in Managua, both working for Jaime Wheelock in the FSLN.

When Pastora was convinced once more to return to war, the Americans, sensing a possible united front, demanded a quick victory. It was time for drama. The CIA decided to venture into mines.

The CIA's motivation was threefold. They wished to prove to the Nicaraguan people that the Americans were serious in their intentions to oust the Sandinista regime—many Nicaraguans were sitting on the fence, waiting to see which of the two great powers, the U.S.S.R. or the United States, would best support its faction. The United States also wished to show their allies that Reagan was serious about getting rid of the Sandinistas. The final hope was that the Nicaraguan economy would be further devastated. The idea was not to actually sink ships but to damage them so that insurance rates would become unaffordable and no one would trade with Managua.

The plan was launched in February 1984 and by April it

was evident the scheme was a total disaster. The CIA was forced to publicly acknowledge that it had been responsible not only for the mining, but also for running the fleet of speedboats off the Nicaraguan coast to plant them.

Members of the Senate leaked the story's details to the press. The reaction in the United States was overwhelmingly negative, as it was elsewhere in the world. The Americans, not the contras, were making war on Nicaragua. The United States was forced to veto a United Nations Security Council resolution condemning the mining. The Sandinistas took the case to the International Court of Justice, which agreed to accept it. This created the awkward situation wherein the revolutionary FSLN appeared to be the defender of the international legal order and the decorous Americans the international outlaws.

What angered some of the contras more than the inefficiency of the CIA's operatives was that the CIA had hired Ecuadorian divers to plant the mines. It then informed both contra fronts of the plan. The contras didn't protest the action but they did find it monstrously simple-minded to hire Ecuadorians when the Miskito Indians are among the world's foremost divers.

The Ecuadorians were a disaster. To get to the Nicaraguan Pacific port of Corinto a long highway bridge must be traversed. That bridge was supposed to have been blown away by an Ecuadorian CIA "Latino asset." The diver, who had arrived in a speedboat, became confused and then got lost. He couldn't locate the bridge. In fact, he couldn't find the entire port. His speedboat was carried away by the current and he was forced to radio the mother boat waiting out at sea so he could be rescued by a helicopter.

As a result of all this, the Boland amendment, prohibiting further covert American military action, was passed by Congress in October 1984.

The mining was supposed to cripple Nicaragua and create the impression that the Americans were ready to take dramatic steps to aid their allies. But its immediate consequence was to weaken Maroni's prestige in the CIA. His star was already fading on account of his reliance on the ever troubling Pastora and he now proved to be a convenient scapegoat.

Pastora's star was also waning.

His constant misinterpretation of the rest of the world was one reason. The coup which deposed Honduran General Alvarez in 1984 was a good example. Tension between Honduran army colonels and the domineering general promoted by the Americans had grown so untenable that the colonels launched their coup without the Americans being aware it was happening. Here was a country that wasn't supposed to breathe unless the Americans gave permission. Now its army basically said, screw you—we are an institution, not a single personality.

Alvarez had stretched the limits of his power. Honduran President Suazo was concerned that Alvarez had his sights set on taking over the entire country. In fact, Alvarez was politicking for Suazo's rival in the National Party (Suazo was a representative of the Liberal Party). The discontent in the army was palpable—the week before the coup, at the Honduran air force bases of Palmerola and San Pedro Sula, Americans were surprised to overhear officers speak of Alvarez with hostility.

On the night of March 31, Alvarez was scheduled to deliver a speech at San Pedro Sula to the Association Pro Honduras, a group of conservative businessmen. The next day he boarded his plane to return to Tegucigalpa to celebrate the baptism of a relative. While boarding, an air force officer came out and said to him, General Alvarez, the President wishes to speak to you on the phone. Alvarez responded, sorry, I am getting on the plane to Tegucigalpa and I will talk to him there. The captain insisted the call was important and Alvarez reluctantly returned to the main terminal. His bodyguards waited outside the door while he entered a private office.

Once inside, two junior officers grabbed him, threw him to the floor, and took his pistol. Also in the room was Colonel Walter López, the head of the air force, who led the coup. Alvarez turned to him and said, you son of a bitch, you will pay for this. López responded, you will do no more harm.

Outside, Alvarez' bodyguards were surrounded and disarmed.

Walter López' brother immediately flew Alvarez to Costa Rica, where arrangements had already been made for his arrival.

Signs of the rebellion had spiraled around Tegucigalpa for a week. President Suazo, the air force, and the army were all participants. Perhaps they were the only ones. On the morning of the coup, the head of the CIA mission in Tegucigalpa interrupted a meeting at the embassy to say, I have to leave now; I have been invited to a baptism by General Alvarez. His behavior seemed to say he was not aware of the coup that had already deposed his favorite general.

Alvarez later told Senator Jesse Helms that the Americans were responsible, because they feared he was ready to attack the Sandinistas, forcing the Americans to play out their promised strategy of invading Nicaragua. Ambassador Negroponte was supposedly opposed to Alvarez' plan. Nineteen eighty-four was an election year and Negroponte did not want American involvement in Honduras to surface just before the polls opened. Alvarez also argued that Negroponte had been too quick to hold a press conference to acknowledge the coup, which helped smooth Honduran acceptance of the events.

In the mind of Edén Pastora, all these happenings had little to do with anything except Edén Pastora. He interpreted the coup as an attempt by the Americans to depose his enemy Alvarez, whom he had never forgiven for placing him under house arrest. I was staying with Pastora when he heard the news in his office in San José. He stood up and shouted, we have won the war! Why? I asked. He looked at me, bewildered by my feeble-mindedness. Because, Arturo, that fascist Alvarez always hated me, me the great revolutionary warrior, and as long as he remained in power I couldn't have won. This is proof the United States is behind me. With Alvarez gone, Bermúdez will soon go, and the Northern Front will be mine.

Pastora was wildly off base, as usual. But the Americans were, in fact, planning to allow him one last chance—the opportunity to take over the small town of San Juan del Norte on the Nicaraguan Atlantic coast.

Whoever controlled San Juan del Norte controlled the entrance to the San Juan River from the Caribbean. San Juan had been an important port in the nineteenth century, through which Granada became prosperous by allowing the city direct access to the British traders on the Atlantic seaboard. During the California gold rush the city's fortunes grew again. Those who didn't wish to cross the American continent for the California goldfields took a boat from New York to either Panama or Nicaragua. If they came to Nicaragua, they landed at San Juan del Norte, navigated the San Juan River, and sailed Lake Nicaragua to the port of La Virgen or San Jorge, then crossed the isthmus of Rivas by stagecoach, went on to San Juan del Sur on the Pacific coast, and then up to San Francisco. Over 150,000 Americans went west to California via Nicaragua during the gold rush.

But by 1984 San Juan del Norte was a forgotten town guarded by seventy Sandinista soldiers.

One of the major credibility problems the contras faced in the United States was their failure to take a town. This struck me as odd. Guerrillas by definition don't inhabit or fortify fixed points. But the contras had allowed world opinion to frame their plight in such a fashion. San Juan del Norte was the remedy. The Americans wanted results.

Among those involved in the takeover were Tito Chamorro, the leader of the operation; Carlos Coronel's brother-in-law, Ian; and some of Pastora's most prominent young soldiers, all former Sandinistas. (The number of distinguished young fighters was diminishing rapidly. One of the best of the young men, "Nafre," I thought, committed suicide in San José by driving so recklessly that he finally drove his car off a cliff. Another of the young men, "Manuel," died needlessly in combat when he started toying with a Sandinista sharpshooter by hiding behind a tree, then running from one tree to another like a human target gallery, until the sniper shot him in his stomach. "Malicia," another young boy, one of those who took over the National Palace with Pastora in 1978, died playing Russian roulette. And "Zelayita," who had been fighting since he was twelve, was captured by the Sandinistas and beheaded. His skull was attached to a stick and paraded through town.)

The storming of San Juan del Norte took two days, wasted over a million bullets, and received forty-five seconds on CBS News. The contras' good press was diminished by a report from a colleague of Jack Anderson, based on a piece of information supplied by Carlos Coronel's brother-in-law. He said that the contras took the town only because the United States Navy had bombarded the garrison with light artillery. This clouded the issue as to whether at last the contras had actually won a town on their own. Still others implied that paramilitary help from speedboats operated by the CIA had assisted the contras.

Nonetheless Tito Chamorro, the leader of the attack, became something of a minor hero. Pastora didn't appreciate Chamorro's fame and that sealed, temporarily, Tito's fate as a contra leader.

With San Juan del Norte safely in contra hands, Pastora flew in from San José by helicopter. At least dirty your boots, Pastora's older brother Félix Pedro said to him. The moment Pastora arrived, the waiting press surged forward, although he had taken no part in the operation. Excitement in the camp was so great that Pastora began to talk of a provisional government in exile, appointing ministers. Altercations broke out among his supporters in San José as to who would get which jobs. I was offered the position as chief of the North American Division in the fantasy Foreign Ministry to be run by Alvaro Jérez.

Two days later the Sandinistas retook the town.

Instead of helping Pastora's relationship with the United States, the affair helped to destroy it. Pastora blamed the Americans for leaving him without the means to maintain the town. The glorious moment had lasted one day.

Shortly after the battle of San Juan del Norte, the CIA station chief told Pastora his money would run out within a month.

Pastora summoned an emergency meeting of me, Carlos Coronel, Donald Castillo, and Alvaro Jérez to discuss the situation and to try to ascertain what the actual truth might be. He railed angrily about "the chairs" and their treachery. We had no idea what he meant. The chairs! he repeated. The chairs! The chairs! It took some time to realize what he meant: *tauretes*, the word he was using, is a Nicaraguan term for a chair and is similar in meaning to the Spanish word for chair, *silla*, which in Spanish is pronounced like the acronym CIA. Pastora was blasting the American CIA, shouting relentlessly about the goddamn chairs.

It could not be, Pastora thought, that the CIA really had no more money, that Congress would not extend aid. The CIA? Broke? This doesn't happen in Cuba, he said. Castro does not allow this. The Americans were lying. Pastora was also convinced that the Sandinistas and the Cubans were about to negotiate with Washington. The Americans are selling us out, Pastora said. What else could it be?

His conclusion was that I should go to Washington to determine what was really happening. I had spent a lot of time traveling back and forth from America to Costa Rica and had developed close contacts in both places. I now talked with the congressional aides and discovered that Congress was still fuming over the mining, regarded as a juvenile and embarrassing operation. Many senators, to cover the fiasco, claimed that they had not been briefed by the CIA, although their aides told me that in fact they had been fully briefed. The senators simply did not want to have any link to such a bungled fiasco.

In Washington I received my first direct call from the CIA. While the contra Southern Front was stagnant, the contra Northern Front was growing in strength. It seemed to me that it was imperative for the Southern Front to improve its ties with the Americans.

So I met with "Tomás Castillo," the CIA man who became the station chief in Costa Rica, at Dupont Circle. I was very apprehensive. I was beginning to shift from idealism to cynicism, from supporting both sides to trusting neither, from believing a solution in Nicaragua was possible to believing it was too late.

Castillo and I met for coffee in the pouring rain; despite our opposing world views we talked for hours. Eventually I came to have great respect for the man. He told me to clarify for Pastora why Alfonso Robelo's political party was receiving aid and Pastora wasn't. The MDN would receive $80,000 to $100,000 a month and Pastora was furious. The Boland amendment prohibited CIA money going to military activities. Robelo was involved in the political struggle; he could receive money. This legal explanation made no sense to Pastora.

I in turn tried to interpret Pastora's psychology to Castillo, to explain why it was necessary for all of us to throw "fits of independence." They weren't more than childish tantrums, I said. Quite simply, there was nothing we could do without the Americans. The pique was for our self-image. If any client has any sense of self-esteem at all, he must try to prove to himself that he is not a puppet. Even though every client knows that, in fact, he is being used.

Pastora decided to give another press conference. It was rumored that he had many agendas but the primary objective of the press conference was to fulminate against the CIA and the Americans who set him up for victory in the south and then abruptly withdrew their support. The CIA had opted for Colonel Bermúdez and the men of the north over him, Pastora argued. At the same time, it was said, Pastora would denounce Secretary of State George Shultz and the Americans who were making deals with the Sandinistas. Pastora was the true Sandino who fought both the reactionaries and the communists—and the Americans were the opponents of both sides. Pastora had also heard that CIA agents in Costa Rica were spreading rumors that Pastora had no more military training than an American sergeant, questioning his military ability. This wounded him deeply.

He also wanted to denounce his allies in the south, including Robelo, whom he no longer trusted.

Libya's Qaddafi was angry at Pastora. Tomás Borge was upset. The Sandinistas, internal opponents, and the northern contras all disliked Pastora. If anyone had a motive to assassinate him, and many did, this was the time to try. Someone did. While Rosita, the fat radio operator, was serving Pastora a cup of coffee at the press conference, a bomb exploded, killing and wounding more than a dozen people. Rosita's bulk saved Pastora from death. She was blown to pieces.

According to Pastora, all he could hear from that moment on were the distant moans of the wounded amid the cries of the others. All he remembered was the human mess around him as he was carried off by his bodyguards. I did notice in the photographs of the incident released later that he had the foresight, nonetheless, to flash a victory sign to the cameras as his men carted him off to a hospital in rural Costa Rica.

In the hospital Pastora told others that the CIA had been responsible for the attack. Many wondered why the CIA would bomb Pastora at a time when it was most likely to be blamed on them. The new mind set throughout Nicaragua was that the CIA, no longer demigods, were clods. It was said that, as this assassination attempt had been botched, no more proof was needed of the CIA's responsibility—after all, it botched whatever it touched.

Venezuela's former President, Carlos Andrés Pérez, offered to help his old friend Pastora by sending his personal jet to bring the man to the best clinic in Venezuela. So, when I was called to attend Pastora, I flew to Caracas, where the wounds had been found to be more serious than at first thought. The clinic was surrounded by the elite troops of the Venezuelan army. Several ex-Miss Venezuelas were sent to cheer up Pastora. Others congregated around him, including Victor Meza, a Honduran supporter, Donald Castillo, Carlos Coronel, and later Alfredo César's brother.

Watching him lie in the hospital bed, his face pale and fragile, I was most worried by the wounds to Pastora's psyche. And I was nervous when I saw his wife, Doña Yolanda, wandering about the halls with books on reincarnation.

God saved me, Pastora told me. He had been chosen by God to become a great figure in history, he said, and not even a bomb could destroy him. Nor the Americans.

I kept saying, no, commander, it was not God, it was the bulk of Rosita that saved you. But Pastora would have nothing to do with it. More than ever he withdrew into his self-image.

Meanwhile, standing over Pastora, the César brothers quarreled as to who would become the new head of the Southern Front, since it was obvious to all that the Americans would no longer allow Pastora to hold the leadership. Either Adolfo Calero or Alfredo César would succeed the man. César schemed with Coronel and Tito Chamorro, who had lost an eye in the bombing.

Coronel was rumored to have flown to Caracas only after a clandestine visit to Managua. Pastora's aide, Donald Castillo, was joining forces with Robelo. Of all these people only the Honduran Victor Meza could be trusted. Meza had studied at Moscow University where he had become a Trotskyite. He was expelled from school by the Soviets. A crucial operative in the Sandinista internal front in the 1970s, Meza had always maintained close ties to Pastora. But Carlos Coronel successfully tore Meza away from Pastora, complaining that he was a Honduran, a foreigner, and not a true participant in Nicaragua's fate. Actually Coronel feared Meza would become a rival.

Carlos Andrés Pérez had plans for Pastora also. He wanted to force him to shed his military role for a civilian one. At his first press conference after the bombing Pastora announced he was considering resigning guerrilla life to become a political activist. At that moment Carlos Coronel said to me, Pastora is a child, he needs a father. The Sandinistas are no longer his father, the CIA does not want him as their child. He belongs to Pérez. We must play Father Pérez' tune for now.

Pastora did try one more time to repair his connections with the Americans. He also wanted to see Oliver North, whose star had risen, even as Maroni's had sunk after the mining disaster. But once again Pastora misconstrued everything. He flew to Washington, where he was provided a police escort. He immediately construed this as a symbol of real power; he must have returned to favor, he thought, seeing a few official cars on either side of him as he drove down Massachusetts Avenue.

But at a scheduled meeting at the Roslyn, Virginia, Marriott Hotel Maroni failed to show. Instead only a minor CIA official attended and he reiterated that there would be no more aid for Pastora. Pastora, his hopes recently raised, was again wounded.

I suspect that North wanted as little to do with Pastora as possible, that he had come to the same conclusion as the CIA. He was repelled both by Pastora's erratic personality and by the fact he had once been a Sandinista. Furthermore, North had a meeting with national security adviser Robert McFarlane and Pastora in early 1984. The meeting was, as always, confidential. But when he reached the Miami airport Pastora called everyone to brag, I just came from a meeting with Bud McFarlane. North found it difficult to trust Pastora after that.

North refused to see Pastora. He did, however, give Alfredo César (who by this time was associated with Pastora) a list of people who could be solicited for money, but the list was not as good as the list he had given Calero.

Pastora only got the message when North refused to pay his hotel bill. My father appealed to North to take care of it; he said, like it or not, the man is popular in Nicaragua, he is a wounded warrior, and he is part of our history. It doesn't take a lot to pick up a bill.

North agreed but he never actually did pay up. As always, Pastora offered to sell his Rolex several times before a Nicaraguan friend came up with the necessary money. Pastora then flew off to Costa Rica to plan a new strategy, which was to appeal for money from the American right and the Miami Cubans in competition with Calero. Above all, like all the rest of us, no matter how he did it, his basic tenet was to stay in the game.

7

Our Friends
the Americans

At the beginning of the summer of 1984, Maroni and Oliver North flew to Tegucigalpa, Honduras, to address the directorate of the FDN. At the meeting Maroni told the Nicaraguans that America and President Reagan supported them a hundred percent. Therefore, Maroni continued, considering that the United States was going to back the contras all the way to ultimate victory, it was only fitting that the contra political system resemble that of its benefactor, the United

States. As in the United States, the commander-in-chief of the armed forces must be a civilian rather than a representative of the military. That civilian, Maroni added, should be Adolfo Calero.

Maroni's selection of Calero was hardly surprising but it still disappointed the FDN directorate. Yet of all the members only Edgar Chamorro complained openly. Chamorro was reputed to have retained close ties with the Americans. Now he fretted publicly. How could the Americans have possibly preferred a middle-class Calero over an upper-class Chamorro? And, as Edgar Chamorro was also a man of some conscience, he was upset over the larger issue: how could the Americans have selected Adolfo Calero under any circumstance?

The message was indisputable. Calero followed Maroni and Oliver North to El Salvador and then back to Washington, where North indicated to Calero that he would now share his contacts for raising money.

Calero was being rewarded for his stability and his long-standing relationship with the Americans. He was also rewarded for having supposedly passed a number of lie detector tests.

Those in the CIA who were replacing the fading Maroni belonged to the cult of counterintelligence. Too many agents provocateurs and spies had penetrated the contras' Southern Front, they claimed. It was necessary to clear the contra house of such persons and institute a permanent policy of reliability.

Unlike most of those in the Southern Front, who were introduced to the lie detector a year later in Costa Rica, I was invited to take the test in Washington in the early fall of 1984. "Alberto"—the man who first occupied the vacuum in the CIA following Maroni's departure—approached me and said, Arturo, I am sorry—you have to take this test. This will be a good opportunity for you to prove your loyalties. I agreed.

The test was administered on a rainy September Saturday

in a Hyatt Hotel suite in Roslyn, Virginia. It was nine-thirty in the morning and I was starving—the rules of the detector forbade me to eat during the twelve-hour period preceding the test. A full stomach was said to facilitate deceiving the machine.

Alberto met me in the Hyatt lobby and accompanied me to the room where a frail, dark man ushered me in and sat me at the machine, explaining its use and the nature of the examination while attaching wires over my body.

Throughout the test I was anxious and breathing heavily. The majority of the ten questions centered on my previous alliances in Nicaragua and my current contacts. The final question basically asked whether or not, in my meetings with the CIA, my loyalty was directed fully and totally to the CIA. Very few people passed this question.

I answered, yes, my first agenda is the CIA. The machine registered a lie, which it was. I had my own motives, as does everyone else. The man asked me this one question repeatedly, and each time I failed it.

However, nine out of ten correct answers constituted a pass on the test and I had gotten the necessary nine. I had passed. This thoroughly upset the frail man, who concluded that my heavy breathing was a ruse to trick the machine. For forty minutes he tried to make me fail one of the other nine questions but I kept getting them right. Finally he left the room to talk to Alberto, who was waiting in the room next door.

Alberto was sympathetic. He entered the room and said, Arturo, the man thinks you have been employing some sort of special breathing technique to beat the machine. I said, how could I be holding my breath when my whole body is attached by wires, by a man who hopes I will fail the examination, to an electrical machine which I have never seen before, and all the while I am listening to my stomach growl? Contrary to what you may think of Nicaraguans, this is not a normal state for us.

I see, Alberto said. Basically the man wanted me to pass, since he thought I could help explain the psychology of the contras. He also wanted to get out of the hotel and back home so he could watch Saturday afternoon football games with his family. Another forty minutes passed and the test was readministered. Once more I passed nine out of ten.

The CIA decided no one could participate in any military work with the Americans unless they had passed the litmus test of the lie detector. The test was also required by the new man in the White House, Oliver North, to whom so much power had recently accrued.

I had felt no particular reason to meet North; I saw no reason to believe he might be any different from all the others like him in the Administration. Then a good friend, one of the American network television anchors, urged me to talk with North just as my close friend, the late Denis Volman of the *Christian Science Monitor,* also convinced me of the same. Volman told me how once, on a whim, he had called North at his office at 10 P.M. To his surprise Volman not only reached North but engaged him in a two-hour, off-the-record conversation. Volman was startled that North was still at work, that he would spend two hours talking with him. He also found North naive. Two congressional aides, one a Democrat, one a Republican, also suggested I meet with North. He was more flexible and intelligent, they said, than one might otherwise assume. Furthermore Otto Reich, the first man in the Administration to show genuine sympathy for my father, advised me of the same. Reich was a Cuban-American of Jewish Austrian descent who held the rank of ambassador in charge of public diplomacy for Latin America and the Caribbean. The Administration, he had argued, was losing the war of ideas in Central America. An office was necessary to talk with the press and the think tanks. Reich was allowed to originate the Office of Public

Diplomacy. The American press soon took to calling him the Minister of Propaganda.

Reich said North was the kind of American I should know —the kind who would throw his body on top of a grenade to save the lives of his soldiers—the kind of person Nicaraguans go through grade school imagining that all Americans resemble.

I made some inquiries and found that North was willing to talk with me. He was curious about the relationship with my father, and also that I was a confidant of both Edén Pastora and Carlos Coronel. So in the early fall of 1984 I made an appointment with his secretary, Fawn Hall, to see him.

Before I met North, I first had to meet Hall, who sat just outside his office. She was stunning. We didn't talk to each other but I couldn't stop watching her until I went into North's office.

The moment I met North I liked him. He was a living metaphor for the Empire. His office was also a metaphor, filled with trophies: caps from North Korea, Soviet canteens from Afghanistan, various books on military subjects strewn all over the tables. All of this suggested that the man read, although I never found out if it was true.

North was warm and engaging. He gave the impression that he could laugh at himself and he seemed sympathetic to my exile status. Instead of the scheduled fifteen minutes we spoke for an hour. We discussed the realities of Nicaragua: how after the fall of Tachito everyone wished to become the next Somoza—Nicaraguan ambitions had been repressed for forty-four years, accumulating like wishes on a star. In terms of foreign intervention, we spoke of how no revolutionary movement of any consequence currently existed that had not aligned itself with a foreign power. If Castro had not brought the nine FSLN commanders to Havana in 1979 the Sandinistas would not have achieved unity; they would have continued fighting each other instead of the National Guard.

North wielded power, and I wanted to become the interpreter of Nicaraguan reality for him. Much in the same way that Carlos Coronel became close to the Cubans, because the FSLN did not properly appreciate his contribution to the revolution, I planned to work with the foreigner who ruled over my segment of my tribe—the contras—since I did not feel that the contras fully appreciated me. I had not yet learned that, while you may pretend to use the foreigner as the instrument, in reality you are the instrument of the foreigner.

North sometimes implied he was like a son to President Reagan, that he and the President shared a special relationship. When North first surfaced in our affairs his claim to fame was that he had overseen the 1983 invasion of Grenada. When the operation occurred the Administration's great fear was that American students in Grenada would react badly; that they would criticize the action when brought back to America. North said Reagan had once taken him aside and urged him not to worry. Then, on the day the Americans were flown back to the United States, Reagan asked North to accompany him into a small office to watch the students' arrival. As the students left the plane and kissed the American ground, Reagan said, "See, I told you."

North enjoyed giving tours of the Reagan White House to his friends at night. Once, as he strolled us through the garden, we were talking about Cuba. I described Havana to him and how the government chauffeurs are usually Angola veterans. A term in Africa brings the reward of driving foreign visitors in a Mercedes-Benz and sharing in the special foods consumed by the guests. The drivers, I mentioned, were obsessed by two things: African venereal diseases, which they said make your penis fall off, and poisonous snakes. Snakes terrify the Cubans—the island has no indigenous poisonous snakes.

North's eyes lit up. I have a great idea, he said. We'll load supply planes with poisonous snakes and then we'll drop them all over Cuba. His eyes were serious.

Once North wanted to know why the political left had such a lock on the resources of Hollywood. Wouldn't it be possible to take some of the celebrities away from the left and bring them over to the right? Or at least some of the well-known businessmen? In early 1985 a stranger appeared in Washington, a very smooth man who stayed in an expensive hotel, a man who gave the impression that he was a sophisticated hustler. He was a Hollywood producer. The man approached North with an idea for the contras. The plan was to charter a luxury ocean liner, get the contra leaders onto the boat, and then send them down to Grenada. The script for the passage called for the drafting of a new Nicaraguan constitution agreeable to all the contra participants. The producer would videotape the entire cruise for television. The event, however, never materialized.

North reminded me always of the man he disliked so much—Edén Pastora. Both men were very seductive, very charming, and both lived deeply within the world of inner fantasy. Each considered himself a brave warrior. Each was also capable of great acts of love and also human insensitivity. North regularly complained that Pastora was not concerned with the welfare of his troops—he constantly referred to one incident when Pastora, as he was on his way to becoming a marginal player, organized a group of a hundred men, provided them with only forty bullets each and little food, and commanded them to attack the Atlantic town of Bluefields. The men were eventually massacred. North was furious—yet he too understood and exploited the value of the martyr.

North was a combination of many men. He had a great admiration for the British Empire. He also admired the Communists' tactics. More than any other American I knew, North reminded me of a Cuban agent. He felt at ease with a sense of empire but it didn't matter whose empire it was.

One of his admirers once said that everything about North was exemplary except that he lived in the wrong era and worked for the wrong people. North was the kind of man who always takes the hill. It could be the wrong hill, but he would take it.

As I was developing my relationship with him I was becoming increasingly tired of Edén Pastora and his obsession with himself. I was a baby-sitter for the man and had to listen to his self-aggrandizing pronouncements. I began to think over my relationship to politics—when I was a child, I had been an Agüerista, then, I became a Sandinista, then a Pastorista. I now understood that these men and their movements had all been proponents, not of political ideals, but of personal ambition. The only man who tried to create institutions over personality was my father. But we did not work well together. He distrusted my advice, thinking that ambition, not idealism, was my motive. And, because I was his son, he felt he had to push me aside to prove his willingness to disregard family for loftier goals.

It wasn't ambition that drove me. I knew that if my father ever achieved a position of power, to prove his disgust for nepotism, I would be the first adviser to be dropped from his circle.

On February 21, 1984, the FSLN announced plans to hold an election for the presidency on November 4, 1984, two days before the American election. The Sandinistas were under severe pressure in northern Nicaragua and they were convinced that Congress would continue to provide aid for the contras. They needed outside help and an election would curry favor—not necessarily in Nicaragua, but elsewhere in the world.

The Americans did not take the announcement from Managua seriously. The date posted for the election was nine months away, the war was progressing well for the contras, and anyway, the Americans thought, the Sandinistas might well change their minds.

The election presented the Ortegas an opportunity to solidify their power; one member of the Directorate could now institutionalize the role of President. Borge's clique had remained ascendant over the Ortegas for a short period and Borge assumed that he, not Daniel, was to become the candidate. He was the most senior of the nine, he had suffered the most, he was the more effective orator, and he was better known throughout Europe.

Borge lost. Humberto had developed a strong army, stronger than Borge's police force, and he checked Borge's challenge to his brother. Furthermore, Castro's continuing pro-Daniel line helped the Ortegas. But the decisive tilt to Daniel followed Jaime Wheelock's promise of support, with the proviso that Wheelock would become the next FSLN candidate in the 1990 election.

Within the internal Nicaraguan opposition no one single group dominated sufficiently to pick a candidate. Finally, after much disagreement, the Democratic Coordinadora, an umbrella group of trade unions, political parties, guilds, and businessmen inside Nicaragua, opted for everyone's second choice. The candidate was no one's favorite yet he was the only man who could be trusted by everyone—Arturo J. Cruz, Sr.

My father was working at the Inter-American Development Bank in Washington, D.C. He had not wanted to become involved in a war against the Sandinistas—he simply did not have either the time or the energy. But in mid-1984 he accepted the nomination.

North was now in a dilemma. He wanted to prevent the Nicaraguan electoral process from gaining legitimacy in the eyes of the world. At the same time he was forced to accept my father's candidacy. He was not happy because he feared that my father's participation in the process would strengthen the FSLN's hold on Nicaragua by legitimizing the election, which was bound to be fraudulent, and thus doom the contras' diminishing chances for congressional aid.

North's best hope was that the complicated procedure would be arduous, that my father's energy would be exhausted, and that North could watch both legitimacy and my father disappear from the scene. His suspicion of my father originated from my father's original sin—that he had once been a Sandinista—and from the fact that his resignation from the last of his many Sandinista posts, as ambassador to the United States, had been orchestrated so as to minimize damage to the Sandinistas.

My feeling was that many in the Administration—as well as many in the contra movement—would not have become terribly upset if something disastrous were to befall him. In death, Cruz might prove a useful democratic martyr, the Chamorro of the 1980s.

I could not consider the candidacy a good idea. My father had always felt a profound distrust of personal power and, although he was a man of great personal courage, he never believed in his own leadership. He considered the best governance of his country to be the thirty-year period of Conservative rule in the nineteenth century, when six successive presidents relinquished office voluntarily. This is the only period in Nicaraguan history that is not associated with a *caudillo;* during these years there was not a single political assassination.

My father believed in rule by consensus. Because of his rejection of the nature of our tradition of personal rather than institutional rule, he was alien to our country's political culture. On the other hand, this very rejection was what made him the ideal man in any transition to a valid Nicaraguan democracy. Arturo Cruz, Sr., was a paradox.

When my father first arrived in Managua for his preliminary campaign work he met with the Democratic Coordinadora. They quickly informed him that the figure of Arturo Cruz, Sr., was not of major importance. What was important, they said, was that he was the symbolic candidate of the Coordinadora itself. In other words, we will dictate everything you do and you are the mouthpiece through which we will speak.

The campaign was rife with private goals. The Ortegas wanted to terminate the equality of the nine commanders. North, as well as the other hard-liners in the Administration, wanted the election to take place but without my father's participation. The Coordinadora position was to demand so many conditions as election prerequisites that my father could not participate. The liberals in Congress and the Social Democrats of Europe and Latin America hoped the election would force the Sandinistas to give up on their Marxist ideological project, while keeping their power. They hoped the country would move toward the Mexican, not the Cuban, model.

And then there was my father, alone in Nicaragua, torn between his desire to reach a genuine compromise with the Sandinistas on the conditions under which he could participate in the election and his fear that he might be considered a collaborator by his compatriots, much as previous candidates had played the game of the Somozas.

Although my father was officially the candidate of the Coordinadora, and the Coordinadora was the vehicle through which the Reagan administration operated, he also became the candidate of the Democrats in the U.S. Congress. They supported him in so far as he was willing to participate in the election and they also supported him in trying to make the process more democratic. The Sandinistas were aware, however, that even if they did not compromise on the electoral conditions the Democrats would remain silent, because their principal concern was domestic politics. The Sandinistas knew that the liberals in Congress and the Social Democrats in Europe and Latin America would live with the result regardless. Anti-Reaganism was the most important element for the Democrats in America. They were less interested in democracy in Nicaragua. I slowly grew to disdain the American liberals who agitated so bitterly against Reagan's policy yet remained silent while the Sandinistas repressed any hope of democracy in my country.

The election proceeded awkwardly. The Coordinadora and the Sandinistas could not agree on how it should be run. My father's participation seemed increasingly unlikely. He was spending most of his time outside Nicaragua, on trips designed to persuade the international community that conditions for a fair election did not exist in Nicaragua and that pressure had to be exerted on Managua to improve the electoral environment.

These trips took him to Central America, Colombia, Panama, and finally to Brazil, where a meeting of international socialists was being held in Rio de Janeiro. My father and FSLN Commander Bayardo Arce were invited to the conference as observers.

Orchestrating the meeting was Venezuela's Carlos Andrés Pérez, who wanted Arce and my father to find a compromise. My father's basic concern was to break the monopoly of the Sandinista-controlled state media in Nicaragua. He also wanted freedom to campaign without physical harassment from the Sandinista *turbas*—hired mobs who, in the best Somocista tradition, used physical harassment, stones and sticks, to obstruct my father's campaign. And he wanted more time to campaign.

Historically, even in the era of the Somozas, a Nicaraguan presidential candidate traveled to the capital of every Nicaraguan department; otherwise it was impossible to create any physical presence in each part of the country. Sixteen weeks were necessary for a fair campaign. My father said he would accept less if he was offered access to the state-controlled media and if Arce could call off the Sandinista mobs.

A compromise was reached, thanks to Carlos Andrés Pérez. But then Commander Arce insisted on a sine qua non. For the agreement to work, said Arce, Arturo Cruz, Sr., in the name of the Coordinadora, had to officially agree to the compromise right there in Rio de Janeiro.

My father responded that he did agree to it. He simply had to discuss it with the Coordinadora for final approval. If the Coordinadora did not accept the agreement, he promised that he would resign as their candidate. Arce would, however, have to wait several days.

Arce refused to accept the delay. He had been forced to compromise for Pérez' sake but now he could withdraw his offer, citing intransigence on the part of the Nicaraguan opposition. The truth was that the Ortega brothers could not compromise on the date of the election because their own personal power was at issue. The internal power struggle among the Sandinista commanders was the real force which dictated the shape of the election.

The recalcitrant Arce did not make many friends in Rio. Repeatedly, when Pérez addressed him, he would make a slight slip of the tongue and mispronounce Arce's first name, Bayardo. Pérez would call him "Comandante Bastardo."

In Nicaragua, Costa Rica, and Washington, the assumption was that my father had sold out to the Sandinistas. His associates' worst nightmares had come true. They assuaged each other by admitting they had never trusted him in the first place.

I was the only one with whom my father maintained contact during the meetings; I was currently in San José, Costa Rica, and urged my father to return there on his way to Nicaragua. I had been talking with the CIA's station chief, Tomás Castillo, who was deeply concerned by what he had heard about Rio de Janeiro. He too was convinced my father was selling out.

He wanted to meet with my father directly, to confront him with the charges of a sellout. César took my father to see Castillo at a safe house. My father in turn insisted that Castillo record the meeting; he did not want his words misrepresented to Washington. The meeting was tense but bearable.

The more difficult meeting was the one with my father's allies, the Coordinadora, whose years of indignation spewed out: the fact that my father had once been a Sandinista; that he, not they, had been invited to the meeting in Rio; that he was the presidential candidate. Still he was ultimately able to explain his proposal for the election. After some deliberation, the others agreed to the compromise.

The FSLN, however, declared this acceptance was tardy and thus unacceptable. My father, who had never officially registered as a candidate, now had no need to register at all. In this way the last opportunity for a compromise was lost.

The Sandinistas ran against carefully chosen opposition candidates and racked up sixty percent of the vote.

After the election my father confounded everyone further. He argued that the election was a fait accompli and Daniel Ortega was now the President of Nicaragua. He hoped that Ortega would be the President of all Nicaragua, not just the Sandinistas. He called Ortega "the President," which was something the rest of the opposition refused to do. They considered my father's move a grievous mistake, one which legitimized the election. And my father offered the new President Ortega a period of grace, to see how he would behave. Let's not dispute this election until there is reason to dispute the President, he said.

During the election period Calero and Pastora had joined forces to collaborate against my father. They feared that his candidacy would strengthen the civilian option over their preferred military route. When the election was over, however, my father's political stock had increased in value, especially abroad—so much so that other exiles became worried. Even the normally moderate Alfonso Robelo took advantage of my father's "period of grace" speech to minimize his stature. Because if there was someone who could give credibility to the election, and then lose, it was Cruz, Sr.

Adolfo Calero now apparently decided to finish my father for good. He took advantage of a forum organized by *La*

Nación in Costa Rica to stage a debate. My father thought it was only to be an exchange of views and accepted the invitation. I warned him to be wary of Calero but in the end I was confident that, as Calero was not a man of ideas, he had chosen an inappropriate place to attempt to ruin my father. Indeed, Calero was outmaneuvered at the debate.

My father should now have withdrawn from the game. There was no reason for either of us to stay. We had no more allies and we had little hope. But we continued to play because there was nowhere else to go.

The 1984 election provided the Ortega brothers with clear hegemony over the country. The FSLN was no longer a fragmented movement. Still the country was in turmoil. People were exhausted with the suffering, the shortages, the long lines at the stores. They no longer felt that they knew which revolution they were fighting for. They longed to be able to buy consumer goods, to live a normal life. They were tired of uniforms. It didn't really matter if the uniforms were khaki or olive green. They were tired of heroes. They wanted to become ordinary people.

The Sandinistas needed some public relations successes. They were rewarded on November 6, 1984, when the Reagan administration announced that the Soviets were sending Managua a supply of MiG-21s. Daniel Ortega had announced this himself after a visit from Moscow. Washington used the shipment as further proof of Nicaragua's intensifying menace to America. But the MiGs never arrived, the Administration was publicly embarrassed, and Managua looked once more like the victim of the American giant.

The Sandinistas actually received something more effective than the MiGs: Soviet MI-24 helicopters, the most lethal tool in combating guerrillas. The helicopters allowed Managua to develop a consistent and effective strategy for stopping the contras.

The United States cut aid for the contras in 1984. The majority of their forces were retreating into their sanctuaries on the border between Nicaragua and Honduras. Oliver North's concern now was to establish a private supply network as a temporary measure and to get Congress back into the game. To do this he helped create a new political organization, one that would hopefully attract new congressional aid.

In early 1985 North called me into his office for the first time—usually I had asked to see him. When I arrived he took out a much-fingered map of Nicaragua and began discussing the possibility of liberating a piece of territory in the northeast. He also talked of an American naval blockade along with air cover to prevent Cuba from resupplying the Sandinista army.

Basically he was suggesting for the first time that the United States was willing to intervene. He then discussed the creation of a junta—the coalition that would eventually be called the United Nicaraguan Opposition (UNO). And he wanted to know if I thought my father would join it. I didn't respond because it was impossible to tell when North was talking, bluffing, or disinforming. If he wanted a response he was usually baiting. So I kept silent.

UNO became reality in March of that year. Three leadership positions were created to run it. My feeling then was that we had to be very careful to avoid the impression that UNO was only a civilian front for the military power of Colonel Enrique Bermúdez, Aristides Sánchez, and Adolfo Calero. Unless UNO had real decision-making capability, the American Congress would see it as a facade.

In order to balance the power of Adolfo Calero within the contra I suggested to North that my father serve as coordinator of the UNO directorate, with Pastora also participating in the governing organization. North prevented this arrangement—he wanted power divided among three leaders of equal stature. Pastora declined my father's invitation to join anyway. Officially Pastora said that UNO was too American in origin. The truth was, he wouldn't cooperate because he couldn't run the whole show. Alfonso Robelo, Adolfo Calero, and my father were chosen to head UNO.

Calero was upset by all these events, particularly by the formation of UNO itself. One moment he had been mingling with the millionaires of Palm Beach as the Appointed One, the American choice for commander-in-chief. Now he was being asked to share the stage with his rivals. He complained bitterly to his sponsors in the CIA. And so the CIA agreed to travel to the contra camps in Honduras and tell the rebels to ignore UNO. UNO was only created for Americans, the CIA said. It was for images. Calero, they said, was still the real man.

On the political front, North informed Calero and the rest of the contra leadership that when the contras were victorious any government of transition had to be of short duration. This had to be the case, North said, because the country would require American assistance to rebuild. Unless the new government was democratically elected, Congress would not provide any aid.

I was puzzled by these statements, since the contras were at that moment retreating to their sanctuaries, not advancing on Managua. Talk of victory seemed, at best, very premature. But North's discourse, combined with President Reagan's constant "freedom fighter" rhetoric, implied that the United States was about to come to the rescue of the contra troops.

Those listening to North's rhetoric assumed that some invisible grand strategy was about to deliver Nicaragua to the contras; that the American Marines were terminating the Sandinistas; and that, following the fall of the FSLN, the UNO was to act as a government of transition. The contra army would soon occupy the country to facilitate the withdrawal of the Marines. Victory was around the corner.

The contra leadership became obsessed with controlling the rebel army in the north and creating an effective electoral machinery to take over the country. The irony behind these preparations was that UNO, instead of bringing unity to the contras, created more chaos—spurred on by the illusion of quick victory to be achieved by the Americans. The contras soon developed a campaign mentality to compete for the approaching office of the presidency. In early July 1985 Calero's people organized an event to honor Calero, to show that he was the real *caudillo.* My father and Robelo were not invited. If they showed up, they were told, the audience would be upset—both men had once been Sandinistas.

Alfredo César was not offered a position in UNO. He went in search of Pastora, who had turned down his place in UNO. Along with other minor luminaries from the Nicaraguan political heavens who had been shut out of participation in UNO, they joined forces to create a different bloc opposed to UNO.

Many thought that Alfredo César was the most skillful Nicaraguan politician of our generation. He was capable of a rainbow of alliances; he could juggle a multitude of opposing viewpoints while never appearing to hold more than one at a time. He alone of the country's politicians was conversant with the new language, the new vocabulary, of the 1980s. César could speak as a liberal to American liberals and as a Social Democrat to European and Latin Social Democrats. He was not a major political player within Nicaragua but he was the first Nicaraguan to understand that recognition in Europe outweighed recognition in his own country. He soon became the most internationally attractive of the contras.

César had two objectives. The first was to hold Pastora's hand, while trying to take Pastora's commanders away from him. In the end, the real game in the south was to inherit Pastora's army. For this César needed the CIA. His second objective, despite his personal warmth toward my father, was to rid himself of Arturo Cruz, Sr., since my father was the other moderate in the field and there was room for only one moderate at the top. To do this, César requested and received the help of Adolfo Calero. César moved his residence from San José, Costa Rica, to Miami, Florida—next door to the Calero household. Suddenly Calero and César discovered their wives were cousins. They said they wished the women to develop a close familial relationship. It was, we said, the Conspiracy of the Cousins.

The birth of UNO was marked by an official signing at my father's headquarters in Costa Rica. It created the impression that my father was in command. He wasn't—there was no command at all. I realized we were doomed when even at the signing Calero minimized the document publicly, suggesting that he didn't really believe in negotiation. He also hinted that my father was ready to sell out to Managua. My father did announce publicly that he wanted to go to Managua, but it was to present the UNO document to the FSLN. Managua, however, refused to let him land in the country, pledging to fine any airline that brought him in.

The other problem was that no one in the left wing of the contras was available to sign the document and help legitimize UNO's credentials. Pastora would not do it. Besides, it was no longer possible to consider him a man of the left.

With no other leftists available, I arranged to have Carlos Coronel sign the document. Coronel was trapped. He didn't support UNO but if he wanted credibility with my father's people he had to support my father. And my father was the only game Coronel could still possibly control—the Northern Front in Honduras would have nothing to do with the leftist Coronel and Pastora was almost finished.

The most important reason to embrace Coronel, I thought, was simply that he was a token expression of independence from the Americans. And in spite of his ultimate personal objectives, whatever they were, we could never finally close off Managua as an option. Coronel, still close to FSLN commander Jaime Wheelock, could prove useful.

I later discovered that it was Coronel who united César and Pastora in their alliance against UNO. And when Robelo joined UNO and ejected several of his top advisers, Coronel encouraged them too—the so-called Excluded Ones—to join the Pastora-César axis. Coronel was helping create UNO and also helping to undermine it.

We knew Coronel was a dangerous element yet neither my father nor I could leave him behind. For one thing, my father was swimming in a sea of sharks and Coronel was the canniest shark of them all. And if Coronel hurt anyone, it would be me, not my father. He respected my father too much. Coronel regarded himself as my own father in the art of conspiracy—he was the one who had taught me whatever I knew about intrigue. Therefore, in his odd paternal, proprietary way, he felt he always retained the right to attack me and, if necessary, destroy me.

Stop scheming, North and the CIA ordered. I suspected that all the Americans enjoyed the spectacle of Nicaraguans feuding bitterly among themselves. It reaffirmed their sense of cultural superiority and further justified intervention.

They might as well have told us to stop breathing. Conspiracy is the ancient legacy of Nicaraguan political culture. From independence in the nineteenth century through all the intrigues of the twentieth century, Nicaragua's political history is rife with the sport of overindulgent conspiracy. My enemy today is my friend tomorrow and my enemy the day after, the saying goes. The Nicaraguan tribe is too small, the country's players too few, and all the political chiefs are friends. Why should one of us wield power when another one could?

And so we fight against anyone who emerges over the rest of us. We believe we are all kings.

In Nicaraguan history, instead of civil war resulting from foreign intervention, intervention has often been a result of civil war. Such was the case of the American mercenary William Walker, who was imported into the country in the 1850s to help break the interminable war between León and Granada. At the time León and Granada were led by eminent *caudillos:* Frutos Chamorro from Granada, and Máximo Jérez, the great general of Léon. Frutos Chamorro, the political patriarch of the conservative Chamorro clan, was also half Guatemalan Indian. Because he was illegitimate he was known as "Frutos the Bastard."

Nicaraguan weaponry at the time was pathetic. Two percussion rifles were able to reverse the fate of a war. So when a Honduran general dispatched an Italian artillery expert to aid his Liberal friend Jérez, the Italian's arrival changed the forces of war in favor of León.

The victory overwhelmed Jérez and he began to dream of more than one Italian mercenary fighting by his side in the endless battle to defeat Granada. He invited Walker and his legion of a few dozen men to come to Central America and join his battle.

Walker fought so skillfully, the Granadans were shocked and subdued. When Walker approached Granada, the city surrendered without a fight. He then took the rest of the country, making the Leónese and General Jérez his junior partners. The Leónese were willing to remain faithful to Walker as long as he could keep their enemies the Granadans in check.

This willingness of one Nicaraguan to sell out another Nicaraguan is one reason why a celebrated journalist once said to me angrily, you Nicaraguans deserve communism, for it is the only system that can straitjacket your country.

The Soviets also took advantage of Nicaragua's political climate by playing one Sandinista commander off against the other. They imported Borge to Moscow, then Humberto, then Wheelock, and strove to make them fight for Soviet favors. The Sandinistas were lucky, though—as revolutionaries, they were joined together by an ideological cohesion from which no one could deviate without losing ground in the wider competition for ideological purity. In contrast, the contras were mired in their inherent Nicaraguan anarchical political culture. As we often remarked, at a meeting called by ten contras to discuss the urgency and necessity of independence from the CIA, all ten present would hurry to call the CIA as soon as the meeting was over to inform on one another.

To help sell the faithful Adolfo Calero to America, North hired the public relations team of Richard Miller and Frank Gomez. The two men were irksome and consistently arrogant. My father soon became one of their premier publicity tools. The duo would fly him down to the military camps on the Honduran border, take his photo, and then get him out of the camps as fast as possible so that the peasants wouldn't talk to him, for fear they might discover that Arturo Cruz, Sr., wasn't a raving communist, which is what others had told the rebel fighters.

Miller and Gomez notwithstanding, the contras were losing the international image contest—our criticisms of the Sandinistas were laughed off while the Sandinista publicity machine was successful throughout the world. Oliver North finally asked me to fly to Europe in order to speak to the press, the universities, the congresses to see if I could repair some of the damage. After all, I had been successful as a propagandist for the other side before I left Managua.

Although the mission was to be nominally run by a member of the contra Northern Front, and I was to be the number two, it was clear, North said, that I could run the show. I agreed.

But I added that, although I would accompany the group to Holland, where the political tour commenced, I would not be able to stay long. North wanted to know why and I refused to say.

The reason was that his secretary, Fawn Hall, and I had started dating just that week. After eight months of flirting I had finally asked her out. We went to see a movie together and by the next day we were in love.

One of the stories that Don Enrique had told me in Granada was about the sad fate of Serapio Cabistan. Cabistan was a handsome young man who lived among the best families of Granada in the early nineteenth century. He was the brother of the mistress of my ancestor, Narciso Arellano, the man who married a member of the Chamorro clan.

Cabistan was educated in Europe. When he returned to Nicaragua at the age of eighteen he fell madly in love with a Granadan woman. She was not from a good family and certainly not good enough for the Cabistans. Their three daughters had had affairs but then had not married. Serapio was their last hope for respectability.

Family pressure has always been extraordinary in Nicaragua. Cabistan obeyed his father's wishes and remained loyal to his family. He said good-bye to the woman and never saw her again.

He went mad. The separation from his beloved took its toll almost immediately upon the boy. Only a few weeks after his farewells he was barely able to function. He then lived alone on a hacienda near Catarina for thirty years, spending every moment of his time saying the rosary in French.

I never forgot the story of Cabistan, especially when it came time in my life to choose between love and logic. I decided that I would rather be perceived as mad than to go mad, so I chose to surrender to love.

On Sunday I met with people from the CIA in a Virginia hotel to settle the final arrangements for the trip. I said, once more, that I would go for only five days, that I would be back on Saturday.

I then called Hall and told her to wait for me at four in the afternoon for the Pan Am flight from London at Dulles. She agreed. We had lunch and remained together until the plane departed. Tuesday, Wednesday, and Thursday I worked with the contra delegation and the CIA control officer.

The contra team that went to Europe was actually quite capable; we were able to make some serious inroads in the international perception of the contra. So I informed the CIA officer that I was no longer needed and that I would be leaving the delegation on Saturday to return to the United States.

You really shouldn't do that, the officer replied. No one had ever truly thought I would leave because the operation was serious and I was doing such a good job. The CIA assumed I would fall in love with my own successes and want to stay on.

I said no.

The next day I received a cable from the CIA, saying, PLEASE, ARTURO, STAY.

I said no.

The next day another cable came from higher up in the CIA. It simply said, STAY.

I said no.

Then the new head of the contra project at the CIA sent another cable demanding that I remain in Europe. Again I said no. I called Fawn at her office and told her to ignore anything they might be telling her about me. You be at the airport at 4 P.M., I said.

North was suspicious; I assume he had simply been waiting for the affair to start. Where's Arturo? he asked Fawn. Don't you dare tell him not to come back, she responded. That said all North needed to know.

I left Europe that Saturday. When I arrived at Dulles, Fawn was waiting. We drove to Annapolis and spent the weekend there.

The next Monday I went to see North. The only time we were able to schedule was eight o'clock at night, and he still made me wait outside in the hall for two hours. He turned out to be more understanding than might have been expected. But we both knew I had blown it.

The CIA was thrilled. Fawn Hall had become a potential security risk. Still, for the time being, North protected her. He put his prestige behind us and didn't force us to split up.

The relationship between Fawn and me continued until autumn of 1986. The most difficult part for each of us was convincing the other that our relationship was based on love, not politics. Our conversations never included security interests because we both feared that any questions about North, or Nicaragua, or my father, or the Sandinistas, might indicate that one of us was trying to obtain secrets from the other.

When Fawn was questioned about our relationship by the CIA, she started to worry. Then a White House officer also investigated our relationship. Still North protected her. He expected the issue to disappear because he expected I would disappear too. Like all Nicaraguans, he once said, your emotions surface and fade like your conflicting alliances.

Throughout the autumn Fawn was under pressure but North shielded her, even as his relationship with me deteriorated. More and more of our meetings ended in bitter arguments; he began to think I was unreliable, and assigned a tail to follow me—although I did not discover this until much later—in order to see if I was working for the other side.

The affair with Fawn eventually expired without any outside interference. I threw into the relationship my anguish over the contras and my despair over America. I began to develop a block against speaking English; I felt it was violating my nationality. It is difficult to translate the Latin American experience into American English. The two cultures are too different. The American is rational, individualistic, self-responsible. We aren't. How could I talk to Fawn about the Urbinas, about Uncle David shouting the Spanish dictionary from on top of the roof? Or that no one ever saw a Chinaman die in Granada?

Fawn just thought I was being impossible. We fought terribly. The affair was almost over by the time of the Iran-contra scandal. At the end I decided I really did love her but it was too late and she did not love me anymore.

Much to my disgust, Edén Pastora was openly unhappy with my father's continuing role as the leader of the civilian wing of the contras. Along with Calero, Pastora feared that the civilian option might someday take precedence over his military prescription.

Pastora was also speaking out against his new enemy, Alfonso Robelo. One assassination attempt had already been made on Robelo's life and Pastora was hand-delivering the Sandinistas every opportunity to make an attempt themselves—for if Robelo were killed, Pastora would no doubt be blamed. Pastora was also acting absurdly; at one point he publicly accused Robelo's people of having stolen his submachine gun. Robelo handed over to Pastora what Pastora claimed was the stolen gun, then Pastora changed his mind and said that this was absolutely not his gun, as he was sure that this serial number could not have been his serial number.

Since the assassination attempt Pastora's imagination had been difficult to harness. He thought he was many things and many people, among them, Sandino and Jesus Christ. He began to suspect that he might be invincible, chosen by God. This feeling was reinforced by an incident in the air. Once, flying inside Costa Rica, Pastora's helicopter pilot realized the plane was running out of fuel. They needed to land. No, no, no, no, Pastora said, we don't need to land, we need to reach our destination. He started pushing his body forward, thrusting it back and forth as though the momentum of his physical being was enough to propel the copter to safety.

The craft ran out of fuel and fell to the ground. Luckily no one was hurt. Pastora was convinced that luck had nothing to do with it. The truth was, he couldn't be killed. His proof was that he wasn't dead—a difficult argument to puncture.

At one of my final meetings with him, while he was surrounded by his new top advisers—Karol Prado, Popo Chamorro—I explained all the compromises needed to be made if he was to remain the head of the Southern Front. I told him how the visit to Washington had failed, how he had lost his contact with Carlos Andrés Pérez, and how all his old friends were leaving him.

He then stood up from his chair and responded, I am Edén Pastora and I am standing on a pedestal!

At which I exploded, you are indeed Edén Pastora, but the pedestal you are standing on is a pedestal of shit!

I stalked out of the house fuming and walked around the block several times until I had controlled my temper well enough to return. When I did, Prado made the belittling comment that I had behaved like a maid. In Nicaragua, when the maids fight with their mistresses, they habitually leave the house to simmer for a few hours and then return to continue their work. I looked like a fool.

But being with Pastora made me feel more foolish. I was working with a maniac and could no longer justify my presence in his camp. Three days later I was asked to meet him again in his office. While talking to him, for the last time as a member of his cabal, Prado looked at me and said, now that the ship is sinking, the rats are deserting. He was referring to me and Carlos Coronel.

I responded that the rats weren't deserting the ship so much as they were steering it.

Pastora didn't listen. He launched into another speech about how he resembled Jesus Christ, Napoleon, and, above all, Sandino.

Finally I said, this is it. I have never betrayed you, Edén, and I have always been faithful to you. From this moment onward, I am your competitor.

At the end of August 1985 FDN forces took the town of Trinidad in the region of Chontales. The FSLN's Soviet helicopters, entering into the combat, performed with great efficiency. The FDN could not retaliate against the helicopters, so North was determined to find a military counterbalance. Only the Jorge Salazar task force, working inside Chontales, was able to maintain a constant presence within the country. This part of Nicaragua, the birthplace of Cardinal Obando y Bravo and Emiliano Chamorro, was always a fiercely independent region, the home of small cattle ranchers who historically had preferred to live under no master. But as the rest of the Southern Front was immobile under Pastora's leadership, Managua committed all its troops to one concerted effort against the contras' task force in Chontales.

Something had to be done about Pastora. The question was, how could Pastora go and his troops remain?

Pastora thought he could circumvent the CIA. If Calero could receive money from the right, why couldn't he? He sent his people off to Miami and Argentina—some say South Africa—to locate financial support. Even Castro had raised right-wing money to fight Batista.

Another source of Pastora's revenue was the Sandinistas. At the end of 1985 they engaged in frequent battles with Pastora's troops near the area of The Castle. During the colonial years English pirates used to attack the city of Granada by sailing down the San Juan River and then navigating the lake. To protect the Granadans against the pirates the Spanish constructed a large fort which is still intact.

The Sandinistas would attack Pastora's men near The Castle, take positions, and then retreat. And in retreat they occasionally left a cache of ammunition behind. Pastora would then sweep in and clean up the ammunition, the spoils of this "victory." This convinced observers that Pastora was truly a double agent. Here was the proof: the Sandinistas were supplying him with ammunition.

My interpretation was that the Sandinistas knew that, as long as Pastora oversaw the Southern Front, the front could never be effective. Sandinista intelligence was so good and so constant, it would have been a devastating blow for Managua to lose Pastora as their enemy. So they helped keep him extant.

It was alleged that Noriega was also feeding Pastora

money. Many said this was being done to please the Sandinistas—it was a favor to Managua, to keep Pastora in the game.

The other rumored source of revenue for the Southern Front, after the Americans stopped providing aid, was drug trafficking.

Since the attempt on Pastora's life the César brothers, Alfredo and Octaviano, had become Pastora's allies. Pastora was upset, however, that the Césars were being funded for their political activities by the CIA, while Pastora was not. The Césars explained that they received their money from Venezuela's Carlos Andrés Pérez and others with the proviso that none of these funds were to be used for military purposes. But the Césars were under pressure to deliver something to Pastora to justify their alliance, which depended on their claim that their great diplomatic skills would ease the CIA back into supporting Pastora—despite the fact that the Césars wanted the CIA to back them instead.

Something had to be done for Pastora to keep him in the alliance. The CIA weren't interested in Pastora now. They were happy to do business with Alfredo César, although they disliked Octaviano. According to Octaviano, this was due to a grave misunderstanding.

During the war against Somoza, Octaviano César served in the Southern Front, working in logistics. He had been assigned as an aide to Commander Victor Tirado (one of the three Tercerista commanders, along with the Ortega brothers). Octaviano also claimed he had been a CIA operative, using his special communications equipment to keep the Americans informed of activities between the Sandinistas and the Cubans.

But Octaviano also told me, the Americans suspected these communications were for the benefit of the Sandinistas, not the Americans; that most of the information was disinformation. Octaviano protested that this was never the case, but the CIA didn't believe him and refused to deal with him.

The problem with Octaviano's tale, like so many Nicaraguan tales, is that fantasy and reality could not be differentiated. Octaviano's dream was always to be an intelligence operative: CIA, KGB, Mossad, Cuban, it did not matter which. If he could have dealt with all of them, that would have made him happiest.

In September 1984, Pastora dispatched one of his commanders, Popo Chamorro, to Miami and New Jersey to raise money from Cuban-Americans. Chamorro claimed this trip raised about a million dollars in money, food, and medicine. That same September Octaviano approached Popo, who was also his cousin and involved in a conspiracy to steal the southern army away from Pastora, with a proposal.

Octaviano was familiar with a Colombian millionaire living in Miami. He now showed Popo a picture of three planes —a Panther, a DC-4, and a C-47—and told him that this Colombian was willing to "sell" one of these three planes for one dollar, for the benefit of the cause.

Popo knew this offer was generous but it was not abnormal. In 1983 a similar deal had been arranged between Pastora's people and private donors for the sale of two Hughes 500-C helicopters. Now, Pastora needed the plane badly, so he was not terribly keen on asking questions. Pastora's pilot, Aguado, suggested that they ask for the C-47, and Popo agreed to meet with the millionaire.

At the meeting in Miami Popo and the Colombian, clad in a silk jogging suit, agreed to the deal. But the Colombian then mentioned that the plane was presently located in Haiti. Popo said that they didn't have the money to send pilots to Haiti to get the plane. So the Colombian gave Popo ten thousand dollars to pay for a pilot and gasoline, explaining that he had great sympathy for Pastora's cause and that someday he would expect a favor in return.

Popo completed the mission on behalf of Pastora and the plane was flown to Miami.

Pastora needed the plane to move food, medicine, boots,

and clothing from Miami to his people in southern Nicaragua. Moreover, the CIA was willing to let Pastora collect from Ilopango, the largest air force base in El Salvador, the leftovers of the aid that had been approved before the suspension of aid in the summer of 1984. The CIA was prohibited, by the Boland amendment, from touching the goods, which were nonetheless still legally available to the contras. The C-47 was used to move the goods to one of the many airstrips in northern Costa Rica left over from the last war.

The millionaire was George Morales, a naturalized American of Colombian origin. In March 1984 he had been indicted for trafficking in cocaine and marijuana. Through the contras Morales hoped to buy the good will of the intelligence agencies of the Americans. When he met Octaviano, I can imagine he thought this was the man to establish his connections. I can also imagine Octaviano needing a psychological equalizer and hinting at his multiple connections with the CIA (even suggesting he had been an agent), and referring to his brother's contacts at the highest level of the American government. Octaviano César took Morales to meet Pastora in December 1984.

In January 1986 Morales was again indicted for drug trafficking between the United States and Costa Rica. In his defense he accused Octaviano César of having represented himself as a CIA agent and pleaded his case as an American patriot. The irony was that Octaviano, trying to impress the exile community with legends of his grand CIA connections, was now the victim of his own vivid imagination. As far as I know, in the middle of 1984 Octaviano had no relations whatsoever with the CIA in Costa Rica. And after March 1985 Alfredo César and Tomás Castillo fought and split up their tactical friendship.

At the beginning of 1988 Octaviano received a letter from Massachusetts Senator John Kerry, chairman of the subcommittee investigating the links between the contras and drugs.

Kerry exonerated Octaviano from any wrongdoing with regard to drug trafficking.

Pastora employed three types of commanders on the Southern Front. One was the city commander in San José, with his gun and his briefcase and his huge stomach. There was the river commander, in charge of logistics. The real commander was stationed inside Nicaragua. The operation ran as follows: the city commanders took as much money out of the pot as they could, the river commanders took almost all the remaining money, and the real commanders got what was left. It is my opinion that Pastora's supervision of these men kept them always fighting against one another.

At the most difficult point of 1985 Pastora abruptly purged his city and river commanders. They were, he decided, all in collusion with his conniving ally, Alfredo César. Pastora then asked his Cuban-trained bodyguards to take command of the remnants of his troops. He also offered one of his daughters —one of the Sherman tanks—in marriage to the best of these soldiers, a boy named Ganso. Because of this, Pastora's angry ex-commanders began to conspire against him too.

Someone was needed to replace Pastora and create a new Southern Front, and that someone was needed promptly. He was found in the person of "El Negro" Chamorro, one of the original contra members. Chamorro was bald, very dark, and had the eyes of an eagle. A thin man who seldom ate, he drank considerably. He was the nephew of Emiliano Chamorro, with whom he had been in exile on many occasions. El Negro's fame derived from his leadership in the 1961 attempt to take over Nicaragua's National Guard barracks— the uprising from which my father excluded himself so as not to lose my mother and his family.

Almost two decades later, in 1978, El Negro checked into the Intercontinental Hotel in Managua, climbed up to his room, and then launched a bazooka attack on the bunker across the street from which Somoza was commanding the war. When he was liberated (along with Tomás Borge) after the National Palace takeover, he removed himself to Costa Rica. El Negro, not a talented strategist, was nonetheless brave, honest, and popular. Above all else, he did not have sufficient control of his senses to pretend he was the real commander, but he was a powerful enough symbol to keep the commanders inside Nicaragua from fighting for power among themselves.

Tomás Castillo accepted the appointment. But he considered El Negro an anarchic disaster, one similar to Pastora. He knew, however, that if you couldn't have Pastora, El Negro was second best.

I told North that the whole south was now a poisoned well, poisoned by the madness of Pastora, the conspiracies of Carlos Coronel and the double agents, the rivalries of the historical families, and the poverty of most of the exiles in the south. The Northern Front in Honduras still maintained a strong sense of hierarchy; everyone knew who was in control. It also had enough liquidity to keep the leadership from fighting for limited resources. In the south all was anarchy following the absolute reign of Pastora.

To assure that Calero would remain the master of the contras, North decided Calero, from Tegucigalpa, could buy the Southern Front. The American Congress could not supply El Negro with aid, so his financial support came from Calero. Money was Calero's power. Politics is essentially the art of solving problems and Calero's pocketbook drove up his political stock.

Calero was supposed to provide Chamorro $50,000 a month. According to Chamorro, however, provision of funds was very erratic. Chamorro then began to compete with Pastora as the head of the Southern Front since Pastora simply wouldn't leave.

To the befuddlement of the CIA, despite the competition between the two men, they remained friends. Pastora and El Negro had no intention of ending a lifelong friendship over this small matter. One of El Negro's field commanders, "Chepon" Robelo, was in constant contact with his associates and friends among Pastora's people. Coronel, too, now had access to El Negro since one of Coronel's best friends was Juan Zavala, El Negro's most intimate friend.

Costa Rica was scheduled to elect a new President in February. That new President would start his term in May. His willingness to allow the Southern Front to operate on Costa Rica's border was in doubt. The contras' Jorge Salazar task force was facing more and more pressure from the Sandinistas, and the Southern Front had to be regenerated to relieve the north of the full brunt of Managua's attack.

It was time for El Negro Chamorro to move his six camps, currently sitting by the Costa Rica-Nicaragua border, into Nicaragua. The Americans also wanted the camps moved so that Pastora's men would see the distinguished El Negro march into the formidable jungle, inspiring them to desert Pastora for Chamorro.

Chamorro pointed out to the Americans that this was all good on paper but where were his supplies? We were promised three hundred EG rifles and we have been sent only a hundred and fifty, he said; sometimes Calero gives us $40,000, sometimes $50,000, sometimes nothing. We are a forgotten front, without liquidity. Our morale is low. Given the dense jungle and without new supplies, morale will become worse. What will Pastora's men say when they see us, ragged and dejected?

If we go in, El Negro continued, at least supply us with a minimum of five hundred properly armed and well-fed recruits.

I was the translator summarizing the arguments for El Negro to Tomás Castillo. I could translate the words but even if they had spoken the same language they could not have understood each other.

El Negro then transgressed the boundaries of American

logic. He told Castillo that he would enter Nicaragua only if he could enter Chontales, the area where his Great-uncle Emiliano Chamorro had been born. El Negro wanted to rekindle the legend of the military Chamorro family, to relive the glories of his uncle in his wars against Zelaya in 1904.

Castillo did not accept this argument and the meeting ended. Later, in the Iran-contra hearings, Castillo testified that El Negro Chamorro was a coward, an assessment which misrepresented all that Chamorro and his family symbolized.

During the drive back to El Negro's safe house, he reminisced about the Americans he had known much earlier. To think, he said, that when my Uncle Emiliano was old and needed medical attention he was taken to Walter Reed Hospital. President Eisenhower came to visit him to show his appreciation for the man and shook his hand. What kind of American is this, this Castillo, this imperial sergeant, who doesn't even know who Emiliano Chamorro is?

It was at this moment that I decided that we would always need a mediator for Chamorro. I had no intention of dealing with another Pastora and, though I had a strong emotional attachment to El Negro and his authenticity, I couldn't mediate between him and the Americans as I had tried to do so long and so laboriously for Pastora. I recommended that Carlos Ulvert—an urbane Harvard MBA raised in England and Nicaragua, at ease with both cultures—should be Chamorro's interpreter of the two cultures.

In May 1986 Pastora made one last attempt to maintain his control. It looked as though his field commanders were ready to strike a deal with the Americans, or that they might accept Chamorro. So Pastora talked to Richard Singlaub, the retired American general he met through his contact with Senator Jesse Helms and who, since 1985, had been traveling throughout the world raising money for the contras. Singlaub wasn't able to help in time, however, and it was said that he was pressured to stop raising money for Pastora since the new Southern Front was finally about to happen. Why provide artificial life support to the near dead?

Finally Pastora withdrew from the game. He had lasted two years without official American support, on the basis of his charisma, his skill as a manipulator of symbols, his feudal understanding of his people. Supposedly he also raised money from the Cuban-Americans, and by selling rifles to the Salvadoran and Colombian guerrillas.

When Sandinista intelligence heard that Pastora no longer ruled his commanders, Sandinista troops swept into the river and captured the area. Now that the possibility of an effective Southern Front was real, the Sandinistas closed it up once and for all. Pastora requested, and received, political asylum in Costa Rica. He became a fisherman, as he had been in 1978 before the Sandinistas allowed him his great moment of glory.

8

The Rise and Fall of the CIA

In the summer of 1986 Assistant Secretary of State for Inter-American Affairs Elliott Abrams met with Bill Walker, Deputy Assistant Secretary for Central America; Norma Harms, the desk officer for Nicaragua; "Cliff," the representative of the CIA; and several others to discuss the issue of the Miskito Indians. The question was how to help them achieve unity. The Indians' efforts at rebellion had been continuous, heartfelt, and, like other dissent within Nicaragua, thoroughly disunited and fitful. Brooklyn Rivera and Steadman Fagoth, the two Miskito leaders, fought with each other as zealously as they fought the Sandinistas.

Cliff conjured up one plan after another, all very American, all very CIA-oriented. The State Department argued against these plans. They accused Cliff of possessing only a limited grasp of the situation; they said that he and the CIA had only disdain for the Miskitos' identity.

The problem with you, Cliff, Norma Harms said, is that all you want to do is manipulate and control the Miskitos.

To which a pleased Cliff responded, thank you, young lady. I am paid to do exactly that—manipulate and control.

The prevailing rumor of 1985 was that Cliff, the new man in charge of Nicaragua at the CIA, was more powerful than Maroni had ever been, even though Maroni had been in charge of all Latin America and Cliff only worked for Maroni's replacement, "Tony." But Tony, fully aware of what had destroyed Maroni, never dealt with the Nicaragua mess directly. He allowed his man Cliff a free hand to run the contra operation. Cliff was also said to be a favorite of William Casey's. Actually many CIA agents told us that they were favorites of Casey's—they knew their Nicaraguan allies were impressed by proximity to power.

When Cliff entered the game Oliver North was as much his competitor as the Sandinistas. Cliff wanted to repair the professional luster of the CIA. North wanted to be the American who saved Nicaragua. These two egos soon clashed. Control of American policy was evenly contested between the White House and the CIA. The agency was weakened by its own internal camps: the old guard (Maroni's staff) and the new (Cliff's). The old guard had two choices: they could either dance to the tune of the new man or they could look for protection elsewhere. Some of them turned to North. Costa Rica CIA station chief Tomás Castillo chose this route. Unlike the CIA or the State Department, North did not have his own institutional network. The National Security Council does not have agents all over the world, never having been designated for that sort of work. Castillo and North soon developed a relationship based on mutual need—North wanted the loyalty of people in the region who would be responsive to his demands and Castillo longed for a powerful protector in Washington, D.C.

Most of the other CIA intelligence officers chose to adapt. So when Cliff asked them to jump, their only question was how high?

Cliff had been a lineman at Ohio State University and, though he was in his early fifties, he was thin, dynamic, and tough. He played politics as though it were all a great football game, scoring touchdowns and extra points for the CIA. He was fonder of undercover games than any other agent I ever met—the false beards, the wigs, the trenchcoats, all the trappings that most agents avoid.

A man of green suburban lawns, Cliff was imbued with a strong sense of cultural superiority. He was aware, however, that some sort of symbolic atonement for his lack of knowledge of Nicaraguan culture was necessary, for indeed he knew nothing at all about us or our country. We were told he had been the CIA station chief in Saudi Arabia. His conversations about Third World assets were filled with Arabic terms of speech, references dropped as though all of us throughout the Other World understood Arabic. In order to show he was truly at ease with Third World traditions, he used to order a glass of hot water after a meal, as did—we were later told—the Arabs with whom he had last served. It took months to figure out what it meant. Perhaps Cliff was constipated, we thought. In Nicaragua, drinking a glass of hot water is considered an enema.

Cliff discerned neither shades nor colors. He once idly remarked that he had hated communism from the moment he was born. He had never gone through a crisis of conscience and he was now controlling a people who were in a permanent crisis of conscience.

His long-term objective was to prove he was more capable than North or Maroni. He did not disagree with the others' basic strategy. He simply needed to prove he could manage the strategy more efficiently. He loved the American sense of management. He decided that the application of proper management skills to the contra situation would provide the necessary control the operation had so far lacked.

I always assumed that Cliff hated Oliver North as much as he could summon the emotion to hate anyone. He regarded North as a man of the military interloping within the world of intelligence, an amateur in a highly professional game. The two men became great rivals, but in 1985, with Congress out of the game, the advantage belonged to North.

The first meeting between Cliff, my father, and myself took place in my Washington, D.C., apartment. Cliff arrived accompanied by two people—the soon-to-depart Alberto, and Fred, Cliff's number two at the CIA. Fred was a thoughtful-looking man who used to sit and smoke his pipe and seldom spoke—for good reason, we decided later, because he had nothing to say.

Cliff hated the location of my apartment, which was just off the Dupont Circle area of Washington. He sniffed the air and said he could smell bohemians and communists.

When the CIA men entered the apartment, my father was already seated on my only couch. Alberto sat down next to him. As soon as he did he realized that the couch was the center of the room and that any other chair was inappropriate for Cliff. Cliff realized this too. He stared at Alberto until Alberto stood up and let Cliff sit down on the couch.

My father started to speak. Before he could open his mouth, however, Cliff erupted. He'd come to distribute directions, not to listen to my father talk. His point was that, yes, Cliff was the new game in town, and that, yes, Cliff was now going to assign us new roles in his game. My father and Cliff clashed immediately.

Both my father and I preferred that Alberto remain on the job. Alberto could be as ruthless as either Cliff or Maroni, but he was mentally agile; he had cooperated with North and the State Department and at the same time he had attempted to understand the psychology of the Nicaraguan.

For instance, at the end of 1984 Mario Castillo, Humberto Ortega's ex-right-hand man, appeared in the United States after having quit the Sandinista regime for Spain. Castillo had always been a controversial figure in Managua: a true believer in the free enterprise system who nonetheless had worked closely with Humberto for years. He had served as Humberto's procurer of civilian goods for the Sandinistas' army. His supplies—jeeps, air conditioners, boots, et cetera —were products of America. Castillo used to say he believed in mini-capitalism, in the "Revolution of the Good Life." His influence on the commanders surrounding Humberto was that each decided he needed a similar procurer and soon everyone was a Revolutionary of the Good Life.

Mario Castillo insisted that the Americans should try to make a deal with Humberto Ortega, not Tomás Borge. Humberto was the classical Nicaraguan and thus more in the traditional *caudillo* mold—more of a personality, less of an ideologue. Further, his power base was the army, where many of the top commanders were more loyal to Humberto, the man, than to Marxism and Leninism.

Alberto was interested in Castillo's proposal and the possibility of conversations between Alberto and Humberto was explored. But any such possibility collapsed when Cliff arrived. Castillo was deemed too unmanageable. The CIA controlled its assets via money. Castillo was independently wealthy and could not be indentured to CIA payments.

I was disappointed because I was the first one Castillo had looked up when he arrived in the United States—I had set up a meeting between him and Alberto in Miami. Castillo and I had been friends since my childhood in Granada. My hope was that a channel to the Ortega brothers could be opened up through Castillo and could help ease Managua into a family-oriented dictatorship in the Nicaraguan tradition. Given either a Marxist-Leninist dictatorship or an indigenous Nicaraguan dictatorship, I preferred the latter. I now believed that the confrontation in Nicaragua is between ideology and tradition. If tradition won, I thought, even if it took the form of a Sandinista uniform, Nicaragua won. Such a theory was alien to Cliff, for whom my friendship with Castillo was another indication that I was unreliable. It was a confirmation of my being—in his words—a loose wheel.

That first meeting with Cliff in Washington was a tragedy. It took one hour to realize that we had little to say to each other. My assumption was that the discussion ended with Cliff deciding to omit any Cruzes from all future activity; shortly thereafter I was told by a Senate aide that the CIA decision to work exclusively through Adolfo Calero had indeed been reaffirmed.

Soon after our meeting Cliff decided that each one of the contras had to be tested for loyalty, and all the members of the new Southern Front in Costa Rica involved in military activities were ordered to take lie detector tests similar to the one I had taken.

It was not necessarily an unfair decision: the Southern Front was riddled with double agents, the network of friendship outweighing any sense of ideological cohesion or loyalty. However, these tests, administered in CIA safe houses in San José, Costa Rica, during the fall of 1985, became a sensitive issue. To take the lie detector test, it was said in the Southern Front, was the political equivalent of being castrated by the Americans.

So said Juan Zavala, the friend of El Negro Chamorro and Carlos Coronel, a man of the lesser Nicaraguan landed gentry, whose life had been devoted to fighting the Somozas.

Zavala felt the best testimony of his opposition to tyranny was his history as a combatant, not the ten questions of a CIA machine. How dare these people not trust me? the man asked. I was an anti-Somocista when the Americans were still supporting the dictator. Zavala christened the test the *chimi-chu,* an old instrument of torture used by the Somozas on their enemies, including Zavala.

The Americans had no patience with this kind of stuff. Zavala, who refused to submit to the *chimi-chu,* was thrown out of the contra.

The people who were supposed to pass the test did pass it. The others didn't. Some were never invited to take the test. In fact, another group of rebels was now being created, composed of those who hadn't passed and those who weren't asked and organized by the recent outcast Zavala. It was aided by the ever recurrent figure of Carlos Coronel (who, of course, didn't take the test). Coronel was organizing other outcasts because he didn't want to take the test himself. He would always say, I am willing to take any lie detector test, under any circumstances, any time. The fact is, he never did.

The new rebel outcasts soon denounced everyone: the Russians, the Americans, those who had passed the CIA's test. The United States was wondering how Carlos Coronel could still be playing in their game. They could never fathom how to get rid of him. The more they pressured their people to avoid him, the more valuable became Coronel's stock as a contra: the one whom the Americans feared most was ipso facto the most genuine.

For his part, Coronel never understood at least one important truth about the Americans. He was always impatient to meet the great ones, the ones who truly ran the Empire. He never believed that the American agents he met could compose the real American CIA. They were too stupid, too obvious; he had such a low regard for them and, in his own way, such a high regard for the American Empire.

He became so desperate that he once told me he had discovered the real CIA: James LeMoyne. LeMoyne was a very intelligent correspondent for the New York *Times* who spoke perfect Spanish. Coronel thought he was the most intelligent American he had met—so he must be a CIA talent. Coronel became so convinced, and hopeful, that he courted the reporter, hoping to make him understand that, even though Coronel maintained a strong attachment to Castro, he was still a rational being and therefore pro-American.

In fact, LeMoyne had no relationship at all to the CIA and had written several articles the CIA detested. But Coronel couldn't help but seek a hidden subtext that might give immediate access to power, give insight into imperial intrigue and genius.

The legend in Nicaragua was that Carlos Coronel's brother had died in East Germany, crossing the Berlin Wall. There are those who say Coronel's brother was an East German agent defecting to the West and that he was killed by the East Germans. And there are those who say he was an East German spy killed by the United States. Depending on his mood, Coronel thought either the East Germans or the Americans were guilty. It was all in the family blood, this game of seeking outside antagonists and sponsors, finding strength through dependence on one great power or other, whether it be Castro, America, or Germany. It is an old tradition, a measure of Nicaraguan vulnerability.

Finally Coronel, having exhausted all his options and having been caught between too many alliances, retired to his new home. He moved back to the city of Granada, into the house across the street from the Urbinas, the house in which my grandparents lived thirty years earlier. But the Urbinas are dead. Don Manuel is dead. Only the dentist who married the Mexican and proved to Granadan men that Mexican women are saints is still there.

Coronel took a job as the manager of a state farm, Hato Grande, near Tipitapa, and when people ask him what he is doing with his time he replies that he is waiting for the new canal which will save Nicaragua.

The rebels in the south badly needed boots, food, bullets, rifles, and uniforms. But no American aid was forthcoming. The now famous private network of funds established by Oliver North was employed to appease the rebel commanders in the south. The failure to create a successful supply operation created increasing pressure to drop supplies quickly. The plane carrying the American Eugene Hasenfus was shot down in early 1986 by the Sandinistas, because it never should have gone up that day. The weather was terrible but the urgency to deliver was great.

The private supply network was never as large as the American media assumed. Nor did much of it reach Nicaragua. The only people making profits were those far from the war. In the field, the contra soldiers, the still increasing numbers of peasants coming to the fronts and enlisting, were dying. Their supplies were wretched. Hand grenades exploded in their own hands. Their boots, nicknamed "Calero boots" after their supplier, Calero's brother Mario, were falling apart. The soldiers had no way to defend against the Soviet helicopters.

North helped obtain Sam 7 rockets, through Calero, to help defend ground troops from the Sandinista helicopters. The best missiles on the market were Stingers; Red Eyes were considered adequate and the Sam 7s were the least reliable. But they were better than no missiles at all—or so it was thought. In December 1985 Calero furnished twenty Sam 7s to the Northern Front; their subsequent performance rendered their delivery of questionable value. A soldier would be commanded to carry this heavy weapon on his shoulder for days into the jungle and he was told that this weapon would save him from the Sandinista helicopters. In fact, as often as not the Sam 7 backfired and, rather than blowing away a Sandinista target, it tore off a shoulder.

The Sam 7s were inferior weapons and this set was particularly defective. Many of them nearly killed their users. A prominent member of North's private network who had supplied the weapons explained, when confronted with evidence of the fiasco, that the contra peasants were simply too primitive to understand how to operate the missiles properly.

The assumption among the contras, however, was that this man was buying bad weaponry at modest prices and selling it at a high profit. The soldiers were later provided with Red Eye missiles, which performed properly; proving that their technical skills were excellent. Their shoulders stopped detonating.

By early 1986 it was apparent that the rebel UNO leadership was not working. I believe it was because it was not designed to work. In my opinion, North created UNO only to meet the demands of Congress. His real instrument of control was the person of Adolfo Calero, not the institution of UNO. Even my father realized that UNO was only a front with no strength. In the meetings of the UNO directorate, Calero habitually read the newspapers or talked during any presentation by my father or Alfonso Robelo, clarifying his attitude that the real business of the contra was being conducted elsewhere. When Robelo repeatedly asked how much money was in those bank accounts into which private funds were being channeled, Calero responded with absurd, arbitrary amounts like $720 or $1350.

The key position in UNO was supposed to be its executive secretary, the person who controlled its day-to-day operation and administered its functions. One weekend, when the discussion of reform was at its most intense, North invited Alfonso Robelo to talk over a plan. He wanted to isolate my father with an arrangement whereby Robelo was to support a Nicaraguan exile named Nayo Somarriba as executive secretary. I never found out what happened in that meeting but Robelo was never the same after it.

Nayo Somarriba was a competent administrator, with strong ties to Adolfo Calero. He was a natural choice for North. I respected Somarriba as a man of principle but I opposed his appointment vigorously, telling my father he should support Ulvert instead. Nonetheless Somarriba was chosen. The only consolation was that many of my father's people were incorporated into the structure of UNO, although I later discovered that two of them were covertly working for the CIA.

Somarriba's job was to guarantee that reforms were never implemented. He did his job well.

Perhaps Congress was our answer. El Negro's cultural interpreter, Carlos Ulvert, had been assigned to Washington to lobby for the contras. He was anxious for reform and so he, my father, Alfonso Robelo, and I met in my Washington apartment with members of the American liberal community to discuss reform possibilities. We called them the Gang of Four.

Our goal was to draft a blueprint of change for UNO, to balance the military power of the FDN in Honduras with a strong civilian executive in UNO. Our ultimate objective was to blend the FDN into the structure of UNO. Moreover, we wanted the rebel directorate as a whole—not simply Calero —to have responsibility for the private funds. We also called for the integration of new people into the process: young faces, intellectuals, political cadres, former Sandinistas, people who were aligned with the future, not the past, of Nicaragua. The contras needed, we said, the discipline of managers and the imagination of poets.

To lobby Congress efficiently, we would have to find an ally in the Administration. Elliott Abrams soon became our choice.

Cliff and North were plainly the principal forces in American policy at this point. But Elliott Abrams was slowly emerging from their shadow. An unusually confident man in his late thirties, he had learned to speak Spanish on the job and was fluent by the end of his tenure. Abrams felt like an ally. People, even if they totally disliked him, were always impressed by his intellect.

Abrams effected two immediate personnel changes. The first was to bring Robert Kagan as a special assistant to help reform the contras. Kagan, in his mid-twenties, bright and knowledgeable, was a Yale-educated activist who felt that American power could be used for the good of the world community. He immediately clashed with the CIA's Cliff, who loathed him. Kagan was intellectually fascinated and exasperated by the mysteries of Nicaragua. Cliff wasn't.

Abrams transferred another State Department official named Chris Arcos into his office. Arcos was one of the more remarkable Americans in the whole affair. A Mexican-American, he had served in Honduras with American Ambassador John D. Negroponte. Negroponte did not like Arcos and wanted him out of the country but he sadly knew that only Arcos could comprehend and interpret the Byzantine politics of Honduras. Arcos understood the Hondurans better than any American official. President Suazo was not easy. He once borrowed a helicopter from the American embassy and flew over his opponent's political rallies, personally bombarding the people below with leaflets which accused his opponent of having AIDS. Suazo paved every road of his own hometown but few others. Arcos somehow managed to maintain a constructive working relationship with this man.

Arcos was actually not unlike an American version of Carlos Coronel. He and Kagan were two key talents on the American side.

In August 1986 the U.S. House of Representatives passed a $100 million contra aid bill by a vote of 221–209. The man most relieved by the bill's passage was Oliver North. His private aid network had begun to burn in his hands. He could leave it now.

The great victor, however, was Cliff. Passage of the aid package signified the end of the Boland amendment which prohibited CIA aid to the rebel army. The CIA was more than ready to return to the battle. Cliff took over. Frazzled and exhausted, North took a back seat, which he seemed almost happy to do.

I felt that the one to suffer from the vote would be Calero. When the Boland amendment forced the CIA out of the game Calero had been the first to run from the CIA and join forces with North. But I was wrong. Calero proved to be the big winner. Cliff liked him very much. He described Calero as a "doer" and not one of those Latin American "philosophizers" like Arturo Cruz, Sr.

Alfredo César was also a winner as Cliff, tiring of my father, had decided César was to become the contra of the moderates. Since the creation of UNO, César had entered into a very bitter relationship with the CIA's Tomás Castillo, despite the fact that Castillo and César had recently been allied. But César had been excluded from the directorate of UNO and so became the organization's, as well as Castillo's, enemy. He justified his dissidence on ideological grounds. In UNO, the institution had no weight; only Calero had power.

I had felt strongly that both César and Pastora should be added to the directorate, particularly as the possibility of UNO reform was becoming more and more illusory. But Tomás Castillo and North did not want César, and certainly not Pastora. My dilemma was that I was also willing to take in César without Pastora. But that would place my father in a difficult situation because César might eventually push my father out. I finally sold César's re-entry to Cliff by pointing out that because of Tomás Castillo's loyalty to North, Cliff had no eyes and no ears in Costa Rica. César should become Cliff's personal contra.

Cliff was surprised by my advice. He assumed I was being disloyal to my father. But I had decided that César had to be brought into the game because Robelo was an unreliable ally and my father needed at least some temporary help in his struggle against Calero. He could not do it alone.

Cliff bought the César option and by mid-1986 a channel was opened between the two. César's brother Octaviano was allowed to renew contacts with the CIA for the exclusive purpose of preliminary negotiations regarding the return of Alfredo César. A player once more, Octaviano was in heaven.

Adolfo Calero's relationship to the contra peasant army resembled that of an old Argentine plantation owner who, living elsewhere, would occasionally return home to survey the land and observe the work of his overseers, who were, in this case, Enrique Bermúdez and Aristides Sánchez. We started calling these three men "The Iron Triangle" as they formed the cabal that had so successfully prevented the contra from being reformed.

To weaken this Iron Triangle, we challenged its weakest links: Bermúdez and Sánchez. We did this by attacking the two publicly, reminding anyone who would listen that Bermúdez was a former member of the National Guard and that Sánchez belonged to the conspiracy of the old oligarchy. The basis of the Iron Triangle, we said, was a combination of the old National Guard, the old landed oligarchy, and Calero, the representative of the American government. What kind of revolution could these people lead? How could Americans back men with such a history? How could the urban Nicaraguan masses ever be expected to support us?

Once more we failed to break the monopoly of power. In fact all we did was, for the moment, to force the three into a more tenacious reliance on one another. For the time being Calero became Bermúdez' and Sánchez' defender from outside pressure. The Iron Triangle strengthened.

We tried again. Carlos Ulvert is actually Carlos Ulvert Sánchez, a cousin of Aristides Sánchez. Ulvert suddenly began to comprehend the value of this family connection. The two men came from very different sides of the family: Ulvert was cool, sophisticated, cosmopolitan; the unworldly Sánchez had never even learned English. But why not explore a personal connection with Sánchez?

Like most Nicaraguans, Aristides Sánchez was a great believer in his own family. Throughout his life he maintained a great sense of the family and its place in the history of the Liberal Party in early twentieth-century Nicaragua. The Sánchez family was far superior to Calero's. Sánchez resented working beneath him.

Historical rehabilitation, after all, belongs to both revolutionaries and counterrevolutionaries. Bermúdez, our old enemy the National Guardsman, the former Somocista, was, we now decided, a humble man who simply used the Guard for social mobility, no different from those who had used the FSLN for similar purposes. His mother, after all, had been a domestic servant. And Sánchez, hardly the pathetic pawn of Calero, was a man of noble Nicaraguan sensibility.

My father never quite swallowed our mercurial, politically expedient rehabilitation of these men. It was too precipitous for him even at a time when rapid-fire conspiracies were dominating the war more than gunfire.

But every conspiracy, every machination, every intrigue we launched was thrown off track by the events of November 1986.

I was at home, working on a speech, when Denis Volman, the reporter from the *Christian Science Monitor*, called me on the telephone.

Watch your television, he said.

Why? I asked.

The game is over, he answered.

I turned the television on in time to see Attorney General Edwin Meese announce the beginning of the Contragate scandal. Various members of the Reagan administration were being accused of having sold arms to Iran and then using the monies to finance a covert operation against the

FSLN regime in Managua. I knew immediately that the entire contra affair, all the personalities, the events, the secrets, the alliances, all of it would be discussed and analyzed and assessed in the American media. North would have to go and I thought, Denis may be right. It is over.

Many of us had already felt that North was bound to get caught, not because we understood the system better than he did but because North was always willing to sacrifice his body for the sake of the team. It was inevitable that at some time he would be asked to make that sacrifice.

I also suspected North wanted everything to unravel. How else would the world ever know of his great conspiracies? The one aspect of his job North disliked was his own anonymity. He feared that no one appreciated his genius.

Many people were intoxicated by the contra scandal but more than the liberal Democrats, more than the Sandinistas, more than Moscow, no one could have been more delighted than Cliff. With North finally out of the way, Nicaragua was all his. No one could compete with him for control—although he failed to see that these same events granting him power might soon leave him nothing at all to control.

Cliff's bottleneck to power in Costa Rica had always been the CIA's own Tomás Castillo, the one who had remained loyal to North throughout. Castillo was no longer an obstacle. Everyone in Washington seemed to know Castillo had been involved in the contra scandal and that he had had a strong relationship to North. I realized this as I was asked by the press to double-check these rumors and led some of the leaks concerning Castillo back to the CIA itself.

North's replacement in the Reagan administration was a Cuban-American named José Sorzano, who believed in the CIA as much as in his own job. He provided no competition to Cliff.

From the Nicaraguan perspective the most intelligent response to the affair was that issued by President Reagan himself. It was certainly the response best understood by Managua, with its Empire-based perspective of America. Immediately after the scandal broke Reagan publicly designated North an American hero. An American hero never betrays his own President. Managua felt only North had the means to involve Reagan. He was now the President's own American hero. He would make sure that, however much Reagan had been involved, no one would hear any details.

The Sandinistas knew that the contra scandal would destroy North, that soon secret information would start to flow like a river and that all exiled Nicaraguans would have to be extra wary in all their dealings with the Americans. The Sandinistas conveyed to their country that the American *caudillo*, the cowboy President, the only one who could ever hurt the Sandinistas, had been shot and mortally wounded. Only a miracle could prevent the Sandinistas from remaining in power.

It was true: Reagan was now forced to retreat from Nicaragua. And no one in the White House as close to the President as Oliver North would be fighting for the contras. I had heard many stories of North's recalcitrance, such as the time he wanted Reagan to give a pro-contra speech. White House Chief of Staff Donald Regan intervened, trying to protect the President from what he felt was overexposure in a highly unpopular arena. North entered Don Regan's office and fought for the speech and supposedly refused to leave the premises until Regan relented—such was North's commitment.

The contra army had a limited understanding of these events. But since supplies were about to come through and the American CIA chief William Casey was still in power, the prevailing opinion was that things must be going well enough. In the peasant army's mind the United States was supposed to act as though it were one man, one voice, one person. If one came from America, one agreed with the American President. That was being an American.

This conviction fostered a general attitude throughout Central America that these American people must be one with their great countryman, the *caudillo* Reagan, and thus seldom could secrets be withheld from Americans—it was assumed that Americans already knew anything Central Americans might know. American journalists were often able to break stories throughout the region because their sources assumed the journalists were fully aware of confidences that were in fact leaks.

For instance, the clandestine airstrip in Costa Rica was uncovered when journalists descended upon the pro-contra Guanacaste region of Costa Rica. This part of Costa Rica greatly resembles Nicaragua; the area is hot and dry, unlike the cool, moist Costa Rican highlands. In fact Guanacaste used to belong to Nicaragua until the people in the region annexed themselves to Costa Rica in the nineteenth century to escape the anarchy in their old country. The supposedly temporary annexation is still in effect.

The Bramadero is an open-air restaurant in Guanacaste where the local cattle ranchers gather to eat and talk. One day an American journalist arrived at the Bramadero, searching for clandestine airstrips where planes landed to refuel before making drops inside southern Nicaragua. The Costa Ricans thought, Well, the reporter is an American, he must know about the airstrip. They asked him when the American Marines were landing to fight the Sandinistas. He pretended that indeed he did know all things American, including the location of the airstrip. He asked when the next plane was going to land. They said that night. The reporter agreed this was a fine thing, so the locals said, perhaps he'd like to go see the airstrip. Fine, the reporter said, let's go ahead. Little by little they told him everything he needed to know until he broke the story back in the United States.

At a meeting in Fort Lauderdale, in April 1986, before the contra aid was voted on, the three directors of UNO—my father, Robelo, and Calero—met with Cliff and the CIA to discuss reform. My father demanded that reform begin immediately. Cliff sighed, ready to launch into another long speech. He reminded my father that everyone had to be patient, everyone had to be methodical, everyone had to be circumspect. . . . Enough, my father said, he had heard of nothing but deliberation and patience far too long. Nothing ever happened. And then my father stormed out of the meeting, sick of the CIA manipulation, sick of lies, sick of the sickness of exile politics.

Cliff realized he had miscalculated. His superiors were always upset any time an asset was poorly managed. He panicked. Later that night he sought my father out at his apartment and anxiously agreed to make the reforms his primary consideration.

But Cliff never forgave my father for the outburst and from that moment his first consideration was to get rid of him once and for all.

My father had already decided to resign. He was spent, overwhelmed by the failed presidential election in Nicaragua, the bickering opposition inside Nicaragua, the Americans, UNO, Oliver North, and the imperial sergeants of the CIA. He was exhausted and saw no hope or future. He confided his plans to me in January 1987. I told him he owed Elliott Abrams, who had always treated him with the utmost respect, advance word.

He told Abrams that he wished to leave UNO. Abrams said, fine—but give me some time to handle the resignation properly. Don't go yet.

My father agreed, once more delaying his departure. The others around him felt that Calero should go instead, or that they should turn my father's heartfelt impulse to leave into some sort of political weapon. But there was also the issue of keeping my father financially afloat. He had left a very high-paying job at the Inter-American Bank prior to joining first the Sandinistas and then the contras. Those within UNO had developed organized political parties, through which they accepted their funding from the Americans. My father had never developed a party. He had met his own personal and political needs with a $7000 stipend from North. He had requested that everyone in UNO explain the source of their money and he spoke openly of his $7000. No one else offered to identify their source of cash, which was also the CIA.

I kept urging my father not to accept money directly from the Americans but, like the others, to funnel it through complicated channels. He refused. He did not know that Bosco Montomoros—Calero's right-hand man—had offered the Miami *Herald* the story of my father's payments from North. The *Herald* reporters refused it, thinking the story too self-serving to be accurate. They were upset to discover later that it was all true when it was published in the Washington *Post*.

The media revelation of the $7000 salary was the last straw for my father. Everyone else was taking money but only he suffered for it. He said he felt like a man who, when he joined the contra, had had the political capital of one dollar. Now he had only ten cents. And he planned to take his ten cents and go home.

This time my father did not tell me of his plans to resign. He told only my mother and my sister Consuelo and then he wrote a letter of departure to the Miami *Herald*, explaining his decision. And he was gone.

When my father left, it was assumed by the other players that I was out. My entry into the counterrevolution had always been through my father. Calero, Robelo, and Cliff were all glad to see that access closed, they hoped, for good.

The only position they thought I might retain was to work in a minor capacity for Alfredo César, who suggested this possibility to Cliff. Cliff was not interested.

I refused, however, to walk away from the movement. My father's people in the contra bureaucracy were stranded. I did not want to see them go to work for Calero or César. I

wanted them to find better positions. When Aristides Sánchez' newfound ally and relative, Carlos Ulvert, asked me to
see his cousin, I agreed. Aristides Sánchez and I had a
lengthy phone conversation and discovered we shared more
interests than we'd previously assumed. Such is the process
of tactical alliances.

For one, we too were related. One of my names is also
Sánchez—my grandfather on my father's side was a Sánchez
—and this grandfather, and my grandmother on my father's
side, were Aristides Sánchez' godparents. The long-forgotten
family tie was now resurrected.

I then flew to Miami and met with my distant relative.
Alfredo César was aligning with Adolfo Calero. Sánchez
needed protection from any alliance they might make. I
wanted to become for Sánchez what Father Miguel d'Escoto
was to Ortega—the one who could interpret the meaning of
foreign things to a man of power.

I rethought my image of Sánchez and decided he symbolized a bridge between the traditional Nicaragua of old and
the new Nicaragua still being born. Sánchez was at ease with
the politics of exile, with the traditional Liberal and Conservative parties—which, I realized, were not going to
readily leave the Nicaraguan scene. Sánchez was also sur-
prisingly flexible, open to change, and willing to listen. He
owned the full trust of the rebel commanders and had good
relations with Bermúdez. At the same time he was disliked
by the CIA, who recognized the value of his good personal
relations with the troops but didn't want to make him a real
player. Sánchez knew that Calero was playing the game of
the Somozas, keeping him and his men away from the real
power just as the Somozas isolated the National Guard from
the rest of the world.

Sánchez' friction with the Americans was valuable; I
guessed he could protect my friends and me whenever the
Americans came after us. Ironically, the one person Sánchez
could not protect was Ulvert himself. Ulvert had confronted

UNO's executive secretary, Nayo Somarriba, too often and too openly and so the CIA dispatched David López, an agent who dealt with the contras in Costa Rica, to Miami to meet with Ulvert. Over breakfast López told Ulvert it was time for him to depart, insisting that the reforms for which Ulvert had fought were soon to be implemented. This was partly true; some of the reforms were to be put in place, but only because the CIA was now creating a supposedly "elected" directorate which belonged to them. Ulvert could not be protected anymore. He too was gone.

Meanwhile my father's few remaining cadres and I joined with Aristides Sánchez, who became our protector.

I cannot disguise the fact that a major reason behind these moves was that I wanted to behave in the best Nicaraguan tradition. Our history says that even when the point is reached in a conspiracy when involvement no longer makes sense, there is no reason to leave if revenge is still possible. I no longer had any faith in its leadership. I could leave whenever I wanted. It made little sense for me to remain. But I wanted to tell the Americans that I would leave when I felt like it—they could not push me out.

The point at which the Americans want to exclude you is exactly the moment when the decision to stay is your best revenge.

I was later told that Cliff was dumbfounded when he discovered my alliance with Aristides. He told Chris Arcos, Arturo Cruz, Jr., is like a Houdini—I can't get rid of the bastard.

My participation in all of this would have been much more difficult if I hadn't developed a genuine respect for Aristides Sánchez. He had a sense of perspective; his involvement went beyond his own personal ambitions, which were nonetheless growing. I also respected the men fighting in the field more and more, and Sánchez truly cared for these troops. Perhaps I was growing up somewhat. The game was less romantic. My father was out and I was alone.

My father's resignation was Cliff's final victory. He now had total control of the movement. To prove it, he created a new electoral exile movement which he christened the Nicaraguan Resistance.

The new movement, elected in May 1987, was to have a directorate of Pedro Chamorro, Jr., Alfredo César, Adolfo Calero, Aristides Sánchez, and a woman named Azucena Ferrey, who, it was hoped, would become the Cory Aquino of the contras. (She didn't.) Robelo had warned that he would resign like my father if changes were not made within the contra organization. (He didn't. Instead he too joined the new organization.)

The CIA did not want Sánchez included but he had too much military power to be left out. And they trusted the other directors. Cliff decided that Pedro Joaquín Chamorro, Jr., was the man he would fashion as the leader of the contra, the face to be exported abroad. Chamorro was young and he was the son and namesake of the editor of *La Prensa*, Pedro Joaquín Chamorro, the great martyr whose assassination in 1978 sparked the revolution. Young Chamorro was the perfect publicity vehicle. The CIA were even telling us that, according to their private polls, Pedro Joaquín Chamorro, Jr., was the most popular Nicaraguan political figure; more popular even than Cardinal Obando y Bravo. As far as any of us could tell, the CIA fabricated these polls.

The rest of us had known for years that Pedro Chamorro was a naive young man, lacking in any political savvy. The CIA discovered this too, as he completely failed to live up to their plans. They had not reckoned with Chamorro's unpopularity with both the American press and his Nicaraguan peers. In 1988 he was voted off the exile assembly by his own former allies to keep him from speaking out.

Cliff also sought to make the Nicaraguan Resistance an exercise in popular politics, with new emphasis on the importance of the Assembly of National Resistance. This was a body of self-styled exile "legislators" who Cliff hoped could sell the image of a democratic process. They would select the members of the Resistance. The CIA then proceeded to buy out this so-called democratic Assembly, reproducing the politics of the past with the politicians of the past.

But the Assembly of National Resistance directorate announced that elections were to take place by secret ballot. This meant that instead of Pedro Joaquín Chamorro, Jr.'s election being a unanimous triumph, as the CIA had hoped, he received the smallest total and was barely elected.

At the same time as this new Resistance was being orchestrated, I flew to Honduras, to the domain of the Northern Front forces where I had never been welcome before. The trip was an unambiguous sign that my role had changed and that I was still active behind the scenes. And it proved the power of Aristides Sánchez. He could make roles change.

Sánchez took me down to Honduras primarily to meet Enrique Bermúdez. Sánchez was nervous; he knew the meeting might turn into a debacle. It almost did. Colonel Bermúdez and I met face to face for the first time in the lobby of the Hotel Maya, huddling in a corner, talking for over an hour. The man was disillusioned by the political representation of the contras. He had a large peasant army and still no international credibility. He couldn't understand why this was so.

We were very frank with each other, which is probably why our meeting was inconclusive. I kept thinking that this man embodied the entire concept of the Somocista National Guard. He was not an idiot by any means and I respected him, but the differences in our sensibility were overwhelming. I told him that at one point I had tried to get rid of him and he informed me of his less than positive reciprocal feelings. But we knew that each of us represented some degree of hope for the other and we cultivated the relationship.

The contra military had finally become self-respecting by the summer of 1987, a position which silenced many of their critics. The word in 1986 was that the contras had become too lazy to move. Aid started to flow in late 1986 and by early 1987 the contra army reinfiltrated most of its troops into Nicaragua. The Sandinistas had been laying down a new system of defense to prevent the contras from entering the country, calling it the forward defense. The concept was to accumulate as much power as possible in the border area and seal it off. The contras simply walked through the forward defense.

Furthermore, the contras had obtained Red Eye missiles which gave them the power to knock out the Sandinistas' Soviet helicopters. The FSLN found themselves in a difficult position; they were forced to resort to less effective artillery as their helicopter pilots refused to fly for fear of being shot down. Or, if they did launch a mission, they flew too high above the jungles for their missiles and machine-gun fire to be accurate.

From a political standpoint the members of the new rebel directorate were pleased. The new Assembly was in place, the directorate was in place, and the contras finally felt they had a democratic political representation, giving them, they hoped, the look of legitimacy.

Even Contragate, for a while, looked as though it might not derail the effort after all. Oliver North had turned into that most temporary of phenomena, a media success. The contras were pleased with his performance—although before North spoke on television many in the contra had run away from him. After his performance they were impressed with his ability to project the image of the hero and hoped they might profit by renewed association.

But North's testimony was generating quite a different effect in the other Central American countries.

On July 7 he testified that the Reagan administration had never really meant to invade Nicaragua. He defended the two-track policy of Thomas Enders and said that the United States had never intended to do anything more than apply pressure on Nicaragua so as to democratize Managua.

An invasion of Nicaragua was never a viable possibility, North said.

This assertion contradicted everything the Americans had privately told the other Central American countries. They felt betrayed, especially the Salvadorans and the Hondurans, who had been carrying the burden of American Central American policy. For years the United States had assured these countries that it would defeat the Sandinistas militarily. The countries had believed the Americans. They had waited for the invasion, confident it was imminent. They thought the contra force had been organized by the Americans, not to overthrow the FSLN, but to resolve the standard American problem of how long an invading force could remain in the country.

The native contras could stay. The other Central Americans regarded them as the military apparatus that would facilitate American withdrawal of troops after the invasion had taken place. Now they were being told that the Americans had been lying all along.

North was convincing in his testimony, I think because in this particular case he was telling his version of the truth. He had truly hoped that the FSLN regime would fall from within, that Managua would collapse. He desperately wanted to disprove the long-standing hypothesis that communist takeovers cannot be reversed. An invasion by American Marines would not accomplish a reversal of the trend. The end of communism had to come from within—or to seem as if it came from within.

The other Central American countries were not as ideological as North. They simply wanted the FSLN out of power and out of Central America. It now appeared this would never happen. And, like the Sandinistas, they believed that Reagan would never recover from the wounds he had received. The contras could never get another penny for lethal aid. The shooting was over.

The other effect of Contragate was the rise to power, in the

Central Americans' eyes, of Democratic House Majority Leader Jim Wright. Two leaders were governing America. As Contragate broke, Wright sent the Central Americans a simple message. It said, in essence, that President Reagan was only going to remain in power for another year and a half but that Jim Wright would stay in Congress for a very long time to come.

The Central American leaders quickly reappraised their policy toward the Sandinistas. Costa Rica's President Oscar Arias was the most aware of all that the Reagan years were fading. Or at least at that point the Jim Wright years seemed inexorable. Costa Rica was suffering from economic depression. The previous slump had occurred in the 1970s and the country had recovered only because President Monge obtained a huge amount of foreign aid, especially from the United States, which needed the support of Costa Rica to continue its Central American policy.

Arias, also in need of money and international support, decided to shift from the business of war to the business of peace. He contrived new means of acquiring large amounts of aid from the Democrats. He and the other Central American presidents met in Guatemala City in August 1987 to discuss new ideas for resolving the Nicaraguan conflict.

As they did this, the new contra directorate made its debut in Washington to meet the President and Congress and to prepare the way for a new aid package. While in Washington they talked with Republican Representative Jack Kemp and his people, the friends of Adolfo Calero. In the meeting they heard, for the first time, that White House chief of staff Jim Baker and Jim Wright were at that moment meeting to freeze aid in order to allow the Sandinistas time to democratize.

Abrams and Jorge Sorzano held a meeting shortly thereafter; I attended as Aristides Sánchez' aide. The Americans explained the potential agreement, assuring us all there was no need to worry. But before the Baker-Wright deal went into effect, word came that Oscar Arias' plan for peace in Central America had been signed by all the Central American presidents. They too had heard of the Baker-Wright deal and decided that if the Americans were so weak as to be cutting deals with the Sandinistas, the time was at hand to distance themselves once and for all from the contras.

The Central American peace plan effectively called for the end of the contra movement. Not all the contras, however, heard the call.

9

The End
of the Party

Like many others within the contra leadership, Aristides
Sánchez always believed that my father and I had forged a
magical relationship with the American State Department.
Sánchez could not figure out exactly what that association
was but he knew he didn't have one. His anxiety to create
such a bond affected his entire family, especially his wife
Cecilia. She felt that Sánchez should receive more attention
from the Americans.

In the middle of a hot night in July 1987 the phone rang in my Washington apartment. It was Cecilia. She had just learned that the Cuban exile community was preparing to hold a celebration at the Sheraton Hilton Hotel in Miami to honor the contras. Sánchez' rival, Adolfo Calero, had himself recently arranged a similarly impressive event at Miami's Omni Hotel, to acclaim Calero for saving the honor of Nicaragua in the Contragate hearings. (It was widely perceived that no harm or disgrace had befallen the Nicaraguans in the hearings and Calero was the first in line to take the credit.) Calero's event also helped to solidify his standing within the exile community—and therefore his chances in the mythical election for a future mythical President in a mythical post-American-invasion Nicaragua.

Now another quasi-imperial event was in the offing. Rumors flew through contra circles as to who might represent Washington at this affair. Cecilia Sánchez had heard that possibly President Reagan might attend. Maybe Vice President Bush or Oliver North. At least, the State Department's less glamorous Elliott Abrams.

The first thing I said to Cecilia was that, no matter how tired I was, the one thing I could guarantee her was that those first three people had absolutely no intention of participating.

Well, Cecilia then asked, what if Mr. Elliott Abrams were to come? He would then be the most important American present. We must make sure that he sits at the same table as my husband Aristides.

I told Cecilia that such a seating arrangement was unlikely to occur. The celebration at the hotel was being staged in the name of the contra field commanders, and therefore it was indirectly in the name of Commander Enrique Bermúdez—since the commanders really belonged under his jurisdiction. Bermúdez himself would be giving an opening speech to welcome the commanders. And to applaud his own role. Anyway, perhaps no Americans would attend.

As it turned out, the Cubans hadn't yet lined up anyone to speak. They customarily planned these events on their own and then, feigning panic, called Washington at the last minute to demand the presence of a great American patriot.

Elliott Abrams was not informed of the event until a few days prior, when he felt obliged to accept. Then followed all the questions Cecilia had anticipated. Where would Abrams sit? Adolfo Calero insisted Abrams sit with him. The Cubans supported this decision. But Enrique Bermúdez wanted Abrams with him. The event was in his honor, after all. Aristides Sánchez now wanted Abrams too.

The intrigues over the seating lasted two weeks. Bermúdez' wife entered the affair, plotting against Cecilia Sánchez, who was previously assumed to have been her ally against the more powerful wife of Calero.

Cecilia now insisted Abrams couldn't sit with Bermúdez since he would already be sitting with his field commanders and thus he had the extra support he needed to display his powerful position. And Cecilia reminded everyone that they all opposed Adolfo Calero, the darling of the Reagan administration. He didn't need the support of a good table. Let's all make sure Elliott Abrams does not sit with Calero, or his wife, or too close to their table, Cecilia suggested.

But Cecilia, I said, if the homage is designed for Bermúdez, it is only normal for Abrams to sit with Bermúdez. She disagreed.

The Miami Cubans, when told about the problem, fashioned their own Solomonic seating solution. They decided to provide one huge table of honor, a table so large and so long that it allowed everyone to sit together.

A deeply motivated woman when she so chooses, Cecilia Sánchez did not surrender. This simply isn't enough, she complained. This doesn't distinguish Aristides one bit. All this does is lose him in the crowd.

Okay, I said. I have a solution. I will be flying down with Abrams to Miami. Cecilia, I said, you arrive at the airport exactly when I tell you to and you can be the one who escorts Elliott Abrams into the room. He will enter on your elbow and everyone will know that Cecilia and Aristides Sánchez brought Elliott Abrams to the event. And I will make sure the logistics work as long as you do not tell any of this to anyone.

Cecilia straightaway told her rivals of her victory. We suspected she might and so we never told her the time the flight was scheduled to arrive. The Abrams conspiracy then shifted from the table of honor to picking him up at the airport. But no one knew when the plane was scheduled to land. A huge list of speakers had been prepared as everyone wanted to be listed in the next day's Latin newspaper, *El Diario de las Américas,* as having spoken at the event. To confuse the matter of Abrams' arrival further, I told the others that he could not sit through all of these speeches and he might arrive at any time. How many times can he listen to himself be called a great American patriot? I asked. He only has a few hours.

The day of the affair arrived. We only told Cecilia our schedule at the last minute. She showed up as planned at the airport and it was one of the great victories of her life. Elliott! Abrams!

Aristides Sánchez is a shy man, Cecilia explained to those who needed to know why it was she executed such elaborate plots. Aristides has often been called "The Eye of Cecilia's Hurricane." To make him speak out loud you had to pinch him. He would pay people not to make him talk. He was a man of limits. Cecilia was not familiar with such boundaries. She justified her behavior through history and family. The death of Aristides' mother had affected her deeply. Not because it was an emotional shock, although Cecilia was fond of the woman. Aristides' mother had died from a heart attack. And she was such a self-sacrificing woman, so quiet, so unprepossessing, that she never bothered to say, excuse me, everyone, I am having a heart attack. Instead she refused to create trouble for anyone, they were too busy, they were all having such a nice day. So she simply left the room and walked into another where she immediately died.

Cecilia was terrified that this tendency for obscurity had passed to her husband. To compensate for genetics, she made sure Aristides was a far more prominent person than he ever would have wished to be.

While the battle over seating arrangements raged in Miami, in the field, inside Nicaragua, the contra troops decided that it was imperative to show the world that they could still perform militarily, although only a fraction of the $100 million of American aid given in 1986 was left. Throughout 1987 the contras' military operation had been successful; they wanted to extend their record, especially as a new vote on aid was near.

The contras decided to attack three Sandinista-controlled towns in northern Nicaragua—Siuna, La Rosita, and Bonanza. Each of them was very small and the site of an operating gold mine. Each was also the site of a full Sandinista battalion. To attack these towns with an element of surprise the contra forces were compelled to covertly mobilize more than three thousand combatants. Siuna and Bonanza were soon taken by the contras, but the army was only able to surround La Rosita. Nonetheless, the operation was successful.

Despite this triumph it was clear that the contras were running out of money and supplies. The end of congressional aid sapped contra morale. Just as the rebels' chances for military successes grew in 1984, the CIA had mined Nicaraguan harbors and Congress terminated military aid, destroying the rebels' hopes for impending victory. Now again in 1987, after a year of military triumphs, the American Congress was threatening to cut them off. This time there would be no Oliver North.

Looming over the landscape was the Central American peace plan. One of the basic tenets of the Esquipulas Agreement stated that contra sanctuaries in Honduras had to be removed into Nicaragua. The new area chosen for the rebels was Bocay, where the land was highly inhospitable, similar to the swampy southern jungles: hot, humid, and overflowing with the Río Coco, which separates Honduras from Nicaragua. To transport anything by land from Honduras to Bocay is impossible. A foot soldier needed three weeks to walk from the contra camp at Yamales to Bocay. Moreover almost five thousand refugee peasants already were living on limited supplies of corn, rice, and beans in Bocay. There was no extra food for the armies. Supplies for the troops had to come by air.

The planes used by the contras to make supply drops were in lamentable shape. The few working helicopters were needed to pick up wounded soldiers from inside Nicaragua. Spare parts for all vehicles were running out. Such was the condition of the contra army during the battle over the seating arrangements for Elliott Abrams.

Renewed contra aid was the first issue to be resolved in 1988. With it, the contras could continue; without it, they would die. We have the votes, Cliff said, we can do it. Military aid is a necessity. If this aid comes, we win. Congress won't turn us down. The Nicaraguans surrounding him, including Alfredo César, who most often correctly interpreted international opinion for other Nicaraguans, trusted Cliff's reading. It was difficult for those who still depended on the CIA to accept that Washington didn't know best.

According to Cliff, the contras' previous problems—those posed by the opposition within Congress—had been rectified. The contras' critics had unfairly blasted the contras' military record, accusing them of having won no battles on their own. But the recent contra military performance had been first rate.

Another argument used against the contras was that they were financially corrupt and stole the money given to them by the Americans. Now the financial accountability of the contras was unambiguous. A huge computer system monitored the flow of all aid. In the history of guerrilla warfare there has never been an army with as high a ratio of accountants per commander.

The next argument against contra aid was human rights. It was charged repeatedly and with some reason that the human rights violations of the contras were frequent and reprehensible. And so a human rights commission was established by a mandate of the American Congress to instill the consciousness of rights into the peasant fighters on the battlefield. Marta Patricia Baltodano oversaw the commission. A prominent anti-Somocista, Baltodano had been instrumental in establishing the first human rights commission to oppose Somoza's regime. Baltodano was now anti-Sandinista.

Allegations of contra drug involvement also had surfaced frequently. But the exhaustive investigation that cleared the name of Octaviano César never proved that the contras themselves were involved in drug trafficking in any organized way.

So the CIA was confident it had addressed all the questions which had prevented Congress from providing aid. Alfredo César and his wife, confident of an imminent victory, flew up to Washington to help him celebrate the expected victory vote.

I disagreed with the CIA. I felt it was necessary to make some kind of compromise with Congress on the *kind* of aid that the contras should get in 1988. Even though it was highly desirable to receive "lethal" aid, many moderate Democrats would not support us unless we agreed to accept only humanitarian aid. We wanted any kind of nonlethal aid. Among the contra leadership only Aristides Sánchez was willing to compromise on lethal aid, doing so at the risk that his allies would tell the soldiers he had sold out. He has compromised your safety by denying you weapons, they could say. Sánchez more than anyone understood the symbolism of aid—aid of any sort—that the peasants, besides possessing a very real need for food, boots, and uniforms, also needed to know that the American government was still supporting their cause. Sánchez would take that support any way he could find it.

Cliff insisted there could be no compromise. The package had to include lethal aid or there would be no aid at all.

The Administration thought they could intimidate the opposition in Congress. They were wrong. The Republicans gambled that in an election year it was most important to be anti-communist. The Democrats gambled that in an election year it was most important to be pro-peace. The Democrats won. The House defeated the aid package on February 3, 1988, by 219–211, a closer vote than expected by many of us. Finally, a sense of defeat pervaded Reagan's administration. What was most amazing to the contra leadership was that when they now asked the Americans to explain their fallback position, it was clear that the Administration had never considered one. Father didn't know best.

In March of that year Cliff resigned from the CIA. The supreme manipulator had nothing left to do except declare his victory and exit. Vowing that he had done everything he could to fight communism, he declared that he couldn't do so if Congress wouldn't let him do it properly. He joined a Fortune 500 conglomerate where he now works. He felt he had united the contras, survived Oliver North, and screwed his enemies. He left feeling triumphant.

With Cliff gone no one remained who was strong enough to handle Calero or Bermúdez. William Webster, the new CIA chief, wanted to hear as little as possible about Nicaragua. At the White House, Chief of Staff Howard Baker had decided President Reagan had to forget about Nicaragua. Defense Secretary Frank Carlucci didn't care about Nicaragua. Jorge Sorzano, Oliver North's replacement, was about to resign. Ambassador John D. Negroponte was now serving as a deputy to Colin Powell at the Security Council. He had helped open the contra shop; now he wanted to close it.

Elliott Abrams was left with the illusion that he now represented American policy in Nicaragua. The State Department rhetoric continued but no substance remained.

The contras' military prospects, once promising, now declined dramatically. The plotting intensified. More than others in the contra, the great negotiator Alfredo César was truly shocked by the defeat of the congressional aid vote.

Like the rest of Central America, César believed that the Democrats were going to win the White House in 1988. No longer able to look for protection from his CIA ally Cliff, César looked south to his old protector, Venezuela's influential Social Democrat, Carlos Andrés Pérez (who in 1989 was re-elected to the presidency of his country). César also sought out Oscar Arias and Speaker of the House Jim Wright. His aim was to become the most attractive contra, the one genuinely interested in negotiation and compromise. He wanted to become the contra of the Democrats as much as Calero was the contra of the Republicans.

The new game of Alfredo César relied on the Ortegas' increasingly obvious takeover of the Nicaraguan government, as all powerful Nicaraguan families have tried to do. Perhaps, as the Somozas had needed a René Schick, the loyal opposition of two decades earlier, the Sandinistas now wanted their own chosen antagonist. César wondered if he could become that loyal opposition, the Schick of the Sandinistas. The Ortegas might provide an electoral process whereby César could be elected President. The Sandinistas did not need to go to elections until 1990; they did not intend to let go of the country. But in the process they wished to keep everyone else in the game, as a sign of their democracy. And since the Nicaraguan economy was in shambles, why not bring in Alfredo César, the consummate technocrat, who could improve it, and who also could bring in international aid?

César decided that the Ortegas controlled the country because they controlled the army—and throughout the army were to be found the Sandinista children of the oligarchy, César's former classmates and friends. These people might be highly receptive to him, he thought, and might talk with him. César also believed that the Sandinista officer corps, along with Humberto Ortega, were embarrassed by the economic disaster and that the military would be happy to allow someone from outside the FSLN to take care of the economy. Most Sandinista commanders, he thought, were no longer interested in social reform and ideological revolution. Their concern was to keep their power; the army and Humberto would be happy as long as they were the center of all strategic decisions inside Nicaragua.

I was skeptical as to whether Sandinista Commander Jaime Wheelock would be willing to settle for César's plan. Neither would Borge. Both men were planning their own campaigns to become President in 1990—Wheelock had been promised the job during the last election and Borge felt that the Sandinistas would be forced to run their most popular candidate; he was sure he was that candidate. In the end it was Daniel Ortega who was nominated.

Daniel Ortega traveled to Moscow just after the House voted down aid to the contras. When he returned to Nicaragua he disembarked from his plane in Managua and drove directly from the airport to La Placa de la Revolution in order to address a rally of party militants.

Ortega did not discuss his speech with the other members of the National Directorate. The speech indicated that for the first time since the beginning of the war Managua was willing to meet face to face with the contra leadership.

The Ortegas had been caught by shifting geopolitics. Mikhail Gorbachev, they decided, represented the future of socialist countries. The loser in the new Soviet *perestroika* was Fidel Castro. The era of Cold War warrior Castro, the charismatic young face of socialism, the most acceptable leader, the charming spokesman whom the liberal Americans could love, was ending. At last there was someone in Moscow who appeared more progressive and more willing to negotiate. The Ortegas began to realign with Gorbachev and the politics of *perestroika* over the politics of Castro.

As they did, their rival Tomás Borge spoke fondly of his Cuban brothers. We owe the revolution to our Cuban friends, not the Soviets, Borge said publicly. All the Sandinista alliances shifted. Borge, the Soviets' disciple, was now working with the Cubans. The Ortegas, formerly Cuban protégés, rediscovered the Soviets.

The Ortegas agreed to negotiate with the contras because, when Congress terminated aid, strategic victory was theirs. The contra military offensive was dead. Through the Arias peace plan, they could now seek the second step of the victory, which was to deny the contras sanctuary in Honduras.

The purpose of negotiations, as envisioned by the Ortegas, was to manage the surrender of the contra army and the coopting of their political leaders. The Ortegas also felt that the contra soldiers, watching their leaders talk to the enemy, would believe a pact was being reached. The peasants would then disband. The negotiations were a Sandinista formality to consolidate power, as well as a favor to Jim Wright for having cut off the rebels' aid.

The contras were stymied. They knew that they had to participate in such a dialogue. They had been asking for these talks for years. They could hardly refuse now. But the contras had no power with which to negotiate; they had no strategy, no understanding of what they should negotiate for. The contras arrived at their most important conference without a cohesive plan.

The negotiations were arranged to be held in the small Nicaraguan town of Sapoa, near the Costa Rican border, on the isthmus of Rivas, on March 23, 1988. The contra delegation moved from San José to Liberia in northern Costa Rica, set up quarters, and every day drove from Liberia to Sapoa.

Calero was designated spokesman. (Alfonso Robelo had dropped out of the directorate. Oscar Arias had ordered the three contras living in Costa Rica—Robelo, Chamorro, and Sánchez—to leave unless they resigned all military roles. Chamorro and Sánchez left. Robelo, claiming that his Costa Rican wife was pregnant, resigned.) Calero also controlled the votes of two others: Azucena Ferrey, the woman who had disappointed Washington by not having turned into a Cory Aquino, and Chamorro.

Humberto Ortega assumed the role of chief negotiator for Managua. He chose Commander Joaquín Cuadra to drive him to Sapoa, which indicated the rising power of Cuadra in the FSLN. Humberto was unable to drive himself because he no longer had functional hands. Wounded years earlier in an attempt to rescue the revolutionary hero Carlos Fonseca from jail, his arms tapered off into talonlike appurtenances; he could never perform simple duties which required hands, such as writing. This is why the Nicaraguan defector Roger Miranda, who told the American press in 1987 of Humberto's plan to build a 600,000-strong army, knew so many of Humberto's secrets. Even in his most private meetings Humberto needed a scribe. Miranda took notes for Humberto until he defected with all the information he had collected.

The meetings proceeded slowly until the third day, March 26, when Humberto took Adolfo Calero aside. For over forty-five minutes the two men talked in a corner of the room. After that conversation, Humberto went to talk to his brother Daniel. Humberto then returned and took Calero for a long walk. Calero then came back and announced that Alfredo César and Aristides Sánchez had to agree to disarmament in return for a promise of democracy. He also reasoned that signing the first round of agreements with the

Sandinistas was the only way Congress would approve humanitarian aid for the contra soldiers.

The question never answered was what Calero and Ortega discussed while they were alone. Humberto knew it was necessary to sow conflict within the contra leadership. If the creation of a puppet contra opposition were truly necessary, Humberto would, I believe, have preferred that it be Adolfo Calero rather than Alfredo César. Just as when the time came for Somoza to pick his own puppet opponent, he chose René Schick over Julio Quintana, the less intelligent rather than the more capable man.

The bus returning the contra delegation to Costa Rica was filled, but absolutely silent. The contingent did not understand why they had signed any agreement at all. Was it Humberto's charm? The attention of the world press? The exquisite food and drink? It didn't matter; it was too late. The only consolation was that they could say they had been forced to compromise in order to obtain humanitarian aid from the United States. Now they would also have to explain to their troops that the rebel soldiers would be moved into designated enclaves where they were to be disarmed if the peace process advanced.

Humberto wished to continue the meetings at Sapoa. Calero wanted the talks moved to Managua, despite Humberto's incredulity that the contras would want to negotiate on enemy territory. But Calero wanted to stage a triumphant entrance into Managua to present himself as the next presidential candidate. When the time came, he brought an entourage of sixty-five people along with him. It looked more like a presidential campaign than a negotiating team. As Calero had wished, it appeared as though he were already running for office.

While in Managua, Calero enjoyed, for the first time in his contra career, a lustrous moment of glory with the American press. Instead of Calero, the old man of war, he became Calero, the statesman who wished to end the fighting. A despondent Alfredo César was eclipsed by the attention showered on Calero. César's vanity was wounded. The negotiations had been taken from his hands. All César wanted now was to take the process away from Calero.

Calero's moves were aggressive and confident. He decided it was time to promulgate his next plan, one last maneuver which could bring him total control of the contras, which he had always coveted.

He contrived a plot to eliminate Colonel Enrique Bermúdez from the contra leadership. The mechanism, Calero decided, would be the young dissidents, field commanders who for years had fought the real war and who felt it was time for younger faces to wrest control of the military command. One of these young commanders, "Tono," had been a cadet in the military academy when the Somoza regime was overthrown. Another, "The Preacher," was a Protestant minister in Nicaragua who once had been pro-Sandinista. The most prominent of the dissidents was "Rigoberto," a rural merchant from Jinotega.

I remember once in Miami I was talking to Tono and The Preacher, explaining that I sympathized with their desire to have a greater role in the decision-making process of the contras. But I said that any move against Bermúdez was out of the question while negotiations with the FSLN were taking place. They paid me no heed. They preferred the promises of Calero, who guaranteed that, as in the times of Oliver North, he would find them the resources to continue military operations.

Like most internal contra business, the conspiracy was soon exposed publicly by other contras. The American media's first instinct was to take the side of Calero, who was at that moment equated with the process of peace. Moreover, Calero called for civilian control over the military, and successfully compared Bermúdez to the unpopular Panamanian leader Noriega.

Calero's last antic conspiracy was a move to install Pedro

Joaquín Chamorro, Jr., the maladroit young political leader, as the godfather of the young dissident commanders. Chamorro, who two years earlier had been a fervent supporter of Bermúdez, had recently grown disenchanted with him. Bermúdez had never allowed the younger man to form an alliance with him. In fact Bermúdez once sent him a very public message in which he called Chamorro *"Chamarro"*, which means "bluff" in Nicaraguan Spanish. Bermúdez insisted later it was simply a typographical error. Chamorro, still upset, became a useful pawn in Calero's plot.

Calero's conspiracy might have succeeded if not for an alliance of convenience between Alfredo César and Bermúdez. César needed to weaken Calero. Bermúdez was his only option. Aristides Sánchez, too, joined the César plot against Calero and his young dissident commanders, so as to prevent Calero from winning it all.

In the end the CIA laid this conspiracy in its grave; they felt that Calero had finally gone too far. This was not, the CIA implied, a ripe moment for changes in the military structure. Moreover the venerable Honduran military command already knew Bermúdez, and found him to be a serious, reliable man. The army colonels of Honduras found all this threatening. The dissident commanders were too young, the CIA continued—if this rebellion worked, perhaps another would take place in reaction, and so on. It could mean the final collapse of any semblance of order among the contras.

When the conspiracy ended, Alfredo César tried to force Calero to relinquish the position of chief negotiator. He paid a call on the young Pedro Joaquín Chamorro. It seemed that Chamorro, too, now wished to become the chief negotiator. The contras' National Assembly was soon to re-elect the members of the contra directorate. Chamorro's last election had been quite close. He decided that the position of chief negotiator would help him keep his seat on the directorate.

César, however, convinced Chamorro that they should instead demand a rotating chairmanship, with César leading off and Chamorro going second. Chamorro agreed in return for César's political support.

At the next meeting of the contra directorate Chamorro walked into the room and immediately announced that he felt Calero no longer should maintain his position as chief negotiator—and he proposed César's plan. Everyone present immediately understood—Calero's ally was proposing Calero be replaced. Calero's glasses fell off his face.

Chamorro's plan, supported by himself, César, and Aristides Sánchez, won. Sánchez then excused himself from the rotating position, explaining that he did not wish to be the chief negotiator. He suggested instead that, at the next round of talks, Bermúdez be included. Calero then suggested they not hold the talks in Managua anymore. Chamorro disagreed, hoping to recreate for himself the recent Calero entourage. He won the right to re-enter Managua.

By the third meeting in Managua, Chamorro realized he had been fleeced by Alfredo César. César had no intention of relinquishing anything at all to Chamorro. Chamorro's turn as chief negotiator was never to come. Chamorro, suddenly sponsorless, re-allied with Calero, who had no choice but to welcome the young man back. Badly damaged, Calero resumed his control of the majority of the directorate. But it was too late to retrieve what he had lost.

Bermúdez, whom Calero had not been able to finish off, became Calero's greatest enemy. The first rule of any conspiracy is: once a conspiracy is begun, it is not over until it is won. Calero, losing badly, now had to pay attention to Bermúdez at all times, knowing that Bermúdez' retaliation would come without warning. Calero resorted once more to the pliable young Chamorro, who eagerly informed the directorate, on Calero's orders, that Bermúdez should be replaced by the dissident rebel commander, The Preacher. Chamorro argued that the political directorate, rather than the military, should run the show—a position he had never supported previously.

Calero voted to remove his enemy Bermúdez from power. So did Chamorro. César and Sánchez voted no. The deciding vote was that of Azucena Ferrey. Although Calero's ally, she was alarmed by the magnitude of the resolution. She refused to vote Bermúdez out of his position. Calero lost.

Aristides Sánchez was becoming increasingly infuriated by this constant maneuvering, considerable even by Nicaraguan standards. Pedro Chamorro's blundering lack of finesse enraged him. While the gathering was still in process Sánchez excused himself from the room and telephoned a contact in the CIA, "Big George." Sánchez complained bitterly to George.

Jorgon Sánchez said, you better do something about Pedro Joaquín Chamorro, Jr., soon. He forgets that we are fighting the Sandinistas and only wishes to do battle against his own side. And he does not do that terribly well either.

Big George was another in the bloodline of huge Americans handling Nicaragua; he was over six feet six. But Big George was very unusual for the CIA: he spoke Spanish well and he genuinely seemed to care about the Nicaraguans with whom he dealt. He had been working in Latin America for many years. Although Cliff had found no special affection for the man, Big George was kept on during Cliff's regime because of his real skills.

He listened to Sánchez for a brief moment before erupting in exasperation. Sánchez returned to the room, whereupon Big George called and asked to be put on the speakerphone. He told Chamorro he was an imbecile and ordered him to stop behaving foolishly. This was unusual conduct for Big George, who was generally most calm and respectful when dealing with Nicaraguans. He was too tired of the situation to remember his manners. The tirade was powerful, effective, and entirely humiliating.

It also provided Chamorro with new celebrity. Chastised

by the Americans, Chamorro was at the same time elevated by the insult. He even took to calling himself a nationalist.

The most important result of the CIA's intervention was that Bermúdez was no longer the object of conspiracy. But the contras' last gasps continued to be wheezes of intrigue.

On July 18, 1988, the meeting to elect the new contra directorate was held in Santo Domingo, in the Dominican Republic. Each directorate member was required to run for re-election.

Most members of the exile assembly were furious with Adolfo Calero over his role in the Enrique Bermúdez affair. Even the most conservative of the Conservative Party believed Calero's conspiracies had overstepped the boundaries of decent Nicaraguan intrigue. Calero's position on the directorate was in jeopardy. Furthermore, Bermúdez, rendered nervous by the recent almost successful attempt to depose him, decided that he needed to get elected to the directorate himself. This meant he would have to occupy someone else's seat. Pedro Chamorro, Jr., and Azucena Ferrey were clearly in line to be replaced.

But before the vote could be held the CIA flew to Santo Domingo to join the conspiracies. Bermúdez and Sánchez were asked to tolerate the presence of Calero in the directorate.

"We do not want any problems with this man just now," the Americans said. Our assumption was that, since American elections were imminent, the CIA did not want someone such as Calero, who knew too many Republican Administration secrets, to become upset.

Sánchez and César agreed to the Americans' request and so Calero's re-election was accomplished.

No one helped young Chamorro and he didn't know enough to make himself a dangerous antagonist. Not only was he voted off the directorate, his replacement was Wilfredo Montalván, a man from a humble background, a man who had previously served as an office boy at the Conservative Party offices. It was a major humiliation, Chamorro felt, to be replaced by one who used to labor for the Chamorro family.

Bermúdez was elected, and Azucena Ferrey was replaced by her brother.

Calero returned to Miami and began telling people that he was close to the new CIA chief William Webster, just as he had been close to Casey. The rumor helped resolidify his position.

In Miami the parade of the grand and meaningless celebrations continued. The forces of the historical Liberal Party in Nicaragua had long scattered into discordant factions. Aristides Sánchez was currently the only leading force for the reunification of the party. Cecilia Sánchez insisted that her Aristides be honored for this important position, just as Calero and Bermúdez had received their honors.

And so a celebration was planned at a modest hotel in downtown Miami to salute the Liberal Party's unification, as an excuse to honor Sánchez, and also to mark the anniversary of July 11, 1893, when the great Liberal nationalist General Zelaya had first come to power. The keynote speaker was to be Dr. Aristides Sánchez.

The Liberal Party had been the party of Zelaya, Sandino, and the Somozas. Many of the expatriate Liberals in Miami were Somocistas. The old guard of the party was invited to attend the ceremonies. They sang the Nicaraguan anthem, then the American anthem, and then the Liberal anthem in a conga rhythm. Then Somoza's best friends, his ministers, appeared. No one from the press was asked to attend. It was a night for the living dead.

The first speech was given by Francisco Urcuyo, the man whom Somoza had left behind when his government fell in 1979, the man of the old presidential sash. Urcuyo, introduced by the master of ceremonies as a poet of exquisite sensibilities, stood up and asked the audience for a moment of silence in honor of two particular dead Liberals. Some in the audience complained that other dead Liberals weren't given minutes of silence, so why should these two? And so the minute lasted only a few seconds.

Speech after speech followed, commemorating anything and everything: from the daughters of great Liberals to the heroic victim of the Tegucigalpa assassination, Commander Bravo. At a table to honor Fernando Agüero, the Conservative Party orator who had fought against and then aligned with Somoza, sat a small group of Conservatives. They were incensed that only Liberals were allowed to speak and, when they did, they celebrated each and every victory of the Liberals over the Conservative army. Still they stayed in the room in the name of unity.

Then Aristides Sánchez gave a brief talk. He didn't recall anyone. He didn't demand anyone's death. He delivered a remarkably good speech. The audience was not appreciative. Sánchez talked of the future, to which, he said, we should now be directing our attention. The audience disregarded this testimony. This dying ruling class was an interesting relic of the way things had once been. It had nothing to do with what is, or what will be, Nicaragua.

I attended the ceremony with Xavier Argüello, a former Sandinista. We expected to be booed upon our entrance but the spirit of unity was gracious, so we were, for the most part, ignored. The two of us sat at a remote table and quietly ate and drank and listened to the speeches.

Later, walking around the room, we ran into Kid Galeano, at one time one of Nicaragua's most popular boxers. Galeano was now living in Miami in total anonymity. Xavier recognized him immediately and he was so touched at being remembered that he asked us to sit with him at his table.

We stayed with Kid Galeano for a moment and, as all the speeches ended, the old boxer rose and cheered with the crowd. While in Nicaragua the Sandinistas were struggling to maintain power; while the peasant soldiers were still dying in the jungles; while the Americans were supplying aid and withdrawing it and then resupplying it and rewithdrawing it; while the Cubans were coming and going at will, and the Bulgarians, the Argentines and Soviets and Venezuelans were all having their moments too; and while earthquakes and hurricanes and coups d'état and revolution swept regularly through the land—Kid Galeano reduced his own personal history of Nicaragua to a single phrase. The boxer stood up and cried out loud for anyone to hear, "Long live the National Guard! Long live Somoza!"

I got up and left for the last time. For me, the party was over.

Abrams, Elliott
U.S. Undersecretary of State for Latin American Affairs.

Agüero, Fernando
Popular opposition leader of the 1960s, later coopted by the Somozas.

Aguirres, Francisco and Horatio
Brothers involved in an insider conspiracy against Somoza in the 1940s.

Arce, Bayardo
Vice Coordinator of the Political Commission of the FSLN.

Arcos, Chris
A U.S. State Department official in Nicaragua.

Arellanos
A prominent family involved in politics and education. Narciso Arellano was a nineteenth-century Minister-General and later Minister of War.

Asenjos
One of the wealthiest Nicaraguan families, prominent into the early 1900s.

Bermúdez, Enrique
Former National Guard colonel, now one of the commanders of the Contra.

"Big George"
CIA agent.

Borge, Tomás
A founder of the FSLN, now Minister of the Interior and head of security.

Bravo, Commander
Somocista hero and National Guard leader who was killed in Honduras.

Calero, Adolfo
The most prominent member of the Contra.

Carrión Cruz, Luís
Minister of State for Economic Affairs.

Castillo, Mario
Successful businessman and Ortega supporter.

Castro, Raul
Fidel Castro's brother and Cuban Minister of Defense.

Cerna, Lenín
Childhood friend of the Ortegas and now head of the state security apparatus.

César, Alfredo and Octaviano
Brothers who were Sandinistas, then Contras.

Chamorros
The illegitimate Frito Chamorro founded the Chamorro political dynasty in the mid–nineteenth century. Pedro Joaquín Chamorro was editor of *La Prensa* until his murder in 1978. Violeta Chamorro, his widow, was a member of the original governing junta and now part of the opposition. Pedro Joaquín Chamorro, Jr., was

a leader of the Contras. His brother Fernando is editor of *Barricada*, the official FSLN newspaper. "Tito" Chamorro is a former Sandinista and Pastora field commander.

Coronel, Carlos
Former anti-Somoza, then anti-Sandinista, he is now a leading Sandinista.

Coronel, Carlos
The tactician behind Edén Pastora.

Cruz, Arturo, Sr.
First a Sandinista then a Contra leader.

Cuadras
Pablo Antonio Cuadra was a poet and leader of the Liberal Party in the early 1900s. Joaquín Cuadra is a Sandinista leader and second-in-command of the army.

Darío, Rubén
Poet, national hero, and longtime expatriate, he died in Nicaragua in 1916.

D'Escoto, Miguel and Francisco
Former Somocistas, Miguel is now Foreign Minister and Francisco is the ambassador to England.

Dinorah
Tachito Somoza's mistress.

Enders, Thomas O.
Undersecretary of State for Latin American affairs after Elliott Abrams.

Fagoth, Steadman
Mesquito Indian and Contra leader.

Figueres, José
The President of Costa Rica.

Fonseca Amador, Carlos
A founder of the FSLN.

Guzmán, Fernando
Civilian President in the late 19th century, his grandson is Enrique Guzmán.

Hall, Fawn
Secretary to Oliver North.

Harrison, Larry
Head of AID after the revolution.

Hueck, Cornelio
Influential member of Somoza's Liberal Party.

Kagan, Robert
Advisor to Elliott Abrams.

Lacayos
A prominent family. Oswaldo Lacayo is a Sandinista commander, while his brother Danilo headed Exxon through the 1970s in Nicaragua, and now in Chile.

LeMoyne, James
The *New York Times* Nicaraguan correspondent throughout the 1980s.

López, Julio (Julian)
Head of the FSLN International Relations Department.

López Pérez, Rigoberto
Anarchist poet who assassinated the elder Somoza in 1956.

"Manuel"
Official at the Cuban mission to the United Nations in New York City.

"Maroni"
CIA agent.

Martínez, Harold
Anti-Somoza guerrilla, then Pastora's deputy commander on the Southern Front, now a farmer in Costa Rica.

Montalván, Wilfredo
Former leader of the Conservative Party and now a Contra leader.

Murillo, Rosario
Common-law wife of Daniel Ortega.

"Nafre"
Young poet and Sandinista fighter, later Pastora's bodyguard.

North, Oliver
Lieutenant-colonel in the U.S. Army and staff member of the National Security Council.

Núñez, Carlos
President of the National Assembly.

Núñez, Orlando
Sandinista leader and architect of the land-reform program.

Ortega, Humberto and Daniel
From a conservative provincial family, both have reputations as political risk-takers. Daniel, the elder, is President of the Republic

and Coordinator of the Political Commission of the FSLN. Humberto is the Minister of Defense and commander-in-chief of the Sandinista Popular Army.

Pastora, Edén
From a conservative pro-Chamorro family, he was a Contra leader who refused to be identified as such.

Pedrarias
Conquistador who arrived with two thousand Spaniards in 1514; a national "antihero."

Pezzullo, Lawrence
First American ambassador accredited by the Sandinistas in 1979.

Quintana, Julio
Somoza's last Foreign Minister.

Ramírez, Sergio
The Vice President of Nicaragua.

Rivera, Brooklyn
Mcsquito Indian and Contra leader.

Robelo, Alfonso
Headed the NTN, an independent party that arose at the end of the Somoza reign; then a Sandinista and later a Contra.

Ruíz, Henry "Modesto"
Minister of the International Cooperation.

Salazar, Jorge
Contra leader killed in the early 1980s.

Sánchez, Aristides
From a prominent Liberal family, he was a top Contra leader.

Sánchez, Fernando
Prominent Liberal Party leader in the 1920s.

Sandino, Augusto César
Hero who led the rebellion against the U.S. occupation. He was killed by Somoza in 1934.

Sevilla Sacasa, Guillermo
Somoza's son-in-law and ambassador to the United States.

Solís, Rafael
First Sandinista ambassador to the United States.

Somozas
From a provincial family that married into the gentry, Anastasio (Tacho) manipulated U.S. aid until his assassination in 1956. His

eldest son Luís was killed in 1967; his son Tachito, a U.S. supporter, was killed in 1980 in Paraguay; Anastasio III (Tacho) was a colonel in the National Guard.

Tirado, Victor
One of the less influential commanders of the FSLN.

Torres, Edelberto
Elder statesman of the left, went to Costa Rica after the revolution, close to Pastora.

Torrijos, Omar
Panamanian President who supported the Ortega/Tercerista faction.

Ulvert Sánchez, Carlos
Has occupied several important posts in the Contra reform movement.

Urcuyo, Francisco (Chico)
From a prominent gentry family, he was President of Nicaragua for 48 hours.

Volman, Dennis
Christian Science Monitor Latin American correspondent.

Walker, William
American expatriot elected Nicaraguan President in 1856 and deposed by 1857.

Wheelock, Jaime
Minister of Agricultural Development and Director of the Institute of Land Reform.

Zelaya, José Santos
Liberal despot deposed through U.S. threats of intervention in 1912.

Members of the Sandinista National Directorate/
Commanders of the FSLN

Daniel Ortega	Jaime Wheelock
Humberto Ortega	Henry Ruíz
Tomás Borge	Carlos Núñez
Bayardo Arce	Victor Tirado
Luís Carrión Cruz	

B O O K   M A R K

The text of this book was set in the typeface Aster and
the display was set in Aster Bold
by Berryville Graphics, Berryville, Virginia.

It was printed on 50 lb Glatfelter, an acid free paper,
and bound by Berryville Graphics, Berryville, Virginia.

Designed by Richard Oriolo